Software Project Management: A Practitioner's Approach

Second Edition

E. M. Bennatan

McGRAW-HILL BOOK COMPANY

London · New York · St Louis · San Francisco · Auckland
Bogotá · Caracas · Lisbon · Madrid · Mexico · Milan
Montreal · New Delhi · Panama · Paris · San Juan · São Paulo
Singapore · Sydney · Tokyo · Toronto

Published by
McGRAW-HILL Book Company Europe
Shoppenhangers Road, Maidenhead, Berkshire, SL6 2QL, England
Telephone 0628 23432
Fax 0628 770224

British Library Cataloguing in Publication Data

Bennatan, E. M.
  Software Project Management:
  Practitioner's Approach. – 2 Rev. ed
  I. Title
  005.1068
  ISBN 0-07-707648-6

Library of Congress Cataloging-in-Publication Data

Bennatan, E. M.
  Software project management : a practitioner's approach / E.M. Bennatan.—2nd ed.
    p. cm.
  Includes bibliographical references and index.
  ISBN 0-07-707648-6
  1. Computer software—Development—Management. I. Title.
QA76.76.D47B455 1994
005.1'068'4–dc20   94-5319 CIP

12345 CL 98765

Typeset by Computape (Pickering) Ltd, North Yorkshire
and printed and bound at Clays Ltd, St Ives plc

Printed on permanent paper in compliance with the ISO Standard 9706

'Would you tell me, please, which way I ought to go from here?'
'That depends a good deal on where you want to get to,' said the cat.
'I don't much care where'–, said Alice.
'Then it doesn't matter which way you go,' said the cat.

Lewis Carroll

CONTENTS

PREFACE TO THE FIRST EDITION

This is a book about software project management; it is not another book on software engineering. There are already many excellent reference books on software engineering (see the reference list at the end of this book). The objective of this book is to present software development from the *manager's perspective*, rather than from the *developer's perspective*.

The book concentrates, in a single volume, many modern software management practices and techniques that have been developed and refined over the past decade. Project management is presented as an acquired skill and not a gift from birth. Certainly, project management requires management talent, but this in itself is not enough. The effective application of modern software development procedures requires *professional* managers.

As this is a practical text (and not a theoretical work), many methods and techniques are described without their theoretical basis. However, extensive references are provided throughout the book for those interested in the theoretical background. A comprehensive list of references and recommended reading appears at the end of the book.

Occasionally, the reader may find some text repeated in the book. This occurs in order to resolve what is often called the *five finger* predicament. This condition occurs when each of the reader's five fingers needs to be inserted into a book as place markers while the reader struggles back and forth between chapters in order to cover a specific topic. This book attempts to reduce the need for place markers by repeating a short explanation of any major topic that is referenced, even though the topic is discussed in detail elsewhere.

Throughout the book the items *work month* and *work year* have been used in place of the older items *man month* and *man year*. These terms are discussed in detail in Section 10.5.3.

INTENDED AUDIENCE

Software project management: a practitioner's approach is intended for a varied audience. First and foremost, the text is intended as a reference source for practicing software project managers, and as such it is organized so that a major subject is covered in each chapter (excluding Chapter 1). This is further discussed in the following explanation of the organization of the book.

The book is also intended as a class textbook. Each chapter (except for Chapter 1) is followed by several exercises which cover the technical material discussed in the chapter and which encourage students to put into practice what they have learned. There are also numerous class projects, which are geared toward team solutions that can later be presented, discussed and compared by the teams in class.

Finally, the book may serve as a reference for software engineers who would like to expand their knowledge into areas of technical project management.

PREFACE TO THE SECOND EDITION

The second edition of *Software Project Management* has undergone several changes. Many subjects have been updated and expanded and several new subjects have been added.

Firstly, a new chapter has been added on software project management in a client/server environment. This reflects the trend toward the development of software both *for* and *on* client/server platforms. As client/server systems become more prevalent the special problems they pose (such as the independence of the client or the management of a geographically distributed development team) also become more prevalent.

Methods for measuring the level of a software development organization are also covered, with Carnegie Mellon's SEI five-level scale presented and explained.

The landmark IEEE 1074 standard for software life cycle processes is covered and an overview of the individual processes is presented.

The discussion of the IEEE standards has been updated to reflect the complete suite of IEEE software standards published in 1993.

European software development standards are now also addressed, with emphasis on the ISO 9000 software standards.

Lastly, those readers familiar with the first edition will notice that the numbering of some of the chapters has changed. The client/server chapter has been inserted as Chapter 7, and all subsequent chapters have moved up by one.

ORGANIZATION OF THE BOOK

Generally, the eleven chapters of the book appear in logical order and provide a step-by-step entry into the realm of software project management. A quick reference appears at the end of each chapter in the form of an extended summary. The summary is intended to be used either as a memory refresher or as an initial source of information.

The reader is urged to try some of the exercises at the end of each chapter. These exercises will assist the reader in understanding many of the ideas and techniques presented in the chapter.

Chapter 1 introduces the concept of software project management. The chapter also discusses many of the difficulties experienced by project managers in gaining support from higher management for the introduction of new development procedures. The chapter concludes with a discussion on methods for measuring the level of a software development organization.

Chapter 2 briefly summarizes many common software development problems (later to be elaborated throughout the book). The chapter is divided into two sections. The first section is intended for readers who are unfamiliar with the fundamental problems of software management. The second section is intended for new and experienced project managers alike. This section discusses a method of combating the problems discussed earlier, called risk analysis.

Experienced project managers may choose to skip over Chapter 1 and the first section of Chapter 2.

Chapter 3 discusses software development under contract. The chapter describes how software project contracts are awarded, how proposals are prepared, how a proposal document should be constructed, and how relationships should be established between customer and developer. This chapter also describes the request for proposal (RFP) document and the selection process after the proposals have been submitted.

Chapter 4 describes the basic software development cycle, emphasizing the phased approach to software development. Other methodologies are also discussed (such as rapid prototyping and the Spiral model). The basic phases are described from the project manager's perspective, emphasizing the atmosphere and the problems of each phase. This chapter concludes with a discussion of the IEEE 1074 standard for software life cycle processes.

Chapter 5 presents some of the basic principles of managing people. The chapter singles out some of the specific aspects related to managing software engineers, such as the considerable difference in productivity between software engineers and the temperament of programmers in general.

Chapter 6 addresses one of the most difficult problems of software development: how to manage large software projects. The chapter explains how large projects can be divided into small manageable pieces according to the *divide and conquer* approach.

Chapter 7 introduces the software project manager to the management of projects in a client/server environment. This chapter addresses management issues related to client/server *development* and *target* environments, and discusses the many advantages and disadvantages of each. The chapter also covers design considerations specific to the development of a client/server project.

Chapter 8 describes three of the basic management support functions: configuration control, quality assurance and software testing. The chapter also discusses the relationships between these functions.

Chapter 9 presents a general overview of software development standards. Two standards in particular are discussed in detail: the US Department of Defense (DOD) standard 2167, and the IEEE standards for software development and the ISO 9000 software standards. Other standards, such as the British and European software development standards, are also referenced and compared.

Chapter 10 discusses scheduling and the project development plan (PDP). Several scheduling and planning techniques are described, including the classic Gantt and PERT charts and the work breakdown structure (WBS).

Chapter 11 contains an extensive and detailed description of several methods and techniques for the preparation of estimates. The chapter includes methods for estimating the size of a project and the project development schedule, as well as technical estimates, such as memory and disk requirements. The chapter also explains how experience can be used to improve estimates, and describes how estimates can be refined as project development progresses.

ACKNOWLEDGEMENTS

The US Department of Defense (DOD) standards DOD-STD-267A and DOD-STD-268 and the related Data Item Descriptions have been referenced and quoted with the permission of the US Department of Defense, Space and Naval Warfare Systems Command.

Figures 1.1 and 1.2 and the text in Table 1.1 are copyright © The Software Engineering Institute (SEI), and are reprinted with the permission of The Software Engineering Institute.

The IEEE software engineering standards have been referenced and the following texts have been quoted with the permission of the Institute of Electrical and Electronics Engineers, Inc. (IEEE):

F. Buckley's introduction to the 1984 edition of the IEEE *Software Engineering Standards*.

J. Horch's introduction to the 1987 edition of the IEEE Software Engineering Standards.

The *Synopses of the Standards* reprinted from the introduction to the IEEE Software Engineering Standards Collection, 1993, edition.

IEEE std   729–1983
IEEE std   830–1984
IEEE std 1002–1987
IEEE std   990–1986

All are copyright © the Institute of Electrical and Electronics Engineers, Inc.. 1983, 1984, 1986, 1987, 1993.

I should like to acknowledge the extensive help provided by Amir in the review and compilation of the text. I am grateful for his many useful suggestions.

I should also like to acknowledge Sharon and Talya for not disturbing the writing of this text.

Lastly, and most importantly, I fondly acknowledge the encouragement of Irit, without which this text would never have been written.

E. M. Bennatan

TRADEMARKS

Ada is a registered trademark of the US Government, Ada AJPO.

BYL is a trademark of Gordon Group.

CDC 6000 is a trademark of Control Data Corporation.

LAN Manager is a trademark of Microsoft Corporation.

Macintosh is a trademark of Apple Computer, Inc.

Motif is a trademark of Open Software Foundation, Inc.

MS-DOS is a trademark of Microsoft Corporation.

NetWare is a registered trademark of Novell, Inc.

PC-DOS is a trademark of International Business Machines Corporation.

PDP is a trademark of Digital Equipment Corporation.

Pentium is a trademark of Intel Corporation.

Power PC is a trademark of Motorola, Inc.

SNA is a trademark of International Business Machines Corporation

Sparc is a trademark of Sun Microsystems, Inc.

UNIX is a trademark of American Telephone and Telegraph Corporation.

VAX is a trademark of Digital Equipment Corporation.

VMS is a trademark of Digital Equipment Corporation.

MS-Windows is a trademark of Microsoft Corporation.

Windows NT is a trademark of Microsoft Corporation.

X-Windows is a trademark of the Massachusetts Institute of Technology.

INTRODUCTION TO SOFTWARE PROJECT MANAGEMENT

INTRODUCTION

'Software is a place where dreams are planted and nightmares harvested ... a world of werewolves and silver bullets.' This quote from Brad Cox (Cox 1990) underlines the concerns of software project managers today. How can this werewolf in the guise of software engineering be controlled? Is software development an engineering discipline at all?

Software development can be controlled. There exist methods, techniques, standards and tools, that when applied correctly, promote the successful development of a software project. These are not silver bullets through the heart of a werewolf; there is no magic involved. These methods provide a systematic approach to software development, beginning with the initial planning stages and ending with the delivery of the final software product.

This book is concerned with the application of modern methods to the management of software projects. It presents a practical 'how to do it' approach rather than a theoretical approach, though extensive references are provided for those interested in a description of the theory behind the methods. The main objective is to concentrate, in a single volume, a description of many of the tools and procedures that have evolved for such software management activities as:

- Estimation of project cost
- Preparation of development schedules
- Application of effective development standards
- Preparation and evaluation of proposals

The software project manager is thus provided with the methods and procedures needed to make software development more successful, with the three famous objectives in mind: to develop software:

1. On schedule
2. Within budget
3. According to requirements

This chapter discusses the role of project management in achieving these objectives and proposes a means of gaining support for the introduction of modern software development methodologies. A method is then proposed to determine the starting point; an answer to the manager's question: 'At what level is our software organization today?'

1.1 THE INCREASING DEMAND FOR SOFTWARE

There are few areas of modern technology that do not contain software. This includes automobiles, aircraft, and satellites, as well as elevators, fax machines, televisions and electronic organs. Software runs the social security system, corporate payroll systems, and the heart of the Western economy – the credit card system. Software was used extensively to write and print this book.

The rise in demand for software has become a critical problem. It has generated a rise in demand for software engineers which far exceeds the rate at which software professionals are graduating from colleges. Software development is therefore required to be more productive, more reliable, and generally more successful.

These new requirements cannot be met with the crude development methods of the early days of computers. New methods have had to be devised to improve significantly the way software is developed. The severity of this problem has been recognized throughout the software engineering community. A number of inter-company and international consortiums have been established in the United States, Japan and Europe, with considerable budgets dedicated to finding methods to alleviate (if not eliminate) the problem (see Bennatan 1987).

Cox (1990), in an analysis of the direction software engineering should be taking, visualizes an interesting software industrial revolution. He foresees a day when programmers will no longer code everything from scratch and will assemble applications from well-stocked catalogs of reusable software components. This and other revolutionary concepts, such as automatic software development (see Frenkel 1985), still have a long way to go before they become effective means of software development.

The trend toward computer-aided software engineering (CASE) has produced many automatic development tools,[1] but unfortunately these tools often take up more time than they are worth. In other areas of technology, automatic CAD/CA[2] systems are being used to design and build electronic components, but software development still remains largely a manual effort.

The development environment within which software is developed has undergone some change over the past decade. Distributed development using client/server systems has changed the way projects are developed and managed. However, client/server environments, with their increased level of developer independence, have solved some problems and produced new ones.

Until such time as reusable software and automatic software development begin to replace software engineers, software will continue to be developed by people. In the meantime, the required increase in productivity and reliability, and the general success of software development must remain the responsibility of the software project manager.

1.2 THE ROLE OF MANAGEMENT IN SOFTWARE DEVELOPMENT

Effective project management requires many talents and skills. The IEEE standards (IEE 1987a) provide the following definition of software project management:

---

1. See Tahvanainen and Smolander's *An Annotated CASE Bibliography* (1990).
2. CAD and CAM are TLAs (three letter acronyms) for *computer-aided design*, and *computer-aided manufacturing*.

Software project management is the process of planning, organizing, staffing, monitoring, controlling, and leading a software project.

Clearly, it is no longer sufficient to be a good software developer in order to be a good software project manager. Specific management skills are required from the initial stages of the project, in such areas as:

- *Supervision and control*
  This includes the efficient management of the development team members and requires constant awareness of the real status of their work on the project.
- *Planning*
  Planning is one of the most important management activities and includes the preparation of good estimates, the maintenance of the development schedule and the efficient assignment of personnel.
- *Customer relations*
  In some projects, contact with the customer is a major management activity. This includes documenting the customer's requirements, controlling changes required by the customer, handling the customer's involvement in the development process, providing reports and organizing reviews and product demonstrations.
- *Technical leadership*
  Good technical leadership is usually a desirable quality in effective software management. This often requires the ability to provide guidance in the solution of technical problems that arise during project development. It does not necessarily mean the provision of the actual solution itself.

These areas of management are applicable to all types of high technology project. However, the management of a software project is more difficult, owing to the fact that software development is less deterministic than other areas of technology. This is because software projects are less measurable, more difficult to estimate, and more dependent on subjective human factors.

The history of software development is full of cases where the level of resources required was badly planned and estimated. Software development has long been perceived as a risky business. There have been many cases of software projects exceeding their original budget by two, three, or even four hundred percent. Some have even been abandoned after spending substantial funds, when it became evident that the original budget estimate was nowhere near the true cost of development.

In recent years, an attempt has been made to standardize the software development process and to create a strict development environment in which software projects are easier to estimate and control. However this has led to a new problem: developers complained that they were spending too much time on documentation and too little on the actual development of code.

Clearly, a middle ground should be sought between the two extremes: the freelance-style project, which is impossible to schedule and estimate, and the over-standardized, over-documented project, where an exaggerated effort is spent on overheads and paperwork.

As software development began to evolve into an engineering discipline, new systematic development methodologies began to appear.[3] The goal of these new methodologies was to make software development more successful. If success is to be measured in terms of the three

---

3. See Shaw (1990) for a full discussion of the evolution of software into an engineering discipline.

previously mentioned objectives (on schedule, within budget, according to requirements), then failure should mean the failure to achieve even one of these objectives. However, success and failure are not that easily defined.

Many studies have shown that project failure is also a question of perception (see Pinto and Mantel 1990). A project may be perceived as having failed in one environment while in another it may be perceived as having succeeded. Simply stated, one customer may be pleased with the outcome of a project, while another customer may not. Hence project success or failure is not only related to the three basic development objectives, it is also related to the expectations of the customer.

The ambiguity of the concept of project failure can best be avoided if a single goal is set. This is the goal that the customer sets; not the development team. This means that:

Ultimately, the success or failure of a project is determined by the satisfaction of the party that requested its development (i.e. the customer).

These concepts are demonstrated in the following example.

1.3 AN EXAMPLE

The following example demonstrates several common management errors that can ultimately lead to the failure of a software project. The project starts off with several basic wrong decisions related to the launching of the project, which in turn lead to more wrong decisions as the project progresses.

Technology Associates Inc. (TAI) is a company that specializes in the development and manufacturing of communications equipment. TAI has a large software department which is responsible for the development of software for communications equipment. The manager of the software department learned that corporate management was looking for an outside software company to develop a time and attendance system for TAI.

TAI's software department took the initiative, prepared a proposal to develop the system, and submitted it to corporate management. According to the proposal, two months would be devoted to consulting the personnel department, the financial department, and the department managers to define the requirements for the system. The development team would then develop the system during the following six months (the total development time would be eight months). The software department estimated that a team of four people would be required to produce the requirements and to develop the system.

The idea to use an outside software company was put aside, and the software department's proposal was accepted by corporate management. A development budget was approved to cover two and a half work years, or four people for eight months. The software department proceeded to establish a project team, and selected a project manager from one of the communications projects to lead the team.

As the end of the initial two month period drew near, it became evident to the project manager that much more time was needed to determine and document the requirements. The project manager's options were:

1. Request an extension for the schedule and an addition to the development budget.
2. Use the existing partial requirements.

The department manager wanted to demonstrate that his department was capable of developing both embedded communications software and information systems. Therefore the project manager and his team were urged to choose option 2. This was based on the premise that if the project was late and over budget, it would be considered a failure, and future information systems would then be contracted to an outside software company.

The time and attendance system was developed based on the incomplete information that was accumulated during the initial two month period. When the system was installed, the personnel department found it inadequate because it could not handle two employee entries and exits on the same day. The financial department found that the system only reported hours worked, and not the time of day at which the hours were worked. This meant that overtime could not be calculated correctly.

All the other departments found several major problems with the system. In short, the system fell far short of what the company needed.

The software department proposed correcting the problems and requested a budget for the development of a new improved version. However, dissatisfaction was such that corporate management decided to offer the development of an entirely new system to an outside software company. The software company that was selected successfully developed the system. Surprisingly, this time the cost was *less* than the budget requested by TAI's software department for correcting the problems in the original system.

This (true) example demonstrates several major project management errors:

- Experience in one area of software (embedded communications systems) is not sufficient for the successful development of software in an entirely different area (information systems).
- A project manager should avoid committing to either development schedule or budget before the project has been adequately defined. In most cases, a firm commitment can be given only after the requirements are concluded.
- If the requirements of a project are not met, then adhering to the budget and schedule becomes meaningless.
- A customer or user will not always provide the correct requirements (e.g. interdepartment transfers). It is often the developer's responsibility to ask the right questions in order to collect the necessary information.
- It is sometimes better to develop a new system from scratch than to try to salvage a poorly developed system.

1.4 GAINING ACCEPTANCE FOR NEW DEVELOPMENT PROCEDURES

One of the obstacles that project managers often have to overcome is the lack of support from higher management for modern development methods. Applying effective methodologies is not easy when higher management disputes their need. This leads project managers to a classic dilemma: how to stand up for what they believe is best while retaining their positions as project managers.

Clearly the many methods and techniques described in this book are effective only when they are *used*. The objective of this section is to assist the project manager in gaining acceptance from higher management for the application of new methods.

Higher management (and sometimes other software engineers) occasionally use the following arguments against the use of modern software development methodologies:

1. These methods are all *theoretical*; in the 'real world' things are done differently.

2. Project managers are too formalistic; they request everything in writing and make an issue out of every small change.
3. We don't have time for all this paperwork.
4. We can't afford the luxury of these lengthy procedures. We have always developed software without all this overhead.
5. This is a business, not a university. We will lose money and customers if we start wasting time on all these methods.
6. The methods are good, but unfortunately, now is not the right time to implement them. We hope to be able to use them some day, but not just yet.
7. None of our engineers is familiar with these new methods. It will take too long and will cost too much to start retraining them.

The following are some of the recommended responses to the above arguments.

1. The record of software development in the real world has not been too good. In fact, the old methods have only too often led to disaster. There have been successes, but the hit rate of successes versus failures is much too low.

    Any effective method contains some theory, just as these software development methods do. These methods have been successfully applied by other similar companies, and have produced a drastic reduction in the cost of software development and a significant rise in the quality of software.
2. Orderly written record keeping is beneficial for everyone: the development team, the customer, and higher management. It assures that verbal communications have been understood correctly. If changes and other instructions are not documented and approved, then the development may proceed in the wrong direction. No one can be sure that all changes, large and small, will be remembered later when the project is completed. A documented list of approved changes provides traceability and accountability.
3. This may be a valid claim; paperwork should be kept to a minimum (it occasionally is exaggerated). However, surprisingly enough, paperwork in moderation actually *saves* time and does not waste it. For example, undocumented decisions often need to be repeated and verbal specifications lead to conflicting interpretations. The lack of documentation is usually most time-consuming during the integration and test phases, when the system design is recorded only in the mind of the developers.

    Also, an undocumented project is a nightmare to maintain. After project completion, when the developers disperse, all that is left is the product and its documentation. Without documentation, the product is no more than a mystery.
4. A question to reflect on is: ' . . . and just how successful has our software development really been?' This argument is best challenged with a prepared file of information that documents the problems the company has experienced with previous projects. The objective is to prove that a new approach to software development is not a luxury but a necessity.
5. Arguments are most difficult to challenge when there is an element of truth in them, specifically when a company intends to develop its own new methodology. Though many companies do carry out research in software engineering, this is hardly necessary in all companies. There exist adequately documented methodologies, standards and guidelines (see IEEE 1987b) to enable them to be easily applied in any company, without the need to redevelop them.

    Customers are lost not only due to an extended development schedule, but also due to poor quality and unsatisfied technical needs. The trade-off is heavily inclined toward a longer development schedule in exchange for a better software product.

Also, short development schedules are often misleading, due to the additional time required to correct a poor software product after its first release (see the example in Section 1.3).

6. Why not just yet? Is there any real basis for the claim that a more suitable time will appear later? On the contrary, the more time and effort invested in poor development methods, the more difficult they are to change.

The best way to respond to this argument is to provide business reasons that explain why new development methods should be adopted as quickly as possible. The prepared file, mentioned in the response to argument 4, will be helpful, together with information collected from other companies. The objective is to demonstrate that orderly development procedures will increase the quality of the company's software product while reducing the cost of development.

7. The importance of investing in training rarely needs to be established; this is a widely accepted notion. This argument may be difficult to challenge when new development methods are presented as a *major* change of direction.

The best response depends on the true situation. If the new methods do indeed represent a major change of direction, then most probably the company has been experiencing many software development problems. The responses to arguments 4 and 5 are then appropriate.

If the new methods do not really represent a major change of direction, then this should be demonstrated using data from previous projects. The basic idea is to show that, although several current development procedures are fine, significant improvement can be achieved through the introduction of some new methods.

All arguments against new development methodologies should only be challenged after adequate preparation. This usually means:

● Collecting data on previous software development projects within the company
● Collecting data on similar companies that have adopted new development methods
● Collecting documented reports, texts, and other written evidence (beware of being too theoretical)
● Obtaining the support of other software development experts, either from within the company, or from without

All the data should be studied, and notes should be prepared that substantiate the need for new development methods. The bottom line should be that *the application of new effective software development procedures is in the interest of the company*.

Having gained the necessary approval from higher management, the software project manager can move on to the application of the methods described in the following chapters. The first step, understanding the basic software development problems, is discussed in Chapter 2.

1.5 MEASURING YOUR SOFTWARE ORGANIZATION

It is reasonable to assume that a good software organization will produce good software. The previous section discussed ways of convincing skeptics that this is indeed so. The problem is that it is not easy to define *a good software organization*. Consequently, there is a need to be able to measure a software organization in order to determine just how *good* it really is.

Assuming that the level of a software development organization can be measured, we can also debate how much the level of the organization contributes to the success of a software project. Will a project necessarily fail if the level of the organization is low?

As we shall see, it is all a question of probabilities.

1.5.1 Likelihood of success

As a software project manager you may, from time to time, be confronted by people who will tell you (and your boss) how they developed a software project without using any orderly development methods. And, of course, they will always tell you how they succeeded in producing the software in a fraction of the time it would have taken them had they used an orderly process, the kind that you support.

This can be a difficult situation to combat, particularly in front of a doubting audience. This is because occasionally such unlikely stories are true!

Actually, the explanation is surprisingly simple. Consider, for example the following scenario.

You are crossing Fifth Avenue in New York City during lunch time. Being a reasonably careful person, you first search out a pedestrian crossing. You then wait until the green 'WALK' light comes on, and then, remembering that traffic lights are considered by New York drivers to be no more than a recommendation, you look left then right then left again. Satisfied that all is clear you safely cross Fifth Avenue to the other side.

While you are involved in this exploit, a friend of yours without hesitating, races across Fifth Avenue and surprisingly makes it safely to the other side. He then proceeds to taunt you for wasting time with all the precautions that you took.

You may be tempted for a brief moment to wonder if he is right.

The parallel in software is that occasionally you may rush through a software project without using any orderly development methods, and you may be lucky enough to succeed. However, in most cases, like the person rushing across Fifth Avenue, you will be hit by a bus!

We all know that occasionally people are lucky. But, as a professional engineering manager, you cannot base your project development plan on sheer luck. The business case for developing a software project is based on the fact that there is a reasonable chance for success. If, in throwing care to the wind, you can promise no more that a poor gamble, then it makes little business sense to develop your project. An orderly development process is like an insurance policy; it greatly reduces risk, but for a price. The recent history of software development has demonstrated time and time again that this price is well worth paying.

We can now rephrase more firmly the statement at the beginning of this section:

The better a software organization, the greater the likelihood that it will produce good software.

We can now go back to the question of how to measure the level of a software development organization.

1.5.2 The SEI scale

Measuring a software organization's development capabilities is a means of assessing its likelihood of success in developing a project. Clearly, the organization's development capabilities are not the only factor in determining the likelihood of success, but it is undoubtedly a major factor.

In 1986 Carnegie Mellon University's Software Engineering Institute (SEI) started working on a five-level scale for measuring what was initially referred to as *software process maturity*, and later as *software capability maturity*.

Paulk *et al.* (1993a) and (1993b) explain the objective of SEI's Capability Maturity Model (CMM) as to 'help organizations improve their software process' through 'the progression from an immature unrepeatable software process to a mature, well-managed software process'.

Paulk provides an excellent description of an immature versus a mature software organization:

Setting sensible goals for process improvement requires an understanding of the difference between immature and mature software organizations. In an immature software organization, software processes are generally improvised by practitioners and their management during the course of the project. Even if a software process has been specified, it is not rigorously followed or enforced. The immature software organization is reactionary, and managers are usually focused on solving immediate crises (better known as fire fighting). When hard deadlines are imposed, product functionality and quality are often compromised to meet the schedule.

... On the other hand, a mature software organization possess an organization-wide ability for managing software development and maintenance process. The software process is accurately communicated to both existing staff and [to] new employees, and work activities are carried out according to the planned process.

... In general, a disciplined process is consistently followed because all of the participants understand the value of doing so, and the necessary infrastructure exists to support the process.

The five levels that measure the path from immaturity to maturity are presented in Fig. 1.1 on page 10, while Table 1.1 explains each of the CMM levels.

Table 1.1 SEI software process maturity levels characterized (reprinted with permission of The Software Engineering Institute)

Maturity level	Level description
1. Initial	The software process is characterized as *ad hoc*, and occasionally even chaotic. Few processes are defined, and success depends on individual effort.
2. Repeatable	Basic project management processes are established to track cost, schedule, and functionality. The necessary process discipline is in place to repeat earlier successes on projects with similar applications.
3. Defined	The defined process for both management and engineering activities is documented, standardized, and integrated into a standard software process for the organization. All projects use an approved, tailored version for the organization's standard software process for developing and maintaining software.
4. Managed	Detailed measures of the software process and product quality are collected. Both the software process and products are quantitatively understood and controlled.
5. Optimized	Continuous process improvement is enabled by quantitative feedback from the process and from piloting innovative ideas and technologies.

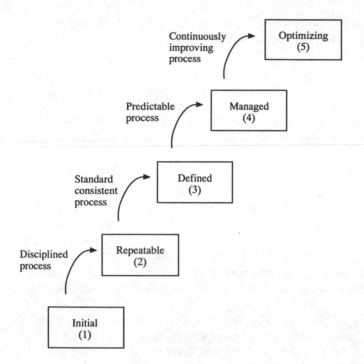

Figure 1.1 The five levels of software process maturity. (Reprinted with permission of The Software Engineering Institute.)

For an organization to be officially designated to have reached a CMM level, it takes a formal SEI assessment with trained assessors, using a formal set of procedures. However, trained assessors can do more than just conduct formal assessments. An organization may choose to train one of its engineers as a formal SEI assessor to guide it as it improves its process and moves up the SEI ladder.

In order for an organization to advance to a higher CMM level it must focus on improvements in *key process areas* (see Fig. 1.2). Each key process area identifies a group of related activities for reaching a set of goals that will enhance the organization's process capability. When the goals for all key process areas for the next CMM level have been achieved, the organization is ready to attempt assessment at the next level.

A good practice is to conduct an informal assessment every six months or so, to evaluate the degree of improvement in each key process area. The main challenge is that the informal assessment must be objective. This is best achieved by taking a strict, uncompromising, approach. Then, if the informal assessment confirms the attainment of the required level, the chances are that the formal assessment will do so too.

Several surveys have been conducted both in the United States and in the Western world to try to assess informally how software organizations are distributed based on the five SEI CMM levels. Though various research papers have reported different results, most assessments agree that in the early 1990s, the large majority (80 to 90 percent) of software development organizations were at level 1. Between 6 and 12 percent were at level 2, and just a few percent were at level 3 and above.

There is broad agreement on the benefits to an organization in reaching levels 2 and 3. This covers both the business case and the engineering justification for moving up the SEI ladder. At

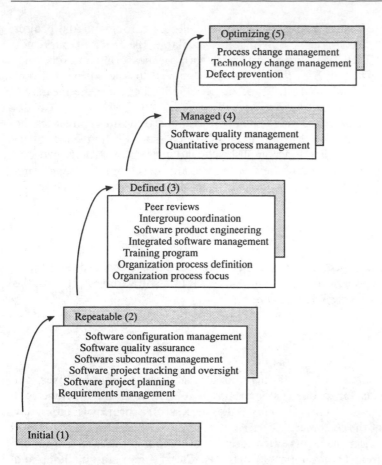

Figure 1.2 The key process areas by maturity level. (Reprinted with permission of The Software Engineering Institute.)

level 2 (*Repeatable*) and above software development can be planned and estimated with a reasonable degree of confidence, and success is not just achieved by chance. At level 3 (*Defined*) the process, with its standards and guidelines, is well defined and is adhered to by all parts of the organization. This produces significant savings because similar methods and techniques are used for all projects throughout the organization.

Levels 4 (*Managed*) and 5 (*Optimized*) undoubtedly also come with a significant set of benefits to the organization. However, there has been much debate as to whether every organization actually needs these levels of excellence. The group that developed IBM's space shuttle program may have been at level 5, but all of IBM certainly was not.

1.5.3 Why measure?

If an organization wishes to improve its level of software development it must have a scale by which to measure itself. It must know where it is, and it must know where it wants to go. It is a well known fact that:

If you cannot measure where you are you cannot demonstrate that you are improving.

Measurements, or as they are called, *metrics*, need to be collected throughout the project development process. The SEI scale is not the only measure available; the IEEE Standard for Software Productivity Metrics (IEEE 1990b) defines a framework for measuring and reporting software productivity. Other metrics, such as IEEE's metrics standard for measuring software quality (IEEE 1990c) address the final product. These metrics, and others, are the means by which the level of a development organization is determined.

So, in most cases it is safe to say that the level of the organization significantly influences the level of the product. Successful software development, just like crossing Fifth Avenue in the anecdote related earlier, may occasionally be accomplished without using an orderly process, but will be much more frequently accomplished with a good development engineering organization. And how do we know if we have a good organization? Well, *good* is measurable.

1.6 SUMMARY

Software development can be controlled. There exist methods, techniques, standards and tools, that when applied correctly, promote the successful development of a software project, with the three famous objectives in mind – to develop software:

1. On schedule
2. Within budget
3. According to requirements

Project success or failure is related not only to these three basic development objectives, but also to the expectations of the customer; one customer may be pleased with the outcome of a project, while another customer may not. Therefore, the success of a project is ultimately determined by the satisfaction of the customer.

One of the obstacles that project managers often have to overcome is the lack of support from higher management for modern development methods. Clearly the many methods and techniques described in this book are effective only when they are *used*.

All arguments against new development methodologies should only be challenged after adequate preparation.

Information on past successes and failures of software development within a company should be collected, together with other written supporting evidence. All the data should be studied, and notes should be prepared that substantiate the need for new development methods. The bottom line should be that *the application of new effective software development procedures is in the interest of the company*.

The better a software organization, the greater the likelihood that it will produce good software. Hence the improvement in our ability to produce successful software is represented by the improvement in the level of our software development organization.

Measuring a software organization's development capabilities produces a means of assessing its likelihood of success in developing a project. In 1986, Carnegie Mellon University's Software Engineering Institute (SEI) started working on a five-level scale for measuring what they referred to as the software capability maturity of a development organization. This scale provides the organization with the means of measuring improvement, and of determining its level of maturity in relation to other software development organizations.

SOFTWARE DEVELOPMENT PROBLEMS

AN OUNCE OF PREVENTION

At a recent course on software project management, one of the participants asked:

> We have several major problems in a project that I am managing. We don't have any orderly documentation, or a development plan, and the project is way over budget and behind schedule. How do I apply all the methods and techniques that I have learned here, in order to get the project back on schedule?

This is not an uncommon situation, where a magical remedy is sought for a near-disastrous situation. Poorly managed projects can run into delays and budget overruns of two or even three hundred percent, and in some cases may even be abandoned. Most modern project management methods are primarily concerned with *preventing* (and not *correcting*) these types of problem.

Preventing problems is easier and less costly than solving them. Effective preventive measures should:

- Locate problems and potential problems early
- Resolve problems before they get out of hand
- Plan ahead for potential problems

Problems become more costly to resolve as the project progresses into advanced development stages. Neglected problems may also propagate into other areas of the project, making them much more difficult to correct. It is therefore important to establish procedures for the early location and correction of problems.

This chapter explains the causes of some of the more common types of software development problem and discusses their effect on the development process. The chapter also discusses the anticipation of problems in order to minimize their impact on the project. Later chapters address methods of preventing the problems described here from occurring.

2.1 BASIC PROBLEMS

There are several basic problems which a project manager is likely to find in any software project. These basic problems are caused by the following situations that can always be expected to occur:

- Inadequate initial requirements
- Dependence on external sources (vendors, subcontractors etc.)
- Difficulties in concluding the project
- Frequent replacement of the development personnel (staff turnover)

Other basic problems are often produced by common errors of management, such as:

- Poor estimates
- Inadequate tracking and supervision
- Uncontrolled changes

The best way to locate a problem early is to go looking for it. Clearly, the first place to look is where problems most frequently occur. For example, frequent and unchecked changes to the requirements specification are notorious as a major source of design problems. Unsupervised subcontractors and vendors are one of the most common sources of surprises, particularly when they report technical problems and delays at the very last moment. For the project manager, knowing where to look is therefore as important as knowing what to do.

2.1.1 Problems related to project requirements

The project requirements specification describes the product to be produced by the development group (see Chapter 4). If the requirements are not adequately specified then nothing short of pure luck will assure that the product meets the needs of the customer.[1] Following are some examples of problems related to poor requirements specification.

- *Features are missing*
  The customer was *sure* that certain missing features would be included in the product, based on informal discussions (often with the wrong people), memos, comments and remarks at meetings, but not based on a formal requirements specification.
- *Unnecessary features have been included*
  The development team was *sure* that the customer would be overjoyed with the extra features that were added to the product (usually without consulting the customer). An example might be the addition of password security access to the system when the customer wanted the system to be readily accessible to anyone.
- *Features that work differently than expected*
  The customer explained the need for a feature inadequately, and so the development team interpreted the requirement according to their own understanding. An example might be a requirement to 'update the database regularly'. The developers produced a system that updates the database once a day, while the customer meant once an hour.
- *Necessary features that nobody thought about*
  The customer is not necessarily a computer expert, and therefore may not be aware that a specific feature is needed. An example would be the need for adequate backups; the customer may assume that backups are unnecessary because if computer service is interrupted (say by a power failure) then the loss of one or two memory resident transactions will not be a problem. However, the customer may not have considered the fact that disk drives can also crash and lose all their data.

---

1. The term customer here is used in its broadest sense to include a formal customer, the marketing department, the users group, management etc.

Clearly, poorly specified requirements are as much a problem to the developer as they are to the customer. The developer, however, is often in a better position to compile the requirements than the customer. Usually, the best requirements specification is the result of a joint effort by both the developer and the customer, with the actual document being written by the developer and being approved by the customer.

2.1.2 Frequent changes

It is extremely rare to find a well planned software project come to a successful conclusion with a requirements specification labeled version 1.0. Changes are inevitable throughout the software development cycle. However, in most cases, the later a change is introduced, the more costly it is to implement.

A reasonable number of changes should be manageable. It is when the flow of changes turns into a torrent that they become a problem. Even a single change can be a problem if it is requested well into the development of the project and if it results in a major change of direction. Excessive changes produce what is commonly referred to as the *moving target syndrome*. The project manager is continually changing direction, and the development team becomes both confused and demotivated.

Changes can disrupt the project if they are not adequately documented and monitored. Changes, in reasonable numbers, must be managed using a systematic change control mechanism. This method, within the configuration control organization, is discussed in Chapter 7.

2.1.3 Estimates and related problems

Good estimates are important, as they form the foundations of a good project development plan. This plan, prepared by the project manager, is produced during the initial stages of the project, and includes estimates related to:

- The project development budget
- The project development schedule
- The required development resources (development staff, development equipment etc.)

Technical estimates are also produced during the design phase, and include:

- The characteristics of the software (estimates of memory size, data base size etc.)
- The characteristics of the required target hardware (estimates of CPU speed, input/output capacity, disk drive capacity etc.)

Estimates are the basis for many technical and management decisions. Poor estimates lead to poor decisions. A poor estimate can be either too high or too low, and the subsequent decisions produce either a waste or a shortage of a development resource. This produces planning errors, such as:

- Schedules that are much too short or highly exaggerated
- Budgets that are much too low or greatly inflated
- Under- or over-staffing

and technical design errors, such as:

- Targeting computers that are much larger (and more expensive) than necessary, or that are incapable of supporting the application being developed

Problems derived from low estimates are usually more critical than problems derived from high estimates. Realizing this, estimators commonly add uncertainty factors (of say 30 percent) to their estimates, assuming that it is better to be too high than too low. However, a high estimate may not cause a project to fail, but it may prevent the project from ever getting launched at all.

Many methods have been developed to produce various types of estimate at different stages of the project (see Chapters 10 and 11). However, even well-prepared estimates can lead to problems if they are not updated on a regular basis. Clearly, better and more complete information produces better estimates. Therefore, as the project moves forward and more information becomes available, estimates should be reviewed and refined. This leads to the reassessment of development decisions, enabling potential problems to be addressed early, before they become critical (see Section 2.2 on risk analysis).

2.1.4 External sources

Project development problems are usually easiest to manage when all the development factors are controlled by project management. This, however, is not always the case. Many projects are dependent on various external sources, such as:

- Subcontractors
- Equipment vendors
- Parallel development projects
- Service providers (maintenance, training, installation etc.)
- Support functions (telephone communications, networks, data providers etc.)

The dependence on external sources must be reflected in the project development plan. This means incorporating within the plan commitments and estimates received from other sources. Consequently, the estimates in the plan can be no better than the estimates received from the other sources.

Reliance on external sources can cause the following problems:

- Schedule delays, owing to late delivery of project components.
- Poor quality and design of development equipment and external project components.
- Incompatible external components, owing to departure by the external developer or vendor from the agreed or published specification.
- Poor product support for external components.

By being aware of these potential problems, the project manager can assure that they are adequately addressed in the contract or agreement with the external source. These problems can often be averted by including in the contract penalties for delays in delivery or flaws in the product (see Chapters 3 and 10). Early warnings can be detected by regularly reviewing the work being developed by the subcontractor and requesting regular progress reports.

2.1.5 Concluding a software project

As all project managers know, projects are difficult to start. Experience shows that they are often no less difficult to end. Toward the end of a project, there is always a tendency for various interested parties to emerge with new requirements, comments, changes, and other last minute activities. This is especially true for *fixed price* projects being developed for a customer under contract (see Chapter 3).

The main problems related to the conclusion of a project are:

- Disputes between customer and developer regarding the interpretation and the provision of all required features.
- Attempts to include last minute changes.
- System failures and design defects located during system installation and test.
- Difficulty in keeping the development team together and motivated. As tension lessens toward the end of the project, there is a corresponding reduction of enthusiasm among the remaining development team members.

It is the responsibility of the project manager to assure the orderly and successful conclusion of the project. This is achieved through detailed planning at the start of the project, and effective project management throughout the project. Specifically, this requires that:

- Acceptance test plans must be prepared, documented and approved by the customer well before the end of the project.
- Staffing levels and assignments must be scheduled, taking into account the gradual reduction in the development team size toward the end of the project.
- The release of the product must be well planned, including packaging, production of documentation, training, installation, and an orderly transition to the maintenance and support phase.

The successful conclusion of a project starts at the other end of the development cycle: at the beginning. Poor requirements specifications, test plans or development plans all lead to major problems at the conclusion of the project.

2.1.6 Staff recruitment and turnover

The difficulty in recruiting development team members is one of the first problems encountered by the software project manager. Before any project can be launched, the initial development team must be established. And the problems do not end once the team is in place. Keeping the team is often as difficult as establishing it.

Frenkel (1985) reports that the demand for software engineers is growing exponentially, while productivity is rising at a rate of about 5 percent a year. US and European universities are not producing software engineers at a rate sufficient to close the gap between supply and demand. In fact, not only is the gap not being closed, it is widening at a concerning rate.

The average amount of time a software engineer remains at a job decreases as the demand for engineers grows. This is not only caused by migration of software engineers *between* companies, but also by migration *within* companies, as these companies attempt to make more efficient use of their engineers. Migration within companies is not only due to the shortage of software engineers but also to their relatively high cost. This means that even in cases where additional engineers are available in the job market, their cost may inhibit additional hiring.[2]

---

2. Basic economic dictates that when engineers are available, their cost should decrease (based on the supply and demand within the job market). However, in recent years the supply of software engineers has never been sufficiently high to cause this effect, except for brief periods of time in isolated locations.

Staff turnover is in itself a major problem. The stability of the development team contributes significantly to the morale and motivation of the team, and thus to the success of the project.

The problems related to staff recruitment and frequent turnover include:

- A significant investment is required in the learning curve and training for new development team members.
- Frequent staff turnover reduces team spirit and negatively affects team motivation.
- Recruitment is often costly and time-consuming, requiring several interviews and possibly recruitment fees.
- Frequent staff turnover produces a lack of consistency in the development of the project.

Of all software development problems, those related to the development team are often perceived as the most critical. The team members are the most important development resource, for it is they who contribute most to the success or failure of the project.

2.1.7 Tracking and supervision

Tracking and supervision are management tasks. When problems arise in these and related areas, they are often the consequence of inappropriate and ineffective project management procedures. One of the most common results is that the project manager is unaware of the existence of major problems at the stage when they can best be contained and corrected.

Effective tracking and supervision require direct contact between project management and the development team (see Chapter 8). One of the major causes of tracking and supervision problems is the *ivory tower syndrome*, where a permanent rift exists between project management and the rest of the development team. This leads to:

- Inaccurate or non-existent flow of information, contributing significantly to poor management decisions.
- Uncoordinated development; this situation is often depicted as one development team developing two different projects. It occurs when uncoordinated and unsupervised development team members proceed in different directions.
- Schedule delays and budget overruns; these are caused by poor estimates based on incorrect information.

Information is the basic ingredient of any type of management. Therefore, poor supervision coupled with an inadequate flow of information are at the core of poor project management. The above three problems describe the general outcome of poor management. The list of resulting problems could just as easily cover almost every type of project development problem. Methods for establishing effective channels of information and well organized reporting procedures are described in Chapter 5.

2.2 RISK ANALYSIS

Foresight is an excellent management quality that can often be cultivated with experience. Indeed, in many cases, problems can be anticipated. In such cases, the manager can plan for the possibility that a problem will occur by estimating its probability, evaluating its impact, and preparing solutions in advance. This is referred to as *risk analysis*, and is an effective means of combating potential development problems.

Performing risk analysis means being prepared. It is a form of insurance, the basic idea being that if a problem occurs, a solution is readily available. Like all insurance, risk analysis usually comes with a price. The cost of preparing for the occurrence of a problem is primarily the cost of having the alternative solution at hand, while the problem may or may not occur. In some cases, the cost may be minimal: the time needed to analyze and document the solution, and the time to track the problem. In other cases the cost may be substantial: for example, the price of an alternative piece of development equipment. In any case, a problem that has been analyzed and resolved ahead of time is far simpler to resolve than a problem that occurs unexpectedly.

2.2.1 Anticipating problems

The first stage of risk analysis requires a review of all project technical and administrative plans in order to identify potential problems. It includes:

- The project development plan
- The requirements specification
- The design specification

All major dependencies in the project development plan are examined and evaluated. Examples may be the dependence on external sources such as subcontractors, vendors and suppliers, and service providers. Problems will arise if external components or services are not provided on time, or if they do not function as expected.

The project design specification is a detailed plan of how the requirements are to be implemented. The implementation decisions involved may contain potential problems. For example, problems will arise if the selected hardware turns out to be inadequate, such as if the CPU is too slow, the LAN is not sufficiently reliable, or the maximum available memory is insufficient.

A list of all anticipated problems is then compiled, identifying each problem and describing the potential effect on the project. Table 2.1 presents an example of an anticipated problem list.

Table 2.1 Example of an anticipated problem list

Problem	Description
1 Late delivery of the development computer	If the development computer is not delivered by June 1, as planned, the integration phase will be delayed.
2 Insufficient memory	The size of the memory resident part of the system may exceed 8 megabytes (the maximum memory size supported by the computer).
3 No operating system expert	The system requires changes to the standard operating system. John Adams is the only OS expert in the company, and he may not be available for this project.
4 System response time too slow	The required system response time to the input may exceed the 5 seconds specified in the requirements.
5 High staff turnover	The schedule is tight with only minimal slack time. If there is more than average staff replacement during development, we will slip the schedule.
6 Communications too slow	The standard communications package is too slow. The design is based on the new binary communications package. This package has never been used with this system, and may not be suitable.
7 Late delivery of the data base subsystem	The data base subsystem is subcontracted to Software Developer Inc. (SDI), who have committed to delivery by April 15. SDI may not deliver on time, thus delaying the final integration and test phase.

The anticipated problem list should be compiled with the participation of the principal members of the project development team. Other people may also be invited to contribute to the list, based on their experience and technical or administrative knowledge. This might include people from other project teams, support groups, the company's legal department or the purchasing department.

While the objective is not to list *every* conceivable problem that any project may experience, it is necessary to identify those problems that should *reasonably* be considered in relation to the project. In any event, the following analysis stage is designed to isolate only those problems that could have significant impact on the project, and that can reasonably be expected to appear

2.2.2 The analysis stage

The analysis of the anticipated problems list requires the evaluation of each problem in order to:

1. Estimate the probability that the problem will occur
2. Estimate the impact of the problem on the project
3. Attribute a measure of severity to the problem

The probability and the impact should be estimated by more than one person. All items on the list are best estimated during a single problem evaluation meeting, to assure that the relative severity between problems is not distorted. The objective is to avoid situations where late delivery by supplier A is estimated at 0.8 by one estimator, and late delivery by supplier B is estimated at 0.6 by another, while both estimators would agree that the probability is equal. Having both persons in the same room at the same time reduces this relative distortion.

A simple and effective way of producing the measure of severity for each anticipated problem is to:

1. Assign an *expectation number* between 1 and 10 based on the probability that the problem will occur, with 10 representing high probability, and 1 representing low probability (e.g. multiply the probability by 10).
2. Assign a number between 1 and 10 based on the impact of the problem on the project, with 10 representing high impact and 1 representing low impact.
3. Multiply the value produced in step (1) by the value produced in step (2) to produce the measure of severity for the problem.

Table 2.2 presents an example of the calculation of the measure of severity, using the anticipated problems described in Table 2.1.

Table 2.2 Example of the calculation of measure of severity

Problem	Expectation	Impact	Severity
1 Late delivery of the development computer	6	5	30
2 Insufficient memory	4	2	8
3 No operating system expert	5	5	25
4 System response time too slow	5	3	15
5 High staff turnover	5	8	40
6 Communications too slow	2	8	16
7 Late delivery of the data base subsystem	3	9	27

Table 2.3 Example of a contingency table

Problem	Severity	Contingency plan	Tracker
5 High staff turnover	40	Allocate bonuses for successful project completion	J. Smith
1 Late delivery of the development computer	30	Request night shift on development system of another project	H. Brown
7 Late delivery of the data base subsystem	27	Design a data base subsystem simulator to be used for integration	W. Alda
3 No operating system expert	25	Locate an OS expert outside the company, and hire as a consultant	H. Brown
6 Communications too slow	16	Contract the company that developed the binary communications package to adapt the package to this project	H. Troy
4 System response time too slow	15	Enter a CPU upgrade agreement clause in the computer purchase contract	Y. Knot
2 Insufficient memory	8	(not considered)	

After the measure of severity has been calculated for each anticipated problem, the list is sorted according to the severity of the problems, with the most severe problem at the top of the list. A decision can then be made that any problem with a severity level less than some value (say 10), will not be considered. The remaining problems are then evaluated and a detailed course of action, called a *contingency plan*, is selected for each problem. The information is then entered into a *contingency table*. For each entry in the table, a member of the development team is assigned as *tracker*, to track the problem, and to alert project management when the contingency plan needs to be put into effect. This stage is demonstrated in Table 2.3.

Risk analysis is first performed as early in the project as possible, but no later than the end of the requirements phase (see Chapter 4). However, risk analysis is not a one-time activity. As the project progresses, additional problems may be anticipated and other problems may need to be removed from the problem list. As new information becomes available, the evaluation of the severity or the probability may be improved. Therefore, the risk analysis tables should be reviewed and updated periodically and whenever a significant event occurs (e.g. a subcontractor announces a schedule delay, or a major design decision is found to be incorrect).

2.2.3 Implementing contingency plans

Contingency plans are implemented in one of the following instances:

1. The anticipated problem occurs, or becomes imminent.
2. The contingency plan requires advance preparation.

Generally, contingency plans can be perceived as plans of action that are shelved for possible later use. However, in some cases, the plan is implemented *before* the anticipated problem occurs, such as the development of a simulator in case the delivery of a critical component is delayed. Then, if the component is delivered on time, the simulator can be discarded.

As an example of the complete process, let us consider a communications project involving a central computer connected by a wide area network to several small computer sites. Two potential problems have been identified:

- The two computers have different architectures that may interpret the designated communications protocol differently (e.g. the order of two byte words may be reversed – LSB MSB instead of MSB LSB).
- The selected phone company may not be able to install test lines in time for the integration phase.

Tables 2.4, 2.5 and 2.6 are the risk analysis tables for the communications project. If the availability of communications lines is delayed this will be slightly more damaging to the project than the incompatible protocol problem. The tracking of this problem has been assigned to William Doo. It is his responsibility to assure that lines are ordered from two other phone companies (for the integration phase only). If the preferred phone company is ready on time, then the orders from the other two companies will be canceled and possibly a cancelation fee paid.

Another engineer, Indira Hope, is responsible for tracking the incompatible communications protocol problem. She must assure that a simple ASCII communications package is ordered for both computers. The cost of the ASCII packages will be wasted if the selected binary protocol works. The alternative ASCII solution will most certainly be much slower, but it will provide a temporary solution until the incompatibility problem is resolved.

Table 2.4 Anticipated problem list

Problem	Description
1 Incompatible communications protocol	The two computers have different architectures that may interpret the designated communications protocol differently.
2 Test line late for integration	The selected phone company may not be able to install test lines in time for integration.

Table 2.5 Measure of severity

Problem	Expectation	Impact	Severity
1 Incompatible communications protocol	5	8	40
2 Test line late for integration	8	6	48

Table 2.6 Contingency table

Problem	Severity	Contingency plan	Tracker
2 Test line late for integration	48	Order line from two additional phone companies.	Will Doo
1 Incompatible communications protocol	40	Use an ASCII communications package.	I. Hope

2.3 SUMMARY

Modern project management methods are primarily concerned with *preventing* (and not *correcting*) project development problems. Preventing problems is easier and less costly than solving them. Effective preventive measures should:

- Locate problems and potential problems early
- Resolve problems before they get out of hand
- Plan ahead for potential problems

There are several basic problems common to almost all software projects. Most of these problems are derived from:

- Inadequate definition of requirements
- Frequent changes
- Poor estimates
- Dependence on external sources (vendors, subcontractors etc.)
- Difficulties in concluding the project
- Frequent replacement of the development personnel (staff turnover)
- Inadequate tracking and supervision

The best way to locate a problem early is to go looking for it. Clearly, the first place to look is where problems most frequently occur. For example, frequent and unchecked changes to the requirements specification are notorious as a major source of design problems. Unsupervised subcontractors and vendors are one of the most common sources of surprises, reporting technical problems and delays at the very last moment. For the project manager, knowing where to look is therefore as important as knowing what to do.

Knowing what to do includes being prepared for the appearance of a problem. In many cases, problems can be anticipated. The project manager can plan for the possibility that a problem will occur by estimating its probability, evaluating its impact, and preparing alternative solutions. This is referred to as *risk analysis*, and is an effective means of combating potential development problems.

Performing risk analysis means being prepared. It is a form of insurance, the basic idea being that if a problem occurs, a solution is readily available. Like all insurance, risk analysis usually comes with a price. The cost of preparing for the occurrence of a problem is primarily the cost of having the alternative solution at hand. In some cases, the cost may be minimal: the time needed to analyze and document the solution, and the time to track the problem. In other cases the cost may be substantial: the price of an alternative piece of development equipment. In any case, a problem that has been analyzed and resolved ahead of time is simpler to resolve than a problem that occurs unexpectedly.

EXERCISES

1. A new cable television service company is preparing to establish service in eight months' time. The company provides service to subscribers for a fixed monthly fee that depends on the extent of the service that they have ordered. The company also screens new movies, each of which can be viewed by a subscriber by telephone request to the company.

The company is now in the process of ordering equipment, purchasing facilities and signing up customers. A software company has been contracted to develop a billing system for the subscribers. The system will interface with the equipment to receive information on new movie screenings, and it will interface with the customer data base for regular monthly billing information.

Prepare a list of the 10 most critical problems that you anticipate in the development of the billing project. Discuss the reasoning behind your selection of problems.

2. Calculate a measure of severity for each of the potential problems you identified in Exercise 1. Explain your assignment of project impact and probability values.

Suggest an alternative method for assigning a measure of severity to anticipated problems that also takes into consideration the cost of preparing the contingency plans.

3. Suggest contingency plans for the anticipated problems you identified in Exercise 1. Consider two different alternative plans for each problem. Consider the cost of each alternative plan, and then select the best one based on the alternative method for assigning measures of severity that you suggested in Exercise 2.

Prepare a contingency table containing the contingency plans that you have selected.

4. Class exercise: divide the class into groups of three or four students. Assign Exercises 1, 2 and 3 to each group. Request each group to present their risk analysis to the rest of the class. Discuss (a) the different anticipated problem lists, (b) the different contingency plans and (c) the different methods for assigning a measure of severity (did any two groups suggest similar methods?).

THREE

SOFTWARE DEVELOPMENT UNDER CONTRACT

THE CUSTOMER–DEVELOPER RELATIONSHIP

Owing to the rapid advances in technology during the last several decades, it has become increasingly necessary for high technology organizations to specialize in specific, well-defined areas. Specialization has not only defined many new branches of engineering, it has also defined areas of expertise within the engineering disciplines. This is especially true of software engineering.

Frequently, organizations that do not specialize in software development hire other organizations that do so to develop software for them. Even organizations that do develop their own software may decide to hire outside specialists in specific areas. IBM hired Microsoft to develop the PC–DOS operating system, because Microsoft had experience in developing microcomputer systems and IBM had not.

This chapter deals with the relationship between customer and software developer, and provides some guidelines on how to avoid the classic pitfalls resulting from conflicting interests. Though many of these problems are common to all customer–developer relationships, some issues are specific to software development. The development of software is much less deterministic and more risky than other areas of technology. This often leads to misunderstandings and disagreements that could have been been avoided if they had been anticipated and contained early enough.

To standardize our terminology, the organization to whom a proposal is being submitted will be referred to as the *customer*, and the organization submitting the proposal will be referred to as the *proposer*. Other terms commonly used elsewhere for the proposer include *bidder*, *vendor* or *contractor* and for the customer *requestor* or *issuer*. The organization submitting the winning proposal, after being selected, will be referred to as the *developer*.

3.1 THE COST-PLUS vs FIXED PRICE DILEMMA

There is often a real or imagined conflict of interest between the developer and the customer. The customer wants to spend less and the developer wants to earn more. As we shall see, a good relationship between developer and customer need not necessarily lead to this conflict of interest.

There are basically two types of contractual relationship between the customer and the developer:

1.   Cost-plus (also called Time and material), and
2.   Fixed price

Most other relationships are some kind of combination of these two.

3.1.1 The cost-plus contract

Cost-plus is a contractual relationship where the developer is paid for the cost of the services provided and in addition is allowed an agreed profit margin. This is rather like renting a car; the customer pays for the time that the car is used (by the hour, day, week etc.), and for any other expenses such as insurance and gasoline. Thus, in a cost-plus contract the total cost of the project is only known after the project has been completed.

As an example, company Alpha may contract software company Beta to develop a system. Company Beta will be paid $80 by company Alpha for each hour invested by their engineers in the project. An additional 20 percent may then be added to cover managerial, secretarial and other office services. Additional expenses incurred by company Beta for the benefit of the project would then be reimbursed by company Alpha. These expenses might cover such areas as:

- Special purpose development equipment (computers, compilers, networks etc.)
- Travel expenses incurred by employees of company Beta for the benefit of the project
- Target equipment procured by company Beta for the use of company Alpha
- Services from other outside sources requested by company Beta for the project

The customer, company Alpha, may require the developer, company Beta, to receive prior authorization before incurring any single expense exceeding $250, and any expense in excess of a $6000 monthly total. Such authorization should always be in writing. This defines a basic cost-plus contractual relationship between the two companies.

In many cases, cost-plus can be the most appropriate way to contract development work. However, there are numerous potential problems. A conflict of interest may arise due to the developer's lack of motivation to complete the project as quickly as possible, or due to the customer's reluctance to authorize additional expenses.

Cost-plus is often appropriate for small undefined projects, when it is difficult to identify the project's requirements in advance. In fact, in many cases the requirements phase of a project is offered as a cost-plus contract, and the remaining phases are contracted at a fixed price. The requirements phase is then used to bring the rest of the project to a sufficiently well-defined state from which it can then be contracted at a fixed price. Occasionally, one company is awarded a cost-plus contract for the requirements phase, and another company is awarded the remaining phases as a fixed price contract.

Cost-plus may be preferred by the customer who wants to retain control of the development process. In some cases, the developer is perceived as an extension of the customer's organization, and the development activities are managed by the customer.

A cost-plus contract should cover the following issues:

- List of persons to be assigned to the project
- Work definition
- The assignment percentage for each person
- Hourly or daily work rate for each person
- Administrative overhead
- Authorized expenses to be reimbursed

- Billing procedure
- Payment procedure
- Termination procedure

The assignment percentage refers to the amount of time each person will be expected to devote to the project. This may be 100 percent for some engineers, and 50–60 percent for experts in specific areas. The assignment percentage may also be quoted in terms of maximum or minimum, meaning that, for example, a quality assurance engineer will devote no more than 20 hours a week to the project, and no fewer than 10 hours a week to the project.

The billing rate may be a fixed rate for all persons assigned to the project, or individual rates may be set for each person or class of people. For example, for each hour worked on the project, the developer will bill $80, irrespective of who worked that hour. Or the contract may stipulate that design engineers bill at $120 per hour, coders at $60 per hour, documentation writers at $50 per hour, and so forth. The most difficult cost-plus contract billing rate method is the individual billing method, where Frank Jones is billed at $90 per hour, John Smith at $75 etc. This means that each time a person is replaced or added to the project, the hourly rate must be renegotiated.

For a software development organization, there can be real advantages in cost-plus contracts. These include:

- No financial or business risk
- Acquisition of knowledge and experience at the expense of another organization

However, as in most cases, these advantages come with some disadvantages, which include:

- Low business profit
- Possible staff discontent
- Reduced control of staff and development work
- Potential friction with the customer due to a lack of well-defined goals and motivation factors
- Contract continuity is not assured

Most employees prefer a clear definition of the hierarchy to which they belong. In a cost-plus contract the employee works within the customer's hierarchy, but belongs to the developer's hierarchy, and this can cause discontent.

In general, from the developer's perspective, a cost-plus contract is a solid, low profit, no risk business relationship.

From the customer's perspective, the advantages of a cost-plus contract are:

- Retention of control over development
- No commitment needed for a full project contract
- A possible reduced business risk (due to the ability to terminate the contract at any time)

The customer's possible disadvantages are:

- Increased development costs
- Customer's assumption of development risks
- Increased involvement in development
- Potential friction with the developer due to a lack of well-defined goals and motivation factors

For the customer, the desirability of a cost-plus contract is difficult to establish. Clearly, this is dependent on the type of project and the conditions under which it will be developed, as well as on other non-technical business considerations.

3.1.2 The fixed price contract

A fixed price contract is a commitment by the developer to provide an agreed product or service for an agreed fee, within an agreed schedule. This is similar to purchasing a bus ticket, where the bus company agrees to take the customer to a specific destination within a published timetable, and for an agreed fee. Of course, travelers can elect to rent a car, instead of purchasing a bus ticket, and then drive to their destinations themselves. However, this may turn out to be more expensive, and requires of the traveler some prior skills and knowledge, such as driving skills and knowledge of the route to the destination. So travelers (or customers) must decide between providing the service themselves and contracting someone else to provide the service.

A fixed price contract can only be applied to a well-defined project. Both customer and developer must be able to define the final deliverable product or service. Once this has been achieved, one of the main weaknesses of the fixed price contract will have been removed.

The advantages of a fixed price contract for the developer include:

- Full control of the development process
- Possible higher business profit
- Commitment for a complete project

The commitment for a complete project is a significant advantage over cost-plus contracts that may end at any time, at the customer's discretion. Of course, fixed price contracts also have some disadvantages for the developer, which include:

- Assumption of business and development risks
- Potential friction with the customer due to:
  - continuing requirement changes
  - project completion criteria
  - interpretation of requirements

A successful software organization will often prefer a fixed price contract. These are usually the projects that build a company's professional reputation, and generate profit to enable growth. Unfortunately, these are also the projects that generate loss, and which often severely harm a company. Stiff competition for an important contract occasionally tempts a company to underbid, which ultimately generates losses for the developer.

It is almost inevitable in any project that the developer will be requested to change the requirements during development. Such changes are usually associated with additional cost to the customer, and are invariably a cause of disagreement between developer and customer. This is often due to unclear or ambiguous requirements, which in turn lead to disagreements regarding the criteria for project completion. This, essentially, returns the contract to an insufficiently defined state.

From the customer's perspective, the advantages in a fixed price contract include:

- A fixed budget for the project
- Most of the development risks are transferred to the developer
- Minimal involvement in the development process

The disadvantages to the customer are:

- Risk of late delivery by the developer
- Reduced control of the development process
- Potential friction with the developer due to:
  -high cost of requirement changes
  -unclear project completion criteria
  -interpretation of requirements

Even though the interests of the developer and the customer may be different, fixed price contracts are still often preferred by both parties. If the project is sufficiently detailed and clear, and if the relationship between the two parties is well defined, then fixed price contracts can be beneficial to both the developer and the customer.

3.2 OTHER CUSTOMER–DEVELOPER RELATIONSHIPS

Cost-plus and fixed price are two of the traditional contractual relationships between developer and customer. There are many variations of these two basic relationships, including various combinations that are tailored to suit specific projects. Some of these relationships are associated with the roles of customer and developer, and attempt to provide more incentives for the developer to support the customer's objectives beyond contractual obligations.

Additional types of customer–developer relationship include:

- Combinations of fixed price and cost-plus
- Joint ventures
- Royalty agreements
- Long-term commitments

We have discussed in Section 3.1 an example of a combined cost-plus and fixed price project, where the requirements are developed at cost-plus and the remainder of the project is developed at fixed price.

Joint ventures are instances where the customer–developer dividing line can become hazy, and many of the previously discussed advantages and disadvantages may not apply. There are many cases where some form of joint venture may be desirable for both parties, such as when the developer wants to retain rights to the product, or when the developer joins the customer in funding part of the development effort.

One way the customer can offer the developer moderate participation in the business aspect of the project is by substituting royalties as partial payment. This generates an added dimension to the developer's interest in the success of the project. The royalties are usually such that the failure of the project would produce less revenue for the developer than a straightforward fixed price contract, and the success of the project will increase the developer's revenue.

Long-term relationships are often important for the developer. In many cases, long-term commitments are also in the customer's interest. This occurs when the developer, by being awarded the initial contract, gains, through acquired knowledge, a major advantage over others for subsequent development work. Clearly, when the developer successfully completes a large and complex project, a significant advantage is then acquired over other companies with respect to future extensions of the project. A long-term commitment may then be of mutual interest to both parties, wherein the customer assures future services from the developer and the developer assures a long-term income commitment.

3.3 THE REQUEST FOR PROPOSAL (RFP)

Software development under contract starts with the selection of the software developer by the customer. A *request for proposal*, or *RFP* (also called in Britain an *invitation to tender*) is the beginning of the selection process. To understand how an RFP should be prepared, we will first review the steps leading up to the decision to request proposals.

In the phased approach to software development the pre-project phase is often referred to as the *conception phase*. This is the stage where the idea behind the project crystallizes and takes form, and decisions are made by the organization on whether or not to proceed with the project. This is also the stage where the organization decides whether the project can be developed in-house, or whether it will be contracted out to another company.

RFPs are not only issued for complete projects; they may also be issued for software maintenance of an existing system, or for a single phase of a project. All well prepared RFPs must contain the same basic information; incomplete RFPs result in incomplete proposals.

3.3.1 Some basic issues

Before hiring the development services of another organization, some basic issues need to be considered:

- What are the objectives of the project?
- Which organizations are to be considered for the job?
- What type of contract will be offered (fixed price, cost-plus etc.)?
- What responses must be received from potential developers so that they can be considered?
- When must the developer selection process be completed?
- When must the project be completed and when must intermediate components be ready?
- Who, within the organization, will be assigned the responsibility of selecting the developer?
- What budget range will be allocated for the contract?

All of the above issues must be adequately addressed before taking the next step: the preparation of the RFP.

3.3.2 Preparation of the RFP

A good request for proposal is one that will draw the best responses (proposals). The preparation of a good RFP often requires the cooperation of many people, each of whom is assigned responsibility for specific sections of the RFP.

An RFP should include the following sections:

1. *Statement of the problem and project objectives*
   This section provides general background information, including a description of the problem that is to be solved. The section should provide all relevant details necessary to understand the problem, including diagrams, reports and examples.
2. *Technical requirements*
   This section describes specific technical requirements of the system, such as:
   - Interfaces to existing systems
   - Data base requirements (such as required capacity, data relationships etc.)
   - Communications and network architecture

- Military, government or other required standards
- Required development methodologies
- Reliability of the system
- Timing constraints
- Programming language
- Host computer

3. *Administrative information*

This section provides information regarding the physical submission of the proposal, such as:

- Who may respond to the RFP
- How to request clarifications or additional information
- Date and location of a scheduled meeting with all potential proposers
- The proposal selection criteria

This section may also contain a provision to the effect that the organization issuing the RFP will not be obliged to select the lowest cost proposal, or any other proposal.

4. *Cost requirements*

All financial issues are addressed in this section. This includes the pricing structure required in the proposal, as well as any specific information that is to be addressed in the proposal (such as justification of costs, or separate pricing for each phase). This section may also specify what type of development contract will be offered (cost-plus, fixed price, royalties etc.)

5. *Referenced documents*

This section contains a list of all relevant documents addressed in the RFP, such as standards, existing system documentation, various product literature etc.

6. *Required deliverables*

This section contains an initial version of the statement of work (SOW). This is mainly a list of the main project deliverables, such as documentation, software, training and any relevant hardware or equipment. This section may also discuss the required warranty for the delivered system.

7. *Required proposal format*

The required standard format for the proposal is described in this section. This includes the required content of:

- The technical proposal
- The management proposal
- The pricing proposal
- The statement of work

An example of a proposal outline appears in Section 3.4.

This section also contains a list of all information that should be appended to the proposal. Apart from the basic proposal (according to the format described above) this may include the latest financial report of the proposer's organization, or the proposer's technical credentials.

8. *Submission schedule and decision schedule*

The critical dates relating to the RFP are described in this section. This includes the latest date for submission of the proposal, and the expected date by which a selection will be made. This may also include a tentative schedule for the completion of the development work.

One of the objectives of the RFP is to ease the task of comparing different proposals. This

Table 3.1 General outline for an RFP

1. Statement of the problem and project objectives
   - description of current state
   - description of the problem
   - support documentation
     - reports
     - diagrams
     - examples
   - objectives
2. Technical requirements
   - interfaces to existing systems
   - data base requirements
   - communications and network architecture
   - military or government standards
   - reliability of the system
   - timing constraints
   - programming language
   - host computer
3. Administrative information
   - who may respond to the RFP
   - how to request clarifications or additional information
   - date and location of a scheduled meeting with all potential proposers
   - the proposal selection criteria
   - other administrative information
4. Cost requirements
   - pricing structure
     - services
     - products
     - procurement
   - justification of costs
   - separate pricing for each phase
   - type of development contract offered
   - cost comparisons of alternative solutions
5. Referenced documents
   - standards
   - existing system documentation
   - product literature
6. Required deliverables
   - documentation
   - software
   - training
   - relevant hardware or equipment
   - warranty for the delivered system
   - development and test tools
7. Proposal format
   - technical proposal
   - management proposal
   - pricing proposal
   - statement of work
   - supplements and appendices
     - financial report of proposer's organization
     - the proposer's technical credentials
     - résumés of key personnel
8. Submission schedule and decision schedule
   - latest date for submission of the proposal
   - expected date by which a selection will be made
   - preferred schedule for the completion of the development work

task can become extremely difficult if all proposals are constructed differently, or if they are based on very different assumptions. Section 3 of the outline refers to a meeting with all potential proposers. This meeting provides an opportunity to assure that all proposers have a common basis of understanding, and results in their proposals being easier to compare. This is also achieved by requiring the standardized proposal format, referred to in Section 7 of the RFP. Table 3.1 contains a general outline of an RFP.

3.3.3 Issuing the RFP

There are three basic methods for distributing an RFP:

- According to a limited distribution list
- According to a broad distribution list
- To all who request it

A limited distribution list contains only those organizations that have been selected according to a specific set of criteria. Various government agencies maintain a list of authorized companies for each class of RFPs. This method precludes organizations that have little chance of being selected.

A broad distribution list includes any organization that has *any* chance of being selected. For an organization to be added to the list, it need only request it. Broad distribution lists may be appropriate for small projects, projects requiring no special expertise, or projects for which few appropriate organizations have been located.

It is not uncommon for initial RFP information to be advertised in the press or in professional journals. These announcements contain a short description of the RFP and invite companies to request a copy of the full RFP. This approach is often appropriate when new potential proposers are being sought.

Whichever distribution method is selected, the organization issuing the RFP must remember that the issuing procedure does not end with the distribution of the RFP. The issuing organization should be ready to provide any additional information and clarifications that may be requested. One way to achieve this, which has already been mentioned, is to schedule a meeting with all potential proposers in order to provide clarifications and to answer any questions. This meeting is also an opportunity for the proposers to tour the target plant and to see at first-hand the problems that will be resolved by the project.

3.4 THE PROPOSAL

The various types of proposal can be divided into two basic categories:

- Solicited proposals and
- Unsolicited proposals

The solicited proposal responds either to a formal RFP or to a specific invitation to submit a proposal, while the unsolicited proposal is usually initiated by the proposer. There are, of course, various combinations of the two, such as the strange but common situation where a company is urged to submit an unsolicited proposal, or when an unsolicited proposal triggers the issuance of a formal RFP.

3.4.1 The unsolicited proposal

Unsolicited proposals are much less formal than the solicited proposal, and they are often no more than a first step leading to more formal negotiations. An unsolicited proposal should contain the following basic sections:

1. Justification for the submission of the proposal
2. A description of the problem that is to be solved
3. A description of the proposed solution
4. A description of the proposer's organization
5. A general overview of the cost of the proposed solution

The justification section is vital, as it explains why the customer should read on. This section may proclaim, for example, that the proposer has developed a new and successful technology that would benefit the customer, and could be adapted to the needs of the customer's organization. The main objective is to provide an answer to the customer's question: 'Why has this company approached me, and why is it to my benefit to read the proposal?'.

Sections 2 and 3 describe the way the proposer's specialized knowledge will be applied to the problems of the customer's organization. This requires the proposer to study the customer's organization in order to assure the proposal provides a *real* solution to a *real* problem.

The precise cost of the solution need not be provided at this stage. An unsolicited proposal is rarely accepted first time around. Its main objective is to generate interest. If the proposal generates sufficient interest, the proposer will be invited to discuss the proposal, and will then resubmit to the customer a more detailed version of the proposal.

3.4.2 Solicited proposals

A solicited proposal is initiated by the customer as a response to a formal RFP or to some other form of invitation to submit a proposal. Contrary to the informal nature of the unsolicited proposal, the solicited proposal is complete and detailed, and its content is often binding on the proposer.[1]

Together with the request to submit a proposal, the customer may also specify exactly how the proposal is to be prepared and submitted. An example of a formal proposal format appears in Table 3.2.

One basic area in which solicited and unsolicited proposals differ is in the need to be competitive. Solicited proposals must be capable of competing successfully with other proposals. This means that the preparation of a solicited proposal must be regarded as a mini-project in itself, and as such requires the formation of a proposal preparation team.

3.4.3 The proposal preparation team

The formation of a proposal board is fundamental to any organization that expects to respond successfully to an RFP. This board designates a person whose job it is to locate suitable RFPs and submit them for discussion, based on a set of guidelines established by the board. These guidelines should address RFPs that:

---

1. The proposal as a binding document is further discussed and illustrated in the introduction to Chapter 11.

- Are within the company's line of business
- Are within specific limits of size (projects that are not too small and not too large)
- Do not obviously preclude the company (e.g. requiring special expertise or security clearance)

Based on its evaluation of the RFPs submitted, the proposal board decides which RFPs will be responded to by the company.

The proposal board then selects a team for the preparation of each proposal. This team may contain a single person, or many team members, depending on the size of the proposed project. The team draws from the experience and expertise of all company employees, and, if necessary, may engage the services of outside experts to assist in the preparation of the proposal.

The basic knowledge required within a proposal preparation team includes:

- Technical knowledge relating to each separate area addressed by the proposal
- Project management, including estimation and planning
- Financial knowledge, including budgeting and finance planning for the whole project
- Familiarity with the customer's organization
- Experience in writing proposals

One member of the team will be designated team leader, or coordinator, by the proposal board. After the team has been assembled, its first two assignments should be:

1. An initial review of the RFP
2. The preparation of a schedule for the completion of the proposal, and the assignment of responsibilities

The preparation of a good proposal costs money, and should be regarded as an investment. If it is done well, it can produce a profit. An inadequate proposal budget will reduce the chances of producing a winning proposal. The members of the proposal preparation team should be dedicated to the task, and they must be provided with adequate resources.

According to Silver (1986), proposals in high technology and aerospace industries are budgeted at around 2 percent of the amount of the contract. However, the range of proposal cost is 1 percent to 10 percent. The higher the cost of the contract, the lower the percentage that is devoted to the preparation of the proposal.[2]

3.4.4 The proposal format

A good proposal should provide answers to six basic questions: *who, what, why, how, when* and *how much*. Responses to these questions simply refer to:

1. *Who* is the organization submitting the proposal?
2. *What* is being proposed?
3. *Why* is the proposal being submitted?
4. *How* will the proposed work be implemented?
5. *When* will it be developed and delivered?
6. *How much* will it cost?

---

2. Silver presents a project contract range of $10K to $2B, with a proposal cost range from 1 percent to 20 percent in the United States, and a contract range of $10K to $1B with a proposal cost range of 1 percent to 10 percent in Europe. With regard to most projects, between $250K and $100M, he presents a proposal cost range of 1.5 percent to 8 percent in the United States, and 1 percent to 2.5 percent in Europe.

The *why* question is important for an unsolicited proposal, and provides the basis for its submission. A response to an RFP would simply state 'This proposal is being submitted in response to Acme Inc.'s request for proposal No.456 of 5 June, . . . '.

The other five questions are addressed in the five main components of the proposal:

1. The technical proposal (*what*, *how*)
2. The management proposal (*how*, *when*)
3. The pricing proposal (*how much*)
4. The statement of work (*what*, *when*)
5. Executive summary

and in the supplements, which include:

- Company background and experience (*who*)
- Qualifications of key personnel
- Exhibits and relevant documents

The executive summary is especially important for large and complex proposals, as not all selection board members will read the proposal. The summary should be between one and six pages in length, and should include references to specific areas in the full proposal which provide more detail.

Tables 3.2, 3.3 and 3.4 present examples of outlines for the technical, management and pricing proposals for a software project.

Table 3.2 Sample outline for a technical proposal

1. Overview of the problem to be solved
2. Overview of the proposed solution
3. Components to be purchased
4. Components to be developed
5. Equipment
   - infrastructure
   - computer hardware
   - communications and networks
   - test and verification equipment
   - other special equipment
   - interfaces to other systems
6. Software components
   - general description of the software system
   - detailed description of each major software component
   - interfaces to other systems
   - data bases
   - use of existing software components
   - reusability of software components to be developed
7. Human engineering and user interfaces
8. Special considerations
   - reliability
   - timing
   - data integrity
   - backup and recovery

Table 3.3 Sample outline for a management proposal

1. Development tools and utilities
2. Development environment
3. Personnel requirements and development team structure
4. Development methodology
5. Development phases
6. Reviews
7. Reporting
   - types of reports
   - report formats
   - reporting frequency
   - distribution list
8. Subcontractors
9. Standards
10. Testing
    - testing stages
    - formal testing procedures
    - error detection and correction
11. Quality control
12. Configuration management
13. Maintenance
14. Schedule
    - major activities list
    - milestones
    - dependencies
    - staffing
15. Risk management

Table 3.4 Sample outline for a pricing proposal

1. Type of contract (fixed price, cost-plus etc.)
2. Development cost by project component
3. Subcontractor costs
4. Procurement costs
5. Overhead
6. Warranty
7. Profit
8. Total project cost
9. Type of financing (negative, positive)
10. Payment schedule
11. Billing and administration

3.4.5 The statement of work (SOW)

The statement of work is the basis of the contract between the proposer and the customer, and is often incorporated into the contract. The SOW contains a detailed list of all work to be performed by the proposer for the benefit of the customer.

The SOW starts as a general list of required deliverables in the RFP. A more detailed version of the SOW is submitted as part of the proposal, and is still considered only an initial description of the work to be performed. The binding version of the SOW is finalized during contract negotiations, or after the detailed project requirements have been completed.

Table 3.5 presents an example of an SOW outline for a software project. The list of items varies considerably, depending on the type of project being developed; for example not all projects include the delivery of hardware components, and not all projects require training or installation.

Table 3.5 A sample SOW outline for a software project

1. Referenced documents
   - requirements specification
   - existing system description
   - customer's RFP
   - developer's proposal
   - vendor's and developer's technical literature
2. Software deliverables
   - functionality (as documented in the requirements specification)
   - list of major software components
3. Equipment and hardware deliverables
   - functionality (as documented in the requirements specification)
   - list of major hardware components
4. Training
   - user courses
   - operator training
   - installation training
5. Market research
6. Procurement
7. Supervision of subcontractors
8. Documentation
   - development documentation
   - user documentation
   - maintenance documentation
   - other technical documentation
9. Testing
   - alpha testing
   - beta testing
   - acceptance tests (ATP)
10. Installation
11. Maintenance services
12. Other services and deliverable items
13. Method of delivery
    - software
    - documentation
    - hardware

The basic guideline for the preparation of the SOW is that any activity, service or product required by the customer, and agreed to by the developer, must be included. This means that there can be no binding work items that were informally *understood*, or agreed to verbally, which do not appear in the SOW. The formal SOW must include all and only the work to be performed. This condition prevents misunderstandings and disagreements later, after the project begins.

3.5 THE PROPOSAL REVIEW AND SELECTION PROCESS

After the proposals have been submitted, the review and selection process begins. This section discusses the review process from a technical perspective. Undeniably, the review process is far from being purely technical. Few proposal selection processes are totally objective. Selection boards are composed of people, all of whom come with their own preferences and inclinations.

In fact, there are many cases where the proposal selection process is totally subjective. This includes cases of personal influence, familiarity and friendship between customer and contractor, unfounded bias in favor of one company, or unfounded prejudice against another. Such situations are difficult to overcome, and often more difficult to discover. These situations can be combated with some degree of effectiveness through psychological sales and marketing techniques that are beyond the scope of this book.

3.5.1 The proposal selection board

A proposal selection board is a group of people appointed to review and evaluate proposals, and to recommend one of the proposals according to a predetermined set of criteria. This may be a set of general guidelines, or an extremely formal set of evaluation factors and procedures.

Many large organizations have formalized the proposal evaluation procedure.[3] This usually includes three separate channels for technical, management and cost evaluation. Each component of the proposal is graded according to a specific evaluation procedure, and a combination of the individual grades produces the final grade for the proposal.

Proposals for small and large projects alike should be evaluated according to a systematic and relatively objective procedure. Based on its evaluation, the proposal selection board then submits its recommendation together with a summary of the data, calculations and evaluations that led to the selection. Frequently, two or three recommendations are submitted, and a second iteration is started with the selected companies to choose the winning proposal.

This list of companies for the second iteration is often referred to as the *short list*, and the second round of proposal discussions is referred to as the *best and final*.

3.5.2 Proposal evaluation method

Most proposal evaluation methods are based on some variation of the weighted technique, where a number of factors score points that are then weighted and combined to provide an overall grade for the proposal.

Silver (1986) suggests a rating technique for each factor that is similar to Table 3.6. Note that the description of the lower ratings takes into account that an opportunity may be provided to the proposer to correct the item being scored.

The rating technique described in Table 3.6 is then applied to each major component of the proposal, and a weighted average is then calculated. As an example, the four major components of the proposal may be weighted as follows:

Technical	35%
Management	25%
Cost	30%
Company background	10%

3. For example, the US DOD has issued Directives 5000.1 *Major Systems Acquisition*, and 4105-62 *Proposal Evaluation and Source Selection*, and DOD FAR Supplement 15.6 *Source Selection*. NASA has issued Directive 5103.6a *Source Evaluation Board Manual*, and FAR Supplement 18-16.608-70 *Proposal Evaluation*.

Table 3.6 A sample rating scale for proposal evaluation

Grade	Rating	Description
9–10	Superior	High degree of expertise knowledge or competence; highly acceptable; comprehensive; leaves very little else to be desired
7–8	Good	Satisfactory level of expertise or knowledge; acceptable; comprehensive; generally does not require additional information or clarification
5–6	Fair	Minimally acceptable level of expertise or knowledge; requires additional information or clarification
3–4	Poor	Below minimally acceptable level; requires considerable improvement; indicates a low level of expertise or knowledge
0–2	Rejected	Lack of capability to perform the work; data cannot be evaluated or not provided

This means that more importance is attached to the technical component of the proposal than to any other component.

The weighted average can be further refined. An additional acceptance criterion may state that any proposal that rates less than 5 out of 10 in any one major component will be rejected, irrespective of its final weighted score. This means, for example, that no matter how good the technical, management and cost proposals are, if the company background is weak, the overall proposal will be rejected.

Table 3.7 presents an example of the weighted items within the management component of the proposal. Similar tables should be prepared for the items comprising each of the major components of the proposal. Both the list of items to be scored and the individual weights may be tailored for each RFP, but this tailoring should be done in advance of the evaluation and selection process. A general master version of the evaluation tables should be maintained as a basis for each new project.

Table 3.7 Management proposal items – evaluation weights

1. Schedule		23%
final completion date	12%	
likelihood	5%	
milestones	4%	
level of detail	2%	
2. Staffing		16%
key personnel	11%	
development team structure	5%	
3. Development control		17%
quality control	7%	
testing	7%	
configuration management	3%	
4. Subcontractors		12%
5. Maintenance		10%
6. Risk management		8%
7. Development methodology		5%
8. Development environment		5%
9. Development tools and utilities		4%
		100%

3.6 SOME ADDITIONAL PROPOSAL CONSIDERATIONS

Software development is much less deterministic than other areas of high technology. It is usually much easier to estimate the factors of a hardware or electronics development project than the factors of a software project. Experience has shown that substantial software project overruns have been much more frequent, and much more extensive, than in other areas of technology. This means that software proposals require special attention in specific areas, such as scheduling, risk analysis, personnel management and costing. These areas are important in *any* area of technology development, but much more so in the development of software.

Both the customer and the proposer must be aware of these and other special peculiarities of software development. The customer should devote special attention to these areas when evaluating proposals, just as the proposer should devote special attention to them when preparing a proposal.

3.6.1 Issues relating to the customer

When preparing an RFP, one of the customer's most common dilemmas is just how much detail to provide. Too much detail may discourage proposers from offering their own solutions, while too little detail may generate unsuitable solutions due to lack of information. The customer usually has some idea of how the problem should be solved. If the customer's ideas are firm, then these ideas need to be detailed in the RFP. However, if the proposers are given the freedom to propose their own solution, then one of these solutions may be considerably better than the one visualized by the customer.

The customer has many other concerns, such as what happens if the requirements change. To what degree will the RFP lock the customer into an airtight solution that will be difficult to change? Or what happens to an urgent project which simply does not provide enough time to complete a good proposal evaluation procedure?

The following is a summary of these and other issues that should be addressed *before* the RFP is released.

1. *The degree of detail*
    Specific problems usually require specific solutions. If the problem is narrow and well defined, or if the customer has a specific solution in mind, then considerable detail should be provided in the RFP.

2. *Evaluating the proposals*
    Objective evaluation of the proposals is not easy to achieve. At least two people should evaluate and score each item in the proposals, and an average should be calculated. If the scores differ greatly, then a third (and even fourth) person should score the item, and the two (or three) closest scores should then be averaged.

3. *Changes to the requirements*
    The formal project agreement between the developer and the customer should allow for a reasonable number of changes (early in the project). This requirement can be included as part of the RFP. The application of the term *reasonable* should take into consideration the customer's valid need to correct errors in the project requirements on the one hand, and the developer's need to avoid disruption of the cost and schedule calculations on the other.

4. *Gaining time*
    The process of issuing an RFP, evaluating proposals and completing negotiations can be

time-consuming. In some cases the project may be urgent, with the development work subject to a critical time frame.

One of the ways to save time is for the customer to permit development work to start immediately upon the selection of the winning proposal. This is usually done by issuing a letter of intent (LOI) to the selected developer. The customer's risk in an LOI can be reduced by limiting the developer to a specific budget until the final contract is signed.

5. *Joint proposals*
    One of the main problems with a joint proposal is the lack of a clear definition of responsibility. Joint proposals must always assign overall responsibility to one party. Other participants in the proposal, such as subcontractors, should be defined.

3.6.2 Issues relating to the proposer

There is no sure method for writing a winning proposal. Questions regarding technical and architectural issues, the inclusion of options, or the submission of multiple solutions depend on the type of proposal and the circumstances within which it is being submitted. The following are some general guidelines for the preparation of a proposal.

1. *The appearance of the proposal*
    The outside appearance of the proposal is almost as important as its content. Few slovenly, haphazard proposals are selected as winning proposals. Significant attention should be devoted by the proposer to the cosmetics of the text, graphics, binding, slides and any accompanying verbal presentations.

2. *Optional requirements*
    An RFP may also include *optional* requirements. These are additional features or capabilities that are not absolutely necessary for the completion of the project, but are what is often referred to as *nice to have*. A proposal that includes the optional features may gain points with the proposal review board.

    Optional features are best addressed within a supplementary section of the proposal, and should be priced and scheduled separately.

3. *All requirements*
    A proposal need not respond to *all* the RFP requirements. It must, however, reference all requirements to demonstrate that they have not been overlooked. Deviations from the RFP must be justified and explained.

4. *Alternative solutions*
    A proposal may include more than one proposed solution. However, alternative solutions must be submitted separately, so that they can be addressed and evaluated separately. Alternatives need not repeat complete sections in the first solution proposed; they can reference them (e.g. 'The development team organization for the Distributed Processing solution will be the same as for the Centralized System solution.').

5. *Professional tools*
    Automated utilities and tools should be used to assist in the preparation of a proposal. Apart from the obvious word processors and spelling checkers, such tools as scheduling packages, design and requirement generators, graphics packages etc. can save a significant amount of effort and time in preparing a professional proposal. A list of tools and utilities is included in a bibliography published by Tahvanainen and Smolander (1990).

3.7 SUMMARY

This chapter deals with the relationship between customer and software developer, and the preparation, submission and evaluation of proposals. It also provides some guidelines on how to avoid the classic pitfalls resulting from the conflicting interests of the customer and the developer. Though many of these problems are common to all customer–developer relationships, some issues are specific to software development.

There are basically two types of contractual relationship between the customer and the developer:

1. Cost-plus (also called Time and material), and
2. Fixed price

Most other relationships are some kind of combination of these two.

Cost-plus is a contractual relationship where the developer is paid for the cost of the services provided and in addition is allowed an agreed profit margin. Cost-plus is often appropriate for small, undefined projects, when it is difficult to identify the project's requirements in advance. Cost-plus may be preferred by the customer who wants to retain control of the development process.

A fixed price contract is a commitment by the developer to provide an agreed product or service for an agreed fee, within an agreed schedule. If the project is sufficiently detailed and clear, and if the relationship between the two parties is well defined, then fixed price can be beneficial to both parties.

There are many variations of these two basic relationships, including various combinations that are tailored to suit specific projects.

Software development under contract starts with the selection of the software developer by the customer. This is usually accomplished by issuing a request for proposal (RFP).

There are two basic categories of proposal: solicited proposals and unsolicited proposals. The solicited proposal responds either to a formal RFP or to a specific invitation to submit a proposal, while the unsolicited proposal is usually initiated by the proposer.

After their submission to the customer, all proposals are reviewed by a selection board. Proposals for small and large projects alike should be evaluated according to a systematic and relatively objective procedure. Frequently, two or three recommendations are submitted, and a second iteration is then started with the selected companies to choose the winning proposal and to produce an agreed development contract.

EXERCISES

1. The Acme Trucking Company has a fleet of 500 trucks, with 30 truck depots around the country. Acme dispatches trucks on delivery routes. Each trip begins at the closest depot to the start of the route that has an available truck, and ends at the closest depot to the end of the route. Acme wants to develop a computerized dispatching system to optimize the use of their trucks.

Discuss the advantages and disadvantages to Acme, and to a project developer, assuming different types of development contracts.

2. Prepare an RFP for Acme's truck scheduling project. Include the Technical requirements section, the Required deliverables section, and the Administrative information section, and an outline for all other major RFP sections.

3. Prepare a proposal to be submitted to Acme for the truck scheduling project. Include the technical proposal, the statement of work, and the executive summary, and an outline for all other major sections (including supplements).

4. Prepare the review and selection method and criteria for Acme's proposal selection board. Assign the weights for the four major components of the proposal and for the weighted items within each major component.

Discuss any special review and selection criteria, such as minimum grades for certain items, or major components.

Explain the reasoning behind the review method that you have described.

5. Class exercise: select one of the RFPs prepared in Exercise 2 as the RFP for the Acme truck scheduling project. Designate three to five proposal preparation teams to prepare proposals in response to the RFP.

Designate a proposal review board to review the proposals and to select the winning proposal.

Discuss the review and selection procedure.

FOUR

THE SOFTWARE DEVELOPMENT CYCLE

VARIATIONS ON A WATERFALL THEME

Software development, just like most other activities, has a beginning, a middle and an end. The end of one development activity is sometimes perceived as being linked to the beginning of a new development activity thus producing a cycle of beginning–middle–end, link, beginning–middle–end, link, and so forth. This view of software development is referred to as the *software development life cycle*.

There are many variations of the software development life cycle. Figure 4.1 presents a simple life cycle that was common during the first few decades of software development. In those early days of software development, the programmer would create programs by iterating from code to fix then back to code, and then to fix again, until something acceptable was (hopefully) produced. At the start of the cycle, there was usually no clear concept of what was required, and the basic development procedure was a form of 'let's see what we can do' approach.

The software development method represented by the development cycle in Fig. 4.1 is often referred to as the *code and fix* method (for obvious reasons). Software development methodologies have come a long way since the days of code and fix, though it is surprising how much software is still being developed this way.

Successful management of any project, especially software projects, requires planning, and planning is impossible with code and fix, which is totally unpredictable. Management of software development within an engineering discipline is based on a much more orderly set of development phases. These phases are not implemented solely by programmers; they require software engineers. In fact, programming has become a relatively small part of the modern software development cycle, as is evident from Table 4.1.

The numbers in Table 4.1 are derived from the general shift in emphasis to software planning (requirements and design) and testing. Commercial data processing systems, with some exceptions, still spend a significant amount of development time in the programming and unit testing phase. Real-time systems are often more complex, and may include extensive hardware/software integration. This usually requires more planning and more integration and testing.

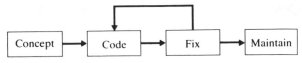

Figure 4.1 The code and fix method.

Table 4.1 Estimated percentage of time spent in each major software development phase

	Planning	Code and unit test	Integration and test
Commercial data processing	25%	40%	35%
Real-time systems	35%	25%	40%
Military systems	40%	20%	40%

Military systems require high reliability and are usually closely supervised by the customer, leading to a significant increase in the time spent in planning.

The data in Table 4.1, of course, represents a generalization; commercial data processing systems can be just as complex as a real-time system (see Section 4.4 for further discussion of this topic).

Figure 4.2 presents the basic phased model of a software development cycle. This model, called the Waterfall model, gets its name from the way in which each phase cascades into the next (due to overlapping), as demonstrated in Fig. 4.3. Some interpretations of the Waterfall model, like the one that follows, combine the top level design and the detailed design phases into a single design phase, and the integration and test phases into a single phase. In fact, there are many variations of the classic Waterfall model, but they are all based upon a systematic transition from one development phase to the next, until the project is complete.

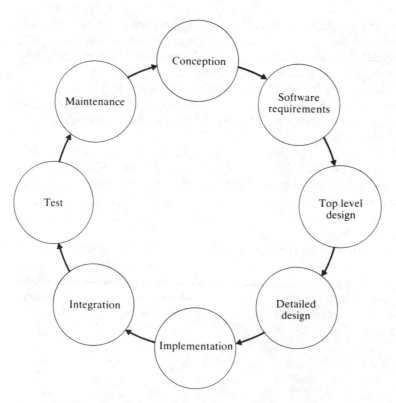

Figure 4.2 The phased model of the software development life cycle.

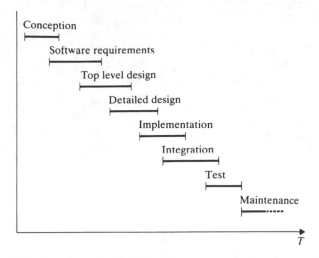

Figure 4.3 The Waterfall model of the software development life cycle.

There are other development methodologies that do not move from one phase to the next like the Waterfall model. Rapid prototyping, for instance, iterates in a mini-development phase until a system prototype is developed (see Fig. 4.4). After the prototype is complete, the Waterfall approach can then be implemented to complete the full system. Rapid prototyping is particularly helpful in projects where the requirements are difficult to specify. The prototype can be used as a tool for analyzing and determining what the requirements should be.

The Spiral model, described by Boehm (1988), is another development method that iterates between the requirements, design and implementation phases. However, the Spiral model continues iterating until the final system is complete. Within each iteration, the Spiral model follows a phased approach similar to the Waterfall model.

Different models may be suitable for different software projects or for different software development organizations. However, a good model must include certain fundamental features. Some of these basic requirements are discussed in IEEE Standard (IEEE 1993) *Standard for Software Life Cycle Processes*. This standard describes the processes that are mandatory for the development of software and specifies the activities that must be included in the life cycle model. This standard is discussed further in Section 4.7.

Most modern software development models, and certainly those following IEEE Standard 1074, include some form of the basic phased model. It is therefore important to understand the different phases and how they relate to one another. This chapter describes some of the management issues associated with the phased model, including the atmosphere and the problems that characterize each phase.

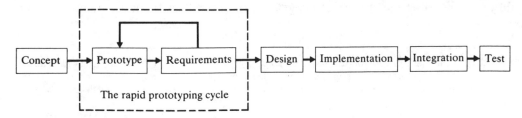

Figure 4.4 Rapid prototyping followed by the phase method.

4.1 THE CONCEPT PHASE

The Waterfall model begins with an initial *concept phase*, during which the need for the software system is determined and the basic concept of the software system evolves. This phase, also named the *concept exploration phase* by the IEEE[1] provides the basis for:

- The preparation of a request for proposal (RFP); the RFP is useful when projects are contracted out to other developers (see Chapter 3).
- The definition of the software requirements (the next phase).
- Initial planning and preparation of estimates; this often serves as an early version of the project development plan.

The concept phase produces two types of project documents:

- The product description
- A concept document

The product description is primarily a marketing document, and is used as a future product announcement or as a general overview of the product. The concept document is a technical document and forms the basis for the main technical activities of this phase (RFP, initial planning). The concept document is also one of the main sources of reference for the production of the software requirements during the next phase of the project.

The concept phase is not a mandatory formal development phase. It is often conducted informally, before any commitment is made to further development of the project.

4.1.1 The atmosphere during the concept phase

The atmosphere of the concept phase is variable, based on the ups and downs of indecision and hesitation. Thus, this initial phase of the project is usually characterized by:

- The desire of the technical staff to get the project moving.
- Lack of full commitment on the part of management; only initial budgets are usually allocated at this phase.
- Frustration of management; due to the inability of the technical staff to provide management with anything more than rough estimates.
- Frustration of the development team; due to the inability of the customer (including management, marketing and users) to provide accurate definitions of the required system.

All these are the product of a lack of commitment by the interested parties. The customer and management have not yet firmly made up their minds about whether they want to go ahead with the project. In addition, they are often not totally convinced of the importance of the concept phase, as there are very few visible results produced. The parties tend to be involved but not fully committed[2] to the project, and therefore expect results without providing sufficient resources.

---

1. The IEEE's *Standard Glossary of Software Engineering Terminology* (Std 729–1983) (1987b), although recognizing the lack of consensus on the phases comprising the software life cycle, presents an example that includes *concept exploration, requirements, design, implementation, test, installation and checkout, operation and maintenance,* and an interesting phase called *retirement*.
2. The concepts of *involvement* and *commitment* are often confused and used interchangeably. A famous anecdote emphasizes the difference between the two: in ham and eggs, the hen was involved, but the pig was committed!

The allocation of a budget is always the firmest sign of commitment to a project, and the larger the initial budget, the firmer the commitment. The procurement of an initial project budget is often the project manager's first major task. This may be achieved as the result of:

- The preparation of a good concept document. A *good* concept document is the result of a comprehensive market analysis and user survey, and it includes a well written overview of the system's functional requirements. This document should also address the feasibility of the project.
- The establishment of a clear need for the system that is to be developed. One of the best ways to gain approval for a development project is to clearly identify and describe the problem for which the project will provide a solution.
- The provision of convincing initial estimates for the development of the project. No organization can commit to an unknown expenditure. If initial estimates[3] cannot be prepared, then at the very least estimates for the requirements phase should be submitted.

4.1.2 Problems during the concept phase

Many problems during the concept phase are due to the difficulty in getting the project to move forward. This, clearly, is the result of the variable atmosphere described in the previous section. This leads to the difficulty in obtaining a binding commitment from the customer and from top management.

The following problems are common during the concept phase:

- Many problems are related to establishing the initial project development team. Locating the right people for the project team is rarely an easy task. Indeed, locating a suitable project manager is not always an easy task.
- A common problem is either the lack or the excess of project leadership. In many cases the concept phase is led by many people; one may be responsible for market analysis, another for estimating, and yet another for producing the concept document. This can cause a lack of coordination between those responsible for the various activities, producing many contradictions and bad initial decisions.
- When an initial team is in place and a rough development plan has been produced, it is not uncommon to find that there are many different ideas as to what the product should actually be. Producing an agreed concept document can often become a major problem. This problem can often be solved through the use of demo systems or prototypes.

Rapid prototyping can be helpful when general agreement on the concept is difficult to reach. Concepts are often easier to consolidate when something concrete can be produced and reviewed by all interested parties.

4.2 THE SOFTWARE REQUIREMENTS PHASE

The software requirements phase, also called the definition phase, is the first formal mandatory phase of software development. This phase provides a detailed description of the software system to be developed. It is according to the requirements specification that the software product is tested at the end of the project to demonstrate that the required product has indeed

---

3. The preparation of estimates is discussed in detail in Chapter 11.

been produced. The requirements specification answers the question *what* while attempting to avoid the question *how*.

The requirements phase forms the basis for:

- The first major system baseline[4]
- The design of the system (the next phase)
- The acceptance test procedures (ATP)

The requirements phase produces one main product document:

- The software requirements specification document

and two project planning documents:

- The project development plan
- The software test plan

The requirements phase formally concludes with the project's first major review: the software requirements review (SRR). It is this review that signs off the requirements specification and formally declares the requirements document as the first approved project baseline.

4.2.1 The atmosphere during the requirements phase

The requirements phase is often perceived as the most important phase of the software development cycle. It is certainly one of the most difficult, due in part to the difficulty in documenting an agreed description of the software requirements. There is always a basic conflict of interest between the customer[5] and the developer. The customer is reluctant to finalize the requirements because of the knowledge that once this is done any further changes may be costly. On the other hand, the developer needs to finalize the requirements as soon as possible because progress will be slow as long as the product is not fully defined; and this too is costly. So the atmosphere of the requirements phase can be characterized as a form of tug of war between the customer and the developer.

Cost-plus contracts, where the developer is paid by the hour or by the day (see Chapter 3), tend to have fewer conflicts of this type. However, cost-plus contracts leave the main responsibility for early closure of the requirements with the customer.

The requirements phase is thus characterized by:

- Conflict between developer and customer in closing the requirements specification
- Disagreements over revised and binding estimates

and also by:

- Confusion due to shifting responsibilities and as yet unstaffed assignments

Closing requirements is not always easy and requires experience, patience and firmness. It is the project manager's job, at some point, to be resolute and decisive in requiring all parties to

---

4. Baselines are discussed in Chapter 10.
5. The term *customer* is used here in its broadest sense and refers to the organization that requested the project, such as an external customer, marketing department or users.

sign off the requirements for the project. This is best achieved by explaining to the customer that lack of closure causes schedule delays, and schedule delays are costly.

4.2.2 Problems during the requirements phase

The occasional conflicts, disagreements and confusion that characterize the atmosphere of the requirements phase are a major source of problems. The list is long, but the most common problems are:

- Frequent requirements changes: during this stage there is often a seemingly endless flow of changes, making it difficult to compile the requirements specification.
- Requirements approval and sign-off: this phase cannot be completed without a formally approved requirements document.
- Requirements feasibility: sometimes this is difficult to determine before the implementation phase.
- Staffing: locating suitable development team members can be a difficult task. Assignment of team members should be completed during the requirements phase.
- Equipment procurement: budgeting and availability problems can disrupt equipment allocation plans.
- Binding estimates: if these have not already been provided, then they should be completed before the end of this phase.

As we have seen, obtaining formal approval for the requirements specification is the most difficult task of this phase. Usually, the requirements evolve gradually, with several draft versions of the specification converging to the final approved document. However, if major changes are introduced continuously, then not only will the document be difficult to compile, the project also will be difficult to plan. In such situations, rapid prototyping can be most helpful in assisting the customer to determine the requirements.

The feasibility of requirements must be determined, when possible, before the requirements are closed. It is always costly to discover unfeasible requirements during later phases of the project.

The feasibility of requirements can be improved by:

- Using prototypes to test requirements.
- Temporarily involving experts in the feasibility analysis procedure.
- Requiring approval for alternate requirements if the original requirement is unfeasible.
- Making vague requirements contingent on certain outcomes (e.g. sufficient memory, or available CPU processing capacity). Whenever possible, vague or suspect requirements should be deleted.

Project planning progresses in parallel to the development of the requirements. Problems associated with the allocation of human and technical resources can delay the project. Finding good team members is always a problem for the project manager. However, once they are located and assigned, adequate development equipment must be available. Therefore problems associated with the procurement of equipment become more severe as the development team grows.

Staffing problems can often be resolved by:

- Using temporary personnel
- Increasing the staff load later
- Training existing personnel

Equipment problems too can be resolved by:

- Using temporary equipment (loaned, or rented)
- Using software simulators in place of expensive equipment
- Obtaining an initial budget to fund basic development equipment

Equipment and staffing problems usually impact the estimates and the schedule in the project development plan. If equipment is late, or if staffing is slow, then estimates will need to be revised and schedules will have to be adjusted. These problems are discussed in detail in Chapter 10.

4.3 THE DESIGN PHASE

During the design phase, the requirements are analyzed and the method of implementation is determined. Just as the previous requirements phase addressed the question *what?*, the design phase addresses the question: how? The response to this question is documented in the software design specification document.

The design phase is often divided into two separate phases: top level design and detailed design. The dividing line between the two phases is set somewhat arbitrarily, based on the level of system decomposition (see Chapter 6). Figure 6.5 presents an example of the division of the design of a system into top level design and detailed design.

One of the advantages in using two design phases instead of one is that the first top level design provides an additional milestone at which the design approach can be evaluated and approved. This is especially important in medium and large projects (e.g. more than 18 work years) where major design errors must be located as early as possible. When a major error is found at the end of the top level design phase it is much easier to correct than if it is found after the whole design is complete. Consider the following example.

A software system is being designed for a specific computer with a basic configuration of eight megabytes of memory, and 256 megabytes of disk space. Memory can be increased in increments of one megabyte, and disk space can be increased in increments of 256 megabytes. The initial design of the system being developed did not fit into the basic memory configuration, and therefore the system was designed to use overlays.

Using overlays was a major design decision, and it impacted timing, complexity, memory utilization, and disk utilization. Many of the subsequent design decisions were influenced by the decision to use overlays. But as it turned out, using overlays was a bad design decision, because disk utilization was also high. That meant that a second 256 megabyte disk drive was needed, and it was significantly more expensive than the additional two megabytes of memory required to overcome the need for overlays.

If the overlay decision is discovered to be wrong only at the end of the design phase then a major rewrite of the whole design will be necessary. The computer configuration may also have to be changed, and the additional 256 megabyte disk drive will have to be returned (assuming the vendor will accept it). However, if this decision is discovered early, during the top level design, then the amount of rewriting will be minimal, and there will be a better chance of changing the computer configuration before delivery.

The design phase provides the basis for:

- The second major system baseline
- The implementation of the system (the next phase)
- Updated development plan

The design phase produces the following documents:

- Design specification (for large projects: top level design specification and detailed design specification)
- Integration plan
- Test case specifications, describing in detail each individual low level test

The design specification document establishes the project's second major baseline. In the case of two design phases, the detailed design specification is regarded as the major design baseline, and the top level design specification is regarded as a secondary baseline (baselines are discussed in Chapter 10).

At the end of this phase, many of the project's unknowns become known, thus providing a significant improvement in the development plan estimates. Various project development parameters, such as the integration schedule and resources, and the actual test cases for the test phase, can now be planned. The updated project development plan can therefore be regarded at this stage as being significantly more reliable.

Hence, in parallel with the design of the system, the following activities are also in progress:

- The development and integration platforms are installed. This includes all the equipment required for system development and integration.
- Estimates are significantly improved.
- Project risk analysis is reviewed and updated.
- The project development schedule is updated.

All the above information is included in a new major revision of the project development plan.

The design phase concludes with the sign off of the design specification document. This usually occurs at a formal design review, referred to as the *critical design review* (CDR). If an intermediate top level design specification is prepared, then this document is signed off at an initial *preliminary design review* (PDR).

4.3.1 The atmosphere during the design phase

The design phase is often a relatively confident and optimistic part of the development project. It is characterized by:

- Enthusiasm: the project gains momentum, budgets have been approved and are now being expended, and a new development team is in place.
- Delays: many changes in requirements and design are introduced, owing to:
  – late ideas
  – unfeasibility of requirements
  – additional new information.
- Confusion: team grows rapidly; project hierarchy and responsibilities are not yet clear.

The design phase, for the project manager, is a period of organization during which the project team structure is finalized and the assignment of responsibilities is completed. These tasks must be completed by the project manager before the end of the design phase, as the confusion that may have accompanied the first two project phases cannot be carried over into the implementation phase.

4.3.2 Problems during the design phase

The main problems of the design phase are related to:

- Technical design issues
- Difficulties in staffing
- Procurement of development resources
- Customer relations

The technical design problems are concerned with both those derived from unfeasible requirements and those due to complex implementation and design decisions. It is during the design phase that all such problems should be resolved, because their resolution will become more costly as the project progresses.

Occasionally, staffing problems are carried over from the previous requirements phase. Some tasks will be hard to staff or slow to staff. It is therefore important for the project manager to attempt to assign people to all project positions as early as possible, even before the actual people are required. In fact, it is good practice to begin assigning people to positions well in advance of the date that people actually join the project.

Many of the problems related to procurement of development resources are also carried over from the previous phase. At this stage of the project, these problems are usually associated either with outside vendors and suppliers or with existing company equipment that is still tied up with other projects. As mentioned previously, many of these problems can often be resolved by equipment rentals or loans. However, the negative impact of such makeshift solutions increases as the project moves into more advanced development stages. In fact, these solutions, if not handled carefully, can lead to new problems:

- Rentals can be costly and can waste substantial amounts from the development budget.
- Loans (or *loaners* as they are often called), can be retracted, leaving members of the development team without the necessary development facilities.
- Temporary makeshift solutions can lead to reduced quality and longer development time. This, in turn, will cause schedule slips.

Some customer–developer related problems may still occur during the design phase. With the requirements now approved, much of the tension has been eased, but when the design phase concludes with a formal review, the customer shares the responsibility for the design. This increases the involvement of the customer in the design phase, and can lead to disagreements on how the system is to be implemented.

These types of problem are best resolved by designating one team member (possibly the project manager), to act as liaison with the customer. This reduces the points of contact between the team and the customer, while assuring that the customer has a single address for all requests and comments.

4.4 THE IMPLEMENTATION PHASE

During the implementation phase the software modules are coded and initial unit tests are performed. Unit testing is carried out by the programmer on each individual module immediately after it is coded. The modules are then approved by software quality control and submitted to configuration control (see Chapter 8 for a discussion of these control functions). Configuration control then releases modules for integration.

A detailed and well-structured design specification leads to relatively smooth and straightforward coding.[6] Thus coding (or programming), which was originally perceived to be synonymous with software development, has become just a single phase in the software development cycle. In fact, the implementation phase is not even the longest phase. A common rule of thumb for estimating the software development cycle phases, uses a 40–20–40 division of effort and time (see Table 4.1). This means that about 40 percent of the time is devoted to specification (requirements and design), 20 percent to implementation (coding and unit testing), and 40 percent to integration and testing.

The current trend is to attempt to reduce the 20 percent devoted to implementation while increasing the 40 percent devoted to specification. One aspect of the reasoning behind this approach is that the earlier development phases are less costly than the later phases. The specification phases usually have lower staffing and less development equipment than the implementation phase. Also, as has often been demonstrated, when more effort is devoted to requirements and design, the integration phase is easier and more efficient.

The implementation phase links the design and integration phases of the system, and usually significantly overlaps each of these other two phases (see Fig. 4.5). Overlapping will often occur when many parts of the system design are completed relatively quickly, leaving some design issues open for quite a while. In such cases, overlapping can shorten the development schedule significantly.

Overlapping of the design and implementation phases requires great care in assuring that only design-complete modules are approved for early implementation. There is a risk that any later changes to the design of these modules may require re-coding, thus wasting resources. There is also the risk of the design being changed without the code being changed. However, these risks are usually well worth taking. With good planning and configuration control, these problems can be overcome.

On the other side of the implementation phase, overlapping of coding and integration is usually less risky, and if planned correctly, can be an excellent time saver. The order of implementation of the modules should be well planned to assure that they are released in the order required for integration. This also means that implementation errors can be located during integration and fed back to the implementation phase.

The implementation phase includes the following main activities:

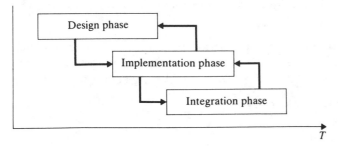

Figure 4.5 Overlapping of phases.

---

6. This is demonstrated by the many attempts to develop automatic code generators that produce code from the design specification (see Balzer 1985).

- The development of the software code
- Preparation for integration and test of the system (the next phase)
- The development of the maintenance plan

Apart from the actual code being written (and hopefully being well commented), some of the other documents that are developed during this phase include:

- The programmer's notebook, documenting coding decisions, unit tests, and resolution of implementation problems
- Maintenance plan and documentation, including all necessary documentation needed for system maintenance
- Initial versions of the user documentation, including reference manuals and operator guides[7]

During the implementation phase the project enters a period of intense activity. The many other activities that are taking place include:

- The design phase is completed early during the implementation phase.
- The integration platform is put in place and integration begins.
- The test bed (test environment and equipment) is put in place in preparation for system testing.
- Risk situations may materialize and contingency plans are then put into action.
- The project plan is reviewed and updated.

4.4.1 The atmosphere during the implementation phase

As we have seen, staffing reaches its peak during the implementation and integration phases. During implementation, the atmosphere is influenced by the many other activities going on in parallel. This atmosphere is characterized by:

- Pressure to get going and show something. This is often the result of a significant increase in the rate of expenditure, with little yet to show for the cost of development.
- Conflicts with the software quality assurance (SQA) and the configuration control organizations. These conflicts are due to increased involvement of these supervisory organizations, and their role in enforcing standards and orderly development procedures.
- Increased development team activity, with little free time left, as the delivery dates become close and more real.

In general, the implementation phase is a transitional period from specification to building. The atmosphere is heavily dependent on the success of the previous specification phases and the expected success of the following integration and test phases. Contributing factors include:

- Requirements may not yet be adequately defined.
- Insufficient resources have been assigned.
- Insufficient development time is available.
- Some technical problems may not yet be resolved.

---

7. Many standards describe the content of the documents produced during a software project. US MIL Std-2167A (DOD 1988a) is particularly comprehensive and detailed. See Chapter 9 for a general discussion of software development standards.

- Management support may be lacking.
- Customer relations may be tense.

4.4.2 Problems during the implementation phase

If the design phase is implemented well, then most technical problems should be resolved by the end of design. If this is not so, then confusion may follow due to the necessity to program and solve technical problems simultaneously. Such situations often fall into the code and fix method (see Fig. 4.1).

Other problems of the implementation phase include:

- Last minute changes: this is a problem which can only be solved by assuring strict and orderly change control procedures.
- Interfacing and coordination between team members: this problem is particularly severe in large projects.
- Controlling and monitoring subcontractors and vendors.

The flow of changes is the scourge of engineering in general and of software development in particular. Clearly, changes must be permitted in moderation, but an unchecked flow of changes can bring a project to its knees. There is also the danger that, in large teams, some team member may be unaware of a particular change.

Communication between team members can be time-consuming. This communications overhead can be reduced in large teams by dividing the project into subsystems, with semi-independent teams assigned to each subsystem. Formal channels of communication are then defined between the smaller teams.

In some cases, subsystems can be assigned to subcontractors. However, controlling subcontractors and vendors may become a full-time job. Verbal and written reports are rarely sufficient; frequent visits to the development sites are often necessary to assure the availability of accurate information. In such cases, the developer becomes the customer in relation to the vendor or subcontractor.

4.5 THE INTEGRATION AND TEST PHASE

During the integration and test phase the software modules are combined into a single system, and the functionality of the system is tested for compliance with the requirements. Integration starts with an initial version of the system that progressively increases in functionality until the full system is assembled. Each test stage then evaluates the performance of the system in order to identify problems that must be corrected before the system can be released.

The integration and test phase provides the basis for:

- The construction of the software system from the various software components
- The integration of the software and hardware equipment
- Determining whether the system has been developed according to the requirements specification
- Establishing the quality of the system

This phase is often divided into two separate and largely parallel phases: the integration phase and the testing phase. In large projects, this division is often necessary, especially when testing is carried out by a separate independent group (the *independent test team*) that works side by side with the developers. In smaller projects, the rationale behind the combination of the two activities into one phase is that integration cannot be successful without extensive testing being carried out in parallel. Therefore, if these two activities are performed by the same team, they are often best combined in a single phase (refer to Chapter 8 for a more detailed discussion of the software test team).

There are many techniques and methods of integration:

- top down
- bottom up

and an interesting approach referred to as

- inside out

The top down approach requires the core of the system (usually the central executive modules) to be implemented first. They are then combined into a minimal system, using empty shell routines in place of the modules that have not yet been implemented. These empty shells of code that return fixed values and are devoid of any logic, are commonly called *stubs*. The stubs are then gradually replaced by the real modules, in a well-planned progressive build of the system, so that each new release of the system provides more functionality.

The bottom up approach starts from the individual modules at the lowest level (e.g. input/ output drivers, formatters, data manipulators and user/machine dialogues) and gradually binds them together in larger and larger groups until the full system is assembled.

The bottom up approach is rarely recommended as a comprehensive integration strategy; in most cases the top down approach is easier and more natural. However, in reality, most successful system integration strategies are a combination of the top down approach with a spattering of bottom up.

Inside out integration is common in the development of large data base systems, when the internal file structures are built first, after which the data processing logic is added, and finally the human interface is added. This approach is best when the system is logically comprised of succeeding layers of functionality, but its main drawback is that the human interface is usually the last to be integrated. This may require writing temporary test code to enable the output to be reviewed. Therefore testing is often slow and difficult with the inside out approach.

Testing starts with integration and continues until the final delivery of the system to the customer. The various types of testing include:

- Integration testing; performed by the system integrators.
- Independent testing; performed by an external test group to assure objective unbiased testing of the system.
- Installation testing. This includes general performance tests required whenever a version of the system is first installed in an operational environment. Many systems include a set of installation tests to assure that the system has been installed successfully.
- Alpha and beta testing. These tests run in the system in a real (non-test lab) environment. Alpha testing tests the system without live data. Beta testing tests the system using live data with constant supervision to correct any problems that may arise.
- Acceptance testing. This is the last milestone of the project, and its successful completion signifies the customer's acceptance of the developed product.

At the conclusion of the integration and test phase all documentation must be complete and ready for delivery, including:

- Maintenance documentation
- Final user documentation
- All updated development documentation
- Test documentation and test reports

In parallel with integration and testing, the following managerial and non-development activities take place:

- Final budgeting of the project; the cost of changes is determined, risk contingency activities are evaluated, and the budget is updated.
- Training is conducted for users, operators, customers, installers, maintenance engineers, and marketing engineers.
- Installation sites are prepared, and the infrastructure for hardware and special equipment is planned and installed.
- The development team size is reduced.

4.5.1 The atmosphere during the integration and test phase

Up to this point in the project life cycle, documents have been written, code has been developed and development equipment has been installed. Except for prototypes, nothing functional has yet been developed. The integration and test phase begins with staffing and budget expenditure at their peak. Integration and testing is therefore often characterized by:

- Pressure to get something working. This began during the previous implementation phase, and now increases. Management has seen little of substance to justify their investment. Any schedule delays at this point can be critical. It is important for the project manager to produce an initial version of the system as soon as possible.
- Pressure to complete the project. This pressure appears towards the end of the project and becomes more intense if schedules begin to slip.
- Overtime. Calendar time is often more critical than development time (e.g. work months). The first solution for schedule slips is usually overtime.
- Conflicts with the customer. At last the customer can see an initial version of what the product will look like. At this point different interpretations of the requirements emerge, and often need to be resolved on a higher management level.
- Frustration. Solutions to integration problems and implementation bugs are often elusive, and may require a return to the design phase.

The integration and test phase is the most difficult to plan. It is also the most important to plan, because so much is actually going on. Many of the pressures of this phase can best be avoided by assuring:

- Good design
- An efficient module coding plan
- A well organized development team
- A good integration plan
- Suitable integration and test platforms

4.5.2 Problems during the integration and test phase

It is during the integration and test phase that most of the development problems appear. Events described earlier in the project as risks now materialize, and other unexpected problems inevitably occur. These problems include:

- Last minute failures: design errors and implementation problems emerge. These are the types of problem that are difficult to uncover without an operational version of the system. They are therefore not discovered earlier in the project.
- Third party problems, including late delivery from vendors and subcontractors and defects in their subsystems and components.
- Last minute changes. This problem exists in all phases but becomes more severe as the project progresses. Changes now become much more costly.
- Budget overruns. This problem is derived from changes and design errors, as well as project planning errors.
- Staff motivation problems. These commonly occur toward the end of the project, during the final test stages.
- Project acceptance problems. This problem is particularly common in fixed price projects (see Chapter 3), when conflicts arise concerning the completion of the project.

Many of these problems can be avoided, or at least their severity can be reduced, by preparing for them early in the project. Just as risk management includes preparing contingency plans in case the risk event occurs, so the severity of any problem can often be reduced by planning for it.

As discussed previously, changes are inevitable, and are best handled through an orderly change control mechanism. This means that no change, without exception, can be accepted unless it is submitted through the change control channels.

Planning for last minute failures and design errors is more difficult. A common solution to these types of problem is to accept that failures and errors are inevitable. This means that they must be taken into account within the project schedule, even though they cannot be identified in advance. The traditional way of scheduling for unknown problems is to add a fixed percentage to the development schedule. A rule of thumb is to *add thirty percent for unexpected delays and unforeseen problems*.

Though a development organization will eventually accumulate the necessary information to define its own schedule contingencies, Table 4.2 is a good starting point. Chapter 11 discusses

Table 4.2 Software project schedule contingency factors

Type of software	Addition to schedule
Small commercial data processing system	10%
Medium commercial data processing system	15%
Large commercial data processing system	20%
Communications system	33%
Scientific systems, compilers etc.	25%
Operating systems	25%
Real-time systems	33%
User interfaces	15%
Hardware/software development	35%

other more complex methods for improving estimates based on the type of project being developed.[8]

4.6 THE MAINTENANCE PHASE

The maintenance phase completes the software development cycle and links the release of the completed software product with the development of a new product. The term *software maintenance* is controversial, because it implies a need to repair a product that has deteriorated. In mechanical or electronic systems, maintenance may require the repair or replacement of failed components, and preventive maintenance may require the service of components to prevent deterioration. However, software does not deteriorate. The vehicle that carries the software may deteriorate, but the software itself will not change[9] without human intervention.

The IEEE definition of *software maintenance* (IEEE 1987b) includes the correction of faults that existed in the software *before* its delivery, as well as changes to improve performance or to adapt the product to a changed environment.

Two other activities that are part of maintenance are:

● Maintaining updated documentation
● Updating user training courses

Unlike hardware maintenance, none of these activities return the software to its previous state. Quite the opposite is true: the objective here is to modify the software.

Modifying software includes all the characteristics of developing software. Modifications need to be formally described, designed, implemented, integrated and tested. And of course, modifications need to be budgeted. It is therefore sound engineering practice to implement the maintenance phase as a series of small software projects.

Configuration control is particularly important during maintenance to manage the various changes to the software, and to control the many releases and versions of the system. This assures orderly periodic releases of the software, and avoids haphazard support and on the spot fixes that can turn into an engineering nightmare.

Project management is not always carried over from the development of the software product development to the maintenance phase. Maintenance requires a much smaller team, and a different type of management. In fact, a single maintenance group can be established to maintain several products, with common management, configuration control, installation and field engineers, and maintenance of documentation.

The documents that need to be updated during this phase include:

● Version release documentation
● Problem reports
● All development documentation
● All user documentation
● Maintenance logs and customer service reports

---

8. The effect of the various schedule factors can be improved by dividing the project into components (e.g. data processing, communications, real-time) and applying the appropriate factors to each different type of component.

9. In some sense software can be seen as changing if, due to a bug or a design error, it modifies itself (called *clobbering*). This can be prevented by storing software in read only memory (ROM).

Maintenance continues for as long as the software product is installed and running. As the system ages, plans are prepared for a new development project to replace the ageing system. At that time maintenance efforts are reduced to a minimum, due to the expectation that all required modifications and bug corrections will be included in the new system.

4.6.1 The atmosphere during the maintenance phase

In many cases maintenance does not provide the challenge of new development. This can lead to an unstable maintenance team, with engineers frequently joining and leaving the team. Nevertheless, maintenance can provide many challenges, such as identifying critical problems, providing solutions and suggesting improvements. In general, the maintenance phase is characterized by:

- A lack of enthusiasm, due, in some cases, to the lack of well-defined technical challenges.
- Pressure to provide quick fixes. In an orderly maintenance environment problem corrections are rarely quick.
- Frustration due to a lack of adequate budgets. Maintenance activities are not always recognized as important, and are therefore often under-budgeted.

4.6.2 Problems during the maintenance phase

As we have seen, software maintenance includes all of the phases of a full development project. Therefore, many of the development problems prevalent during the basic development phases are common also in the maintenance phase. Other problems specific to this phase include:

- Insufficient knowledgeable maintenance engineers; due to the difficulty in recruiting engineers willing to accept maintenance tasks.
- Budgeting problems; associated with new releases of the system.
- Multiple patches on the existing system; after a while even an orderly maintenance procedure can produce a patchwork software system. This often prompts the development of a new system.
- Lack of support equipment and test platforms; this problem too is often the result of insufficient budgets for maintenance activities.

For the maintenance manager, staffing the maintenance team is essentially a problem of creating an interesting and challenging assignment. This can often be achieved by assigning responsibility for a single project, or a well defined part of a large project, to one software engineer. The assignment should include the identification of problems, provision of solutions, and suggestions for improvement, within the engineer's area of responsibility. This approach promotes the engineer's dedication to the assignment and identification with the success of the maintenance effort.

Unlike staff motivation, budget and equipment problems are not primarily dependent on the maintenance manager. Budgets must be secured from higher management, and are often funded by the users of the system being maintained. Monthly or annual fees are a common way of budgeting maintenance.

The gradual evolution of a patchwork system has no real solution other than the eventual development of a new system. However, the many difficulties associated with a continuously evolving system can be significantly reduced by implementing an orderly configuration control program. As we have seen, maintenance without configuration control can become extremely difficult to manage.

4.7 IEEE STANDARD 1074: A STANDARD FOR SOFTWARE LIFE CYCLE PROCESSES

Strictly speaking, the maintenance phase is not the final phase in the life cycle of a software product. The final phase, often called *retirement*, heralds the end of the software's productive existence. Of the many life cycle models that deliver software from conception to retirement, the best are those that have well-defined processes associated with them.

A well-defined set of processes can be associated with many different software development life cycle models. In fact, one of these initial processes may be the selection of the best suited model from a set of candidate models. These required activities are described in the IEEE Standard 1074 (IEEE 1993) for software life cycle processes.

IEEE Standard 1074 was first published in 1990, with the stated purpose of defining the processes that are required for the development and maintenance of critical software. For non-critical software, the developer can tailor the standard to the level of the software project being developed.

Standard 1074 describes the mapping of activities into the chosen life cycle and the identification and documentation of standards and controls that govern the life cycle. This is achieved through six sets of processes:

- Life cycle model selection
- Project management
- Pre-development processes
- Development processes
- Post-development processes
- Integral processes

Standard 1074 does not define how the activities related to each process are to be implemented; it describes what the activities are. The implementation of the processes is defined by the project manager when selecting the specific life cycle model to be used.

The following sections provide an overview of the processes described in IEEE standard 1074.

4.7.1 The selection of the project software life cycle model

Standard 1074 starts with the definition of a process for selecting the life cycle model that will be used to develop a specific project. The selection process includes two basic activities:

1. The identification of candidate software life cycle models
2. The selection of a suitable project model

The first activity is involved with the evaluation of several models which may be appropriate for the project to be developed. New models may be constructed by combining elements of other models. It is important to understand that a development organization may have more than one software life cycle model, but only one model may be selected for a specific project.

The second activity takes into account the characteristics of the software product to be developed (interactive, batch, transaction processing etc.) and of the project itself (requirements easy or difficult to define, development constraints etc.). The decision to be made is based upon which model will best support the management of the project.

Finally, and most importantly, the model selected must be capable of supporting the required processes and activities further described in standard 1074.

4.7.2 Project management processes

The project management processes cover the initiation, monitoring and control of the project throughout the life cycle.

Project initiation refers to those activities that apply the 1074 standard to the selected model. This process also includes the allocation of project resources and the establishment of the environment within which the project will be developed. These activities are then laid out in an an organized software project management plan.[1]

The project monitoring and control process covers risk analysis (see Chapter 2), monitoring of milestones and budget (see Chapter 10), the maintenance of records, and the implementation of a problem report method. This is an iterative process which continues throughout the project life cycle.

4.7.3 Pre-development processes

The pre-development processes include early project tasks that precede the main-line development activities. These are the activities, often performed by the project manager before the team is in place, that set up the structure for the project.

The first pre-development process is the *concept exploration process*. All projects are initiated with the identification of an idea or a need for a system to be developed. This is often referred to as the *initial requirements*. The concept exploration process also considers potential solutions. This is an initial early glimpse into the design phase, to provide some basic insight into the type (and cost) of possible solutions.

Another pre-development process is the *allocation process*. This process provides an early assessment of the allocation of functions and is needed for projects that require the development of both software and hardware. The process provides an initial mapping of the main project functions into hardware and software. This process also supports initial project planning based on the type of expertise that will be required and the resources that will be needed for implementation.

4.7.4 Development processes

The development processes as defined in IEEE standard 1074 cover three of the classic project phases described earlier in this chapter. They are:

- *The requirements process*
  This process covers all activities related to the production of the software requirements, the definition of interface requirements, and the prioritization and integration of the individual list of requirements.
- *The design process*
  This process covers all activities related to the conversion of the requirements into

---

1. The format for the software project development plan is discussed in Chapters 9 and 10.

architectural design, the analysis of information flow, design of database and interface requirements, and the selection of algorithms.

- *The implementation process*
  This process covers the transformation of design into code. It includes the creation of test data, coding, operating documentation and integration.

4.7.5 Post-development processes

The post-development processes include the processes needed to install, operate, support, maintain and retire a software product.

The installation process covers the following list of activities:

1. Plan installation
2. Distribute software (load the software on the storage media)
3. Install software (on the target platform)
4. Load data base
5. Accept software in functional environment (acceptance)
6. Apply updates (if required)

The operation and support process involves user operation of the system and ongoing support. Support includes providing technical assistance, consultation with the user and recording user support requests.

The maintenance process is concerned with the resolution of software errors, faults, failures, enhancements and changes. These activities also require the application of a software life cycle for the development of the changes that correct or enhance the software system.

The retirement process involves the removal of an existing system from active support or use by ceasing its operation or by replacing it with a new system.

4.7.6 Integral processes

The integral processes are the processes needed to ensure the completion and quality of project functions. They include:

- The verification and validation process
- The software configuration management process
- The documentation development process
- The training process

The training process is especially important, as it assures the correct operation of the finished software product. Customer personnel have to be qualified to install, operate and maintain the software. Training is therefore equally important for technical support staff and for customers (or users) alike.

4.8 SUMMARY

The software development life cycle includes all software development phases from the initial concept to the final delivery of the system. There are various different approaches to the software development cycle, including the primitive *code and fix* method, various iterative methods (such as rapid prototyping), and the phased approach.

The phased approach to software development divides the development life cycle into:

- The concept phase
- The requirements phase
- The design phase
- The implementation phase
- The integration and test phase
- The maintenance phase

The phased approach (also called the Waterfall model) is included within most other software development methodologies. In fact, there are many variations of the classic Waterfall model, but they are all based upon a systematic transition from one development phase to the next, until the project is complete.

The Waterfall model begins with the initial *concept phase*, during which the need for the software system is determined and the basic concept of the software system evolves. This is followed by the requirements phase, which provides a detailed description of the software system to be developed. The requirements phase provides the project's first major baseline.

After the definition of the requirements, the design phase analyzes the requirements and determines the method of implementation. The design phase is often divided into two separate phases: top level design, and detailed design. The dividing line between the two phases is set somewhat arbitrarily, based on the level of system decomposition. The system design provides the second major project baseline.

During the next phase, implementation, the software modules are coded and initial unit tests are performed. The modules are then approved by software quality control and submitted to configuration control. Configuration control then releases modules for integration.

During the integration and test phase the software modules are assembled and the system gradually takes form. The system is then tested for compliance with the requirements specification.

Finally, the maintenance phase completes the software development cycle and links the release of the completed software product with the development of a new product. Software maintenance is involved with the correction of faults that existed in the software *before* its delivery, as well as changes to improve performance or to adapt the product to a changed environment.

A well-defined set of processes can be associated with many different software development life cycle models. These required activities are described in the IEEE standard 1074 for software life cycle processes. Standard 1074 does not define how the activities related to each process are to be implemented; it describes what the activities are. The implementation of the processes is defined by the project manager when selecting the specific life cycle model to be used.

EXERCISES

1. A large aircraft manufacturer has decided to permit engineers to work from their home. The engineers will be provided with a terminal and a modem, and they will dial in to the company's computer from home.

The aircraft manufacturer needs a communications and monitoring software package to manage the work being performed by the engineers. The package must include a sophisticated security feature that will prevent unauthorized people from dialing into the company's system, and will activate various alarms if unauthorized access is attempted. The system must also monitor the hours worked by the engineers from home, and it must provide resource sharing of common data files and software utilities. Finally, the package must contain both an on-line and a batch mode report feature to provide information on the use of the system by engineers from their home.

Analyze the software package and consider various methodologies for implementation. In particular, compare rapid prototyping with the Waterfall approach. Explain the advantages and disadvantages of each approach for this project.

2. Consider the overlapping of phases when applying the Waterfall method to the system described in Exercise 1. In particular, consider the overlapping of the implementation phase with the design phase.

Prepare a plan to code the modules so that the implementation phase can begin as early as possible. Explain which modules can safely be coded first, and discuss the possible risks.

3. As in Exercise 2, consider the risks of overlapping implementation with integration.

Prepare a plan to integrate the software modules so that integration can begin as early as possible. Explain which modules can safely be integrated first, and discuss the possible risks.

Compare the use of a top down integration plan to a bottom up plan and an inside out plan. Describe which approach you would recommend for this project.

4. Discuss the main problems that you anticipate in the development of the system described in Exercise 1. In particular, consider the problems associated with the definition of requirements. Who is the customer?

Also, consider the integration and test problems in this project, and discuss the expected requirements changes. How will these problems best be handled?

5. Consider at least six additional features and improvements for the system described in Exercise 1. Prepare a long-range maintenance plan that includes new releases of the system with bug corrections and some new features in each new release.

The dial-in phone costs for the engineers have been overlooked, and cannot be reimbursed by the system. Propose a solution to this problem and schedule it in one of the new releases of the system.

6. Consider several different types of life cycle model that may be applied for the development of the project described in Exercise 1. Which of the IEEE 1074 standard processes are of particular importance for this project? Can any of the 1074 processes be tailored?

FIVE

PRINCIPLES OF MANAGING SOFTWARE ENGINEERS

ARE THEY REALLY ANY DIFFERENT?

According to many studies, managing software engineers is more difficult than managing engineers in most other areas of technology. The typical software engineer (if such a person exists) is often characterized as being both artistic and logical, as well as possessive and temperamental. These traits can be found in any group of people, but they appear to be more prevalent among software engineers.

Software engineers are also widely diverse in their level of productivity. As far back as 1968, Sackman *et al.* documented the enormous difference in productivity between software programmers. Sackman reported productivity ratios of up to 25:1 for programming and 28:1 for debugging. All of the programmers taking part in the experiment were familiar with the application areas of the programs, leading Sackman to interpret the results as a range of their competence.

Sackman's results may be somewhat extreme. However, in an average project it is not uncommon to find productivity ratios of 1:5. One of the targets of modern day software engineering has been to reduce this startling range of productivity among software developers. This has been done through more organized and systematic software development, much to the displeasure of the gurus at the high end of the productivity range. These software development methodologies have also reduced the impact of other human traits on the development process. This is achieved through the introduction of extensive documentation, reports, development standards and status meetings. These procedures, however, are but a few of the means for managing people.

People are managed through an organizational structure. This hierarchical structure is based on the four cornerstones of management: delegation, authority, responsibility and supervision (see Fig. 5.1). Delegation bestows authority, and authority produces (and requires) responsibility. Both authority and responsibility require supervision, and effective supervision requires a suitable organizational structure.

Most projects are organized as teams, with each team assigned specific functions within the project. Different types of project require different types of team structure, as for example a team of junior programmers requires a technical team leader while a team of experts may require only an administrative team leader. It is the project manager's responsibility to select the structure best suited for the project.

This chapter deals with these people management issues. The main emphasis throughout the chapter is on software project related issues. For a more general discussion on methods of

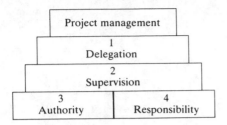

Figure 5.1 The four cornerstones of management.

managing and motivating people, the reader is referred to an interesting text compiled by the *Bureau of Business Practice* (1981).

5.1 THE SOFTWARE PROJECT ORGANIZATIONAL STRUCTURE

There are many ways to organize a software project. The larger the project the more critical the organizational structure becomes. Badly organized projects breed confusion, and confusion leads to project failure. Figure 5.2 describes the basic structure of a project in which below the

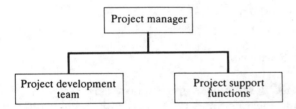

Figure 5.2 Basic structure of a development project.

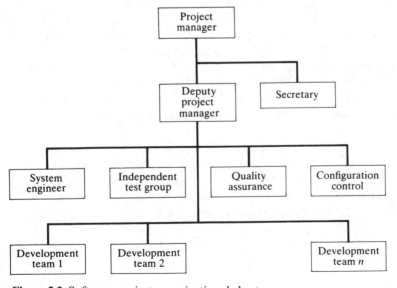

Figure 5.3 Software project organizational chart.

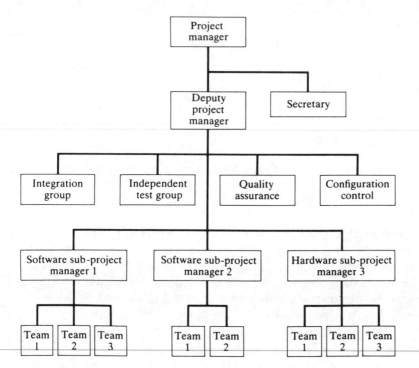

Figure 5.4 Large hardware/software project organizational chart.

project manager are just two general functions: development and support. This very basic software project structure was not uncommon in the 1950s and 1960s. It is still a valid project structure for very small projects (up to five developers), though occasionally it can still be found today in larger projects.

Figure 5.3 describes a detailed organizational chart including all major support functions. This organizational structure is suitable for large projects (with a staff exceeding 20). Smaller projects may not require a deputy project manager or separate configuration control and quality assurance groups (see Chapter 8 for a detailed discussion of these topics).

Very large projects (exceeding a staff of 40) can often be managed more easily by dividing the project into sub-projects. Figure 5.4 presents the organizational chart for a large project. This chart includes both software and hardware development teams, and an integration group that is responsible for hardware/software integration as well as integration within each group.

As an example, consider the organization of a large satellite project. The project manager is in fact responsible for a number of projects: the ground control station, the rocket and the satellite itself. The software for all of these sub-projects is managed within a single project office. Each sub-project is then managed by a sub-project manager. An organizational chart similar to the one described in Fig. 5.4 can be applied to the satellite project; the resulting chart is described in Fig. 5.5.

Clearly the project's organizational structure is dependent on the type of project being developed. Some of the issues that must be considered are:

● Project size: the larger the project, the more important the organization. Large projects

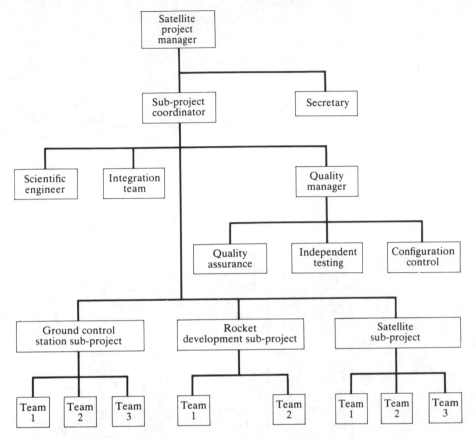

Figure 5.5 Satellite project organizational chart.

have significant human communications and coordination overhead, and therefore require more support functions.

- Hardware/software development projects. The simultaneous development of hardware and software is not easy. Planning, integration and testing are much more complicated, and require dedicated support groups.
- High reliability systems. Any system that is sensitive to issues of reliability (such as military or life-saving systems) requires a major effort in quality assurance. Quality is also an important consideration in many marketable software products (e.g. communications packages). These types of project require a separate quality assurance organization.
- Corporate structure. The project's organization is largely dependent on the overall structure of the company within which the project is being developed. Many of the project support functions can be provided by centralized groups within the company. In fact, basic services, such as financial, secretarial and legal services, are commonly provided by the parent or corporate organization.

Corporate structure usually dictates one of two basic types of project organization: matrix or pyramid. Figure 5.6 describes the structure of a matrix organization (compare this to the pyramid structure in Fig. 5.4). Within a corporate matrix organization, the project manager

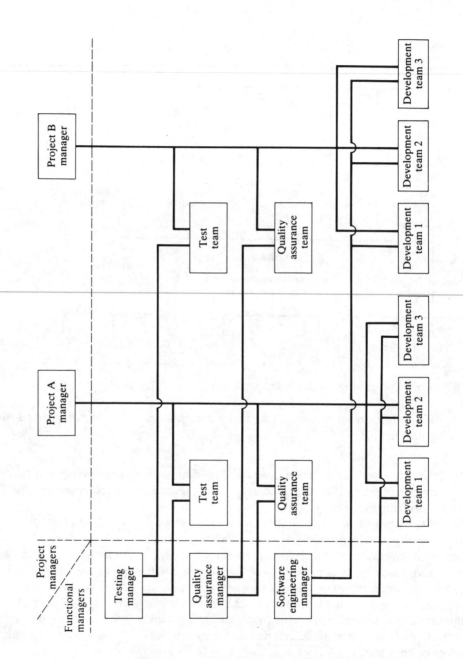

Figure 5.6 Matrix organizational chart.

manages the technical activities of the project staff, while his or her involvement in non-technical personnel issues (e.g. salary reviews, promotion, training) is minimal.

The advantages of a matrix organization are:

- More expertise: a matrix organization can maintain experts in specific fields (communications, data bases, graphics etc.) who are then assigned to different projects. A single project cannot always afford the luxury of maintaining experts in all fields.
- Flexibility: it is easier to move people around from one project to another. This results in better utilization of the available expertise.
- Emphasis on managing the project: the project manager is freed of many of the staff management tasks, leaving more time to concentrate on the technical aspects of the project.

However, matrix organizations also have significant disadvantages:

- Fewer management measures. One of the primary tools for generating motivation, promotion, is taken out of the hands of the project manager. The manager has little influence on the developer's salary and professional role in the organization.
- Lower staff loyalty. All employees like to know exactly who their superior is. In a matrix organization, an employee has more than one superior. This causes a division of loyalty, and a weaker bond between employee and manager.

These disadvantages often outweigh the advantages of the corporate matrix organization. Motivation is a major factor in the success of a project, and anything that undermines motivation is usually contrary to the best interests of the project. Unfortunately, the best interests of the project do not always completely coincide with the best interests of the company.

Pyramid organizations provide a clear, well-defined hierarchy in which all individuals know their own position and the positions of those above and below them. When promotion and status play a major role in generating motivation (and they often do), then the pyramid organization is most effective. Many other factors generate motivation: sense of achievement, praise and peer esteem are just a few (refer to Section 5.4 for further discussion of these topics). Though promotion and status are not always the most effective motivators, a project manager should rarely relinquish *any* effective management tool. Therefore, from the perspective of a single project, the pyramid organization is often the best.

5.2 THE TEAM STRUCTURE

Except for very small projects (fewer than five developers), software projects are best organized into small development teams. The ideal size of a development team is between four and six developers. Larger teams restrict the ability of the team leader to function also as a developer, and thus increase management overhead and limit the team leader's technical involvement in the project.

Teams provide the project manager with many advantages, including:

- Easier and better management: the team structure easily supports delegation of authority.
- More effective exchange of information and ideas, due to broader familiarity within the team of each team member's tasks.
- Teams reduce the possibility of engineers becoming irreplaceable by sharing knowledge within the team. No single person becomes the only source of critical information.

- In small projects, there is stronger identification with the project. In large projects, developers tend to feel that they are just one of very many, and that their contribution to the project will go unnoticed. Smaller, more cohesive, teams can generate more dedication.

5.2.1 The team leader

The team leader serves as the main channel of information between the project manager and the team members. This does not mean that there is no direct communication between the project manager and the team members. However, if all communication was direct then this would defeat the main purposes of the team structure: effective delegation of authority and responsibility (see Fig. 5.1).

The team leader's role is:

- To represent the project manager, via delegation of authority
- To represent the team to the project manager
- To represent the team to other project teams and organizational functions

The team leader may also have other responsibilities, depending on the type of team structure. Figure 5.7 presents examples of two different team structures (these team structures are discussed later). All team leaders lead administratively; not all team leaders lead technically. Chief engineer teams require technical leadership which, in turn, requires technical seniority. Both democratic and chief engineer teams require administrative team leadership.

It is the project manager's responsibility to select the teams and assign the team leader roles. This can (and usually should) be done in consultation with other experienced team leaders and senior project members. The team structure and assignment of key tasks is part of the project development plan, and should be completed as early as possible in the project development cycle (for a detailed discussion of the development cycle see Chapter 4).

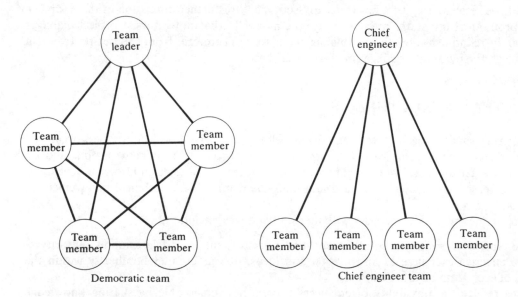

Democratic team   Chief engineer team

Figure 5.7 Development team organization.

Team leaders should first be selected on the basis of their basic leadership abilities. If this ability is not inherent in the individual's character, then training will rarely be enough. A common error is to promote a good engineer to become a bad team leader.[1]

Team leadership is, first and foremost, a management function, and as such requires training. All team leaders should be formally trained in the basic management skills needed both for managing the team and for interfacing with project management. A capable, well-trained team leader becomes a successful extension of the project manager.

5.2.2 Democratic teams

Strictly speaking, democratic teams do not have a *leader*; the function of the team leader role is more that of coordinator. In democratic teams, team leaders assign a small part of their time to:

- Representing the team in communications with the project manager and other teams
- Coordinating activities within the team
- Handling other administrative tasks, such as reports, scheduling and monitoring activities

All technical decisions within a democratic team are made by the whole team. The team leader convenes meetings at which critical or urgent issues are discussed, but all team members take part in the decision-making process and assume responsibility for the outcome.

Democratic teams are often appropriate for groups of senior, experienced developers. The role of team leader then reduces the administrative overhead by assigning all the team's administrative tasks to a single team member.

The democratic team structure is particularly unsuitable for mixed groups, or groups comprised mainly of junior developers. In both these cases clear leadership is required.

5.2.3 Chief engineer teams

Chief engineer teams (also called chief programmer teams) provide clear leadership for the development team. The team leader's role is that of both coordinator (as in the case of democratic teams) and technical mentor. In complex projects, team leaders may be required to devote as much as 50 percent of their time to technical and administrative activities.

The main activities of the chief engineer team leader are:

- Assigning tasks and responsibilities to the team members
- Supervising the work of the team members
- Providing advice and guidance to the team members
- Administrative and coordination activities (similar to the democratic team leader)

Chief engineer teams are appropriate for mixed teams and teams that are mainly comprised of junior or inexperienced developers. The team leader functions as a first level manager, and therefore should have adequate training in basic management techniques.

Chief engineer teams can also be successful in teams of senior and experienced developers, but the role is often unnecessary. When this structure is applied to a team of experienced engineers, it becomes doubly important for the team leader to have basic management skills, without which friction can develop between the team members and the team leader. In this respect, leading a team of experienced professionals is more difficult than leading a team of beginners.

---

1. See *The Peter Principle*, Peter and Hull (1970), for an interesting discussion of this phenomenon.

5.2.4 Expert teams

Expert teams are small teams that are established to solve specific problems within a project. An expert team may be established during project development when a complex problem arises, and the team may then be disbanded when the problem is solved. In some cases, expert teams may support the project throughout the development cycle. The objective of an expert team is to concentrate expertise in a specific area of the project.

As an example, consider an automatic bank teller system with two major subsystems; the bank's central computer and the remote automatic teller. The development plan for these two subsystems has assigned the development of each subsystem to a separate team, but the size of the project cannot justify a separate integration team. The two teams have performed initial subsystem testing and integration using simulators. However, when the two subsystems are integrated together, the communication between them fails.

There is always a danger in such situations that each of the two teams will look for the problem in the other team's work. Even when the two teams cooperate well, differences in implementation (or in design) may make it difficult for the problem to be resolved. As the schedule begins to slip, this becomes a major concern to the project manager.

In such cases, the project manager may decide to establish an expert team to resolve the communications problem. The team would comprise two communications experts (possibly from outside of the project staff) and two project engineers, one each from the two teams. This expert team would then concentrate its efforts on resolving the problem as quickly as possible, while the other two teams resume other development activities. After the communications problem between the two subsystems is resolved, the expert team can be disbanded.

In some respects, independent test teams and quality assurance teams can be viewed as expert teams (see Chapter 8 for a discussion of these topics). Independent test teams function primarily during the integration and test phases of the development cycle. The quality assurance team is an example of an expert team that functions throughout the project's development cycle.

An expert team frequently has highly experienced engineers. In such cases the team would most probably be constructed as a democratic team. In the preceding example, the team may be either a democratic team or it may be led by a senior communications expert.

5.3 BASIC REPORTING TECHNIQUES

For the project manager, it is essential to be constantly informed of the true status of the project. This is achieved by assuring the regular flow of accurate information from the development teams. Many of the methods of acquiring information are not objective and rely on the accuracy of the reports provided by the project developers themselves. They include:

- Periodic written status reports
- Verbal reports
- Status meetings
- Product demonstrations (demos)

Product demonstrations are particularly subjective, because they demonstrate only what the developer wishes to be seen. The project manager needs objective information. Such information can often be acquired from reports produced by support groups, such as:

- Quality assurance reports
- Independent test reports

Although reports and meetings are indeed useful sources of information, nothing can replace direct contact between the project manager and the development staff. Frequent informal talks with the developers are excellent sources of information, especially when held in an informal atmosphere (and not in the project manager's office).

The project manager must keep on constant guard against an error commonly referred to as the '90/50 syndrome', which states that 'it takes 50 percent of the time to complete 90 percent of the work, and an additional 50 percent of the time to complete the remaining 10 percent of the work'. This means that project developers will begin to boast quite early that they have 'almost finished' their tasks. Unfortunately, there is a great difference between 'almost finished' and 'finished'.

Finishing a task – writing documentation and polishing off the last few problems – often takes longer than developers anticipate. This is because these activities produce very few visible results, and developers tend (wrongly) to associate work with results. Therefore, managers can obtain more information from developers by asking them how long they estimate it will take to finish, and not how much of their work has been completed.

5.3.1 Status reports

Status reports should be required from *every* member of the development team, without exception. The reports should be submitted periodically, usually weekly or bi-weekly, and should contain at least the following three sections (see Fig. 5.8):

1. *Activities during the report period*
    Each subsection within this section describes a major activity during the report period. The description of each activity should span two to three lines. Activities should be linked to the project task list or work breakdown structure (WBS) (see Chapter 10 for a description of the WBS).
2. *Planned activities for the next report period*
    Each subsection within this section describes a major activity planned for the next report period. The description of each activity should span one to two lines.
3. *Problems*
    Each subsection within this section describes a major problem that either occurred during the report period, or that was reported previously and has not yet been resolved. This means that problems will be repeatedly reported until they are resolved. In particular, this section must explain why this report's Section 1 does not correspond to the previous report's Section 2.

All reports should also contain:

1. Date of report
2. Report period (e.g. 3 July to 10 July 1992)
3. Name of report (e.g. Communications team status report)
4. Name of person submitting the report

The preparation of a periodic status report should take about 20 minutes, but not longer than 30 minutes. Developers should submit their status reports to their team leader. The team leader then combines the reports of the team into a single status report, while maintaining the same report structure. This activity should take the team leader about 30 minutes, but not longer than 45 minutes (this is easily done when the reports are prepared and submitted by electronic mail).

Each team leader submits the team status report to the project manager. The individual status reports need not be submitted; these should be filed and submitted to the project manager only on request.

From: John Doe, Team Leader
To: Frank Smith, Project Manager
Date: 15 June 1993

User interface team: weekly status report
for the period 5–12 June 1993

1. Activities during the report period:

1.1 The design of the user help screens (activity 3.12.6) was completed on schedule. The design specs were submitted to configuration control.

1.2 Coding of the command pass through modules (activity group 5.12) continues, and is currently behind schedule by about 1 week.

$$\vdots \qquad\qquad\qquad \vdots$$

2. Activities planned for next week:

2.1 Coding of the command pass through modules (activity group 5.12) will be completed, and unit tests will be started.

2.2 Two members of the team (Ed and Joan) will attend a two day course on the programmer's interface to the new user interface package. This is an unscheduled activity that was approved at the last project meeting. This will not delay the schedule, due to the early completion of the command pass through modules (see Section 1.2 above).

$$\vdots \qquad\qquad\qquad \vdots$$

3. Problems:

3.1 The user interface package we originally planned to use was found to be inadequate for the project. Two team members will study the new proposed package (see Section 2.2 above). If the new package is also found to be unsuitable, then this will severely impact our development schedule.

3.2 One of our team members (Jack Brown) has been using an old VT100 terminal instead of a workstation for the past two weeks, due to the acute shortage of workstations. This is the reason why Jack's task 5.12 was not completed this week, as scheduled.

Figure 5.8 Example of a weekly status report.

The project manager also receives status reports from other project support personnel such as the project systems engineer or the deputy project manager. The project manager then prepares the project status report by combining the individual reports received into a single three-part report. The project status report is then submitted to top management.

Project status reports are not necessarily submitted at the same frequency as internal project status reports. Project reports may be submitted bi-weekly or monthly.[2]

5.3.2 Project status meetings

Project status meetings should be held periodically, usually once a week. A good time for status meetings is either at the end of the last day of the week, or at the beginning of the first day of the week. Status meetings also contribute to the atmosphere of order and control within the project, and should be held regularly, at a fixed time. Participants who cannot participate in the project status meeting may, with the project manager's approval, delegate participation to another member of their team.

The project manager prepares for the status meeting by reviewing the status reports submitted by the key project members (particularly scrutinizing the problem section). Therefore the status reports should be submitted at least two to three hours before the status meeting.

Project status meetings are attended by the key project members. The meeting begins with a report of project activities and general issues by the project manager. Then each participant should be given about five to ten minutes to report on the activity of his or her team or area of responsibility. The discussion of problems should not be restricted to the person reporting the problem and the project manager. All problems may be addressed by all participants, with possible assistance offered between team leaders, thus making their experience available throughout the project. It is not the project manager's role to provide solutions to the problems, but rather to guide the team members toward solutions.

Solutions should be worked out whenever possible during the status meeting. Any problem not resolved within five minutes should be postponed for discussion by the relevant parties after the status meeting.

The proceedings of all project status meetings must be recorded. Verbatim minutes are not required, though the following items should appear in the record:

1. Date of meeting
2. Name of meeting
3. Present (list of participants)
4. Absent (list of absent invited participants)
5. Action items (name, action, date for completion)
6. Major decisions and items discussed

The record of the project status meeting should be typed and distributed as soon as possible, but no later than by the end of the day. This is particularly important when there are action items to be completed on the same day. When the project is sufficiently large to justify a secretary, then the record will be taken and typed by the secretary. In smaller projects, the project manager can rotate this task each week between the participants.

---

2. Chapter 10 discusses further how status reports are used to update the project development schedule.

5.4 GENERAL GUIDELINES FOR MANAGING SOFTWARE ENGINEERS

Many of the guidelines in this section are equally applicable to all types of engineer. However, owing to the diverse characteristics of software engineers discussed at the beginning of this chapter, good management techniques are more important in the management of software than in most other areas of technology. Therefore a basic guideline for software managers is that education in the area of modern management methods, particularly in the management of people, is essential for success. This is true for team leaders and project managers alike.

Management by agreement is preferable to management by edict. It is always best to have an engineer *accept* the assigned task. This provides what is commonly referred to as *ownership* of the task, and increases the motivation of the engineer significantly. In order to achieve this, engineers should be assigned tasks that they want whenever this is possible. When this is not possible, the project manager should candidly describe the options available and explain to the engineer why specific tasks are not available.

Responsibility must always go side by side with authority. All project staff members, no matter how junior, must be given authority to act within their area of responsibility. Quality assurance engineers must have the authority to approve or reject product components, and development engineers must have the authority to make design decisions related to the components that they are developing. However, no authority is absolute, and higher level personnel within the project must constantly review these decisions and step in when they feel an error is being made.

As a general rule, only outright errors should be corrected. This leads to one of the basic rules of project development: *a better way of doing something is not sufficient grounds for change*. In other words, if the manager feels that he or she could have made a better decision, but the current decision is acceptable, then the decision should not be changed.

Ownership is not related only to tasks, but also to the schedule and resources that go with the tasks. All schedules should be agreed to by the implementors. In fact, schedule estimates should be prepared together with the implementors. This assures a commitment by the implementor or developer to adhere to the schedule.

Lastly, motivation is the single most important factor in the successful management of the development team. Motivation can be encouraged in many ways:

- Salary and remuneration
- Advancement (promotion)
- Working conditions and environment
- Interest in the assigned work
- Peer esteem
- Appreciation
- Promoting a sense of achievement

Many managers make the mistake of assuming that the prime motivator is salary. This is not so. The most effective motivators are sense of achievement and appreciation (see Giegold 1982). This means that it is important to explain to the development team members just how important their work is to the project and the company (and possibly to the country or humanity as in the case of the development of a medical support system). People are highly motivated when they believe that they are doing something important.

Appreciation is also a high motivator. For the project manager to call someone into his office and say 'thanks, you have been doing a great job' can do wonders. Other ways of showing appreciation are by issuing letters of appreciation with copies to higher management and to the personnel department, or by sending employees who have made an extraordinary effort on a weekend vacation. All these will increase motivation, not only for the individual employee being thanked, but for others throughout the project.

5.5 SUMMARY

Managing software engineers is more difficult than managing engineers in most other areas of technology. Software engineers are widely diverse in their level of productivity. In an average project, it is not uncommon to find productivity ratios of 1:5. One of the targets of modern day software engineering has been to reduce this range of productivity among software developers through more organized and systematic methods of software development.

There are many ways of organizing a software project. The most suitable project organizational structure depends on the type of project being developed. Large and complex projects require large organizational structures. Irrespective of project size, software projects should be organized into small development teams. Ideally, a software team will contain four to six developers, and will be led by a team leader.

There are three types of software team:

- Democratic teams, which are led administratively by the team leader. Technical decisions are made by all members of the team.
- Chief engineer teams (or chief programmer teams), which are led by an experienced senior engineer, whose responsibilities are to lead both administratively and technically.
- Expert teams are established to resolve special problems within the project. They may be disbanded when the special problem is resolved.

For the project manager, it is essential to be constantly informed regarding the true status of the project. There are many methods of acquiring information; most rely directly on the provision of information by the developers. However, frequent informal talks with the developers are also excellent sources of information, especially when held in an informal atmosphere (and not in the project manager's office).

Motivation is the single most important factor in the successful management of the development team. Many managers make the mistake of assuming that the prime motivator is salary. This is not so. The most effective motivators are sense of achievement and appreciation. People are highly motivated when they believe that they are doing something important and when they feel that their effort is being recognized.

EXERCISES

1. You are project manager for a communications project linking all the stores in a large department store chain. Each store currently has its own computer, connected to the checkout registers. The management of the chain wants to install a central computer in the main office, and to connect all the store computers to the central computer via a wide area network. The central computer will receive real-time information on the transactions at the stores and will update a central inventory data base.

Prepare a pyramid organizational chart for the store communications project. Explain the structure you have chosen, and why it is better suited than other possible organizational structures.

2. Plan the flow of information within the organization that you have proposed in Exercise 1. Which reports will be required, and how often will they be submitted? Which status meetings will be required, and how often will they be held? Who will attend?

Suggest a varying frequency for the status reports and the status meetings, according to the different phases of development.

3. Prepare a matrix organizational chart for the project described in Exercise 1. Compare it to the pyramid structure you proposed in Exercise 1; which is more suited to the project? What are the advantages and the disadvantages of each organizational structure for this project?

4. Propose the structure of the development and support teams for the project described in Exercise 1. Explain the structure you have chosen. Do you foresee a need for any expert teams during the development of the project?

5. Class project: divide the class into three or four groups of students. Assign Exercises 1, 2 and 4 to each group. Have each group present their solutions to the class.

Compare the solutions proposed by each group. Discuss the differences between the solutions.

HOW TO HANDLE LARGE PROJECTS: DIVIDE AND CONQUER

LARGE NEED NOT MEAN DIFFICULT

Many complex objects can be viewed as a collection of numerous simpler objects. An appropriate example would be a complex chemical compound that is formed by various molecules, each of which is formed by combining various atoms. The atom, though itself divisible, can be regarded as the smallest particle of a chemical substance.

In a similar way, a complex project can be divided into simpler components. While the full project may be difficult to manage, each component will be easier to handle. Software projects can be decomposed into smaller components in order to provide better estimates of the amount of work involved, or in order to monitor the activities of the various development teams.

The decomposition of a software project is one of the software project manager's first tasks. However, the method of decomposition may differ, depending on the project manager's actual objective. A functional decomposition of a project may not be the same as a design decomposition. A functional decomposition divides the project into its basic components from a user's perspective, while a design decomposition divides a project into its basic programming components or modules.

This chapter discusses methods for effectively managing complex software projects, and presents methods for decomposing projects into manageable components. The various types of project decomposition are also discussed, and the objectives of each type of decomposition are explained.

6.1 STEPWISE REFINEMENT

Intuitively, it would not appear reasonable to attempt to identify all project components in a single step. Clearly, an iterative procedure that would gradually provide more detail would be easier to use. Iterative methods of this kind are called *stepwise refinement*, as the decomposition is further refined in each succeeding step.

Figure 6.1 presents a general illustration of stepwise refinement. The system is initially divided into three top level components. In turn each top level component is further divided into lower level components, and so forth, until the lowest decomposition level is reached.

In a stepwise decomposition of a project, each component decomposes into the components directly below it, so that each step of the decomposition describes the full system, but at a different level of detail. In Fig. 6.1, components 1, 2 and 3 comprise the complete system. For

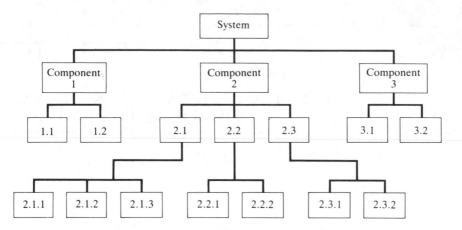

Figure 6.1 Software decomposition by stepwise refinement.

more detail we take the next decomposition step, and find that components 1.1, 1.2, 2.1, 2.2, 2.3, 3.1 and 3.2 now represent the whole system.

A stepwise refinement diagram looks similar to a hierarchical system chart. However, it is important to understand that stepwise refinement is basically different because the diagram's building blocks are different. A hierarchical system diagram describes the hierarchical relationship between components, so that each component in the diagram actually corresponds to a real component in the system. However, in a stepwise refinement diagram, a higher level component is only a name conveniently given to a group of real components that appear below it.

In Fig. 6.2(a) the Controlled access system software has five low level software components: Visitor identification, Door lock control, Access file manager, Illegal access identification and Alarm activation. Each of these five modules may correspond to an actual software module.[1] The two high level components, Access control and Alarm system, do not exist as actual software modules, and only appear as names given to the two groups of lower level components.

Figure 6.2(b) describes the same Controlled access system software, but this time it is represented as a hierarchical chart. Here, each component in the diagram represents a real software component. The System executive main Loop component calls three other components: Visitor identification, Door lock control and Alarm activation. The Visitor identification component calls two components: Illegal access identification and Access file manager.

6.1.1 Functional decomposition

The functional decomposition of a software project is a division of the system into its operational components as they are seen by the user. Functional decomposition is part of the requirements phase of a project. The objective of this phase is to define all the characteristics of the system from the user's perspective.

Let us consider an automatic bank teller system. The ability to communicate on-line between the remote automatic tellers and the bank's central computer in order to provide updated account information is a functional characteristic of the system. This will usually be defined

---

1. This is, of course, a simplification of a real system. In reality, these five low level components would be further decomposed into lower level components.

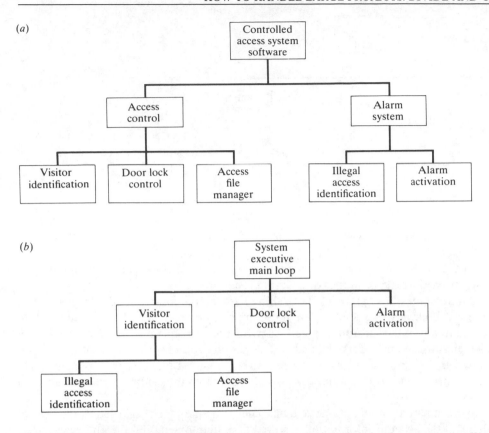

Figure 6.2 (*a*) Decomposition of high level components into low level components; (*b*) a hierarchical structure chart.

during the requirements phase of the development cycle. However, the method of transmission between the automatic teller and the central computer is not a functional characteristic of the system, as this is internal to the design and implementation of the system and is not apparent to the user. The method of transmission, including the communications protocol, will usually be defined during the design phase of the development of the system.[2]

Figure 6.3 presents an example of the functional decomposition of an automatic bank teller system into lower levels of functional components. In Fig. 6.3 we have determined that there will be a customer data base, which could be viewed as a design decision. This is unavoidable. The functional decomposition is rarely completely devoid of all design considerations. As we will see, the functional decomposition is often a starting point for the initial design of the system.

6.1.2 Design decomposition

The design decomposition of a software system is a division of the system into lower level components that coincide with the actual software components of the system. In a full design

---

2. Implementation decisions may occasionally be dictated during the requirements phase, and are referred to as *implementation requirements*. This may include such features as the type of object computer, the programming language to be used, or the method of communications to be used. It is usually better to delay implementation decisions until the design phase whenever possible.

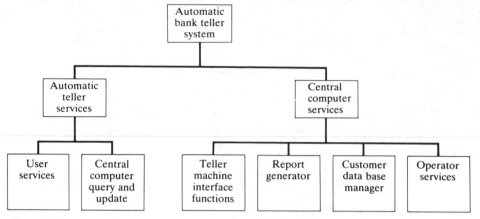

Figure 6.3 Automatic teller system – functional decomposition diagram.

decomposition of a software system, the lowest components correspond to programming modules (usually procedures, subroutines or program functions).

Just as the requirements phase precedes the design phase, so the functional decomposition of a software system will usually precede the design decomposition. The functional decomposition will often provide much of the information necessary for the subsequent division of the system into the implementation components. In fact, the functional decomposition is often a good place to start when designing a software system, as the major functional components of a system will often correspond to the initial division of the system into subsystems or high level components.

Two of the main functions of an automatic bank teller system may be regarded as the central computer, where all the account information is stored and maintained, and the automatic teller machines that interface with the customers. The communications network that links the central computer with the teller locations may be defined as an additional high level component. This, then, would naturally be the first division of the system from a design perspective: (1) the automatic teller subsystem,[3] (2) the central computer subsystem and (3) the communications network facility.

Figure 6.4 presents an example of the design decomposition of an automatic bank teller system into lower levels of design components. On the third level, the Automatic teller component decomposes into the Hardware interfaces, and the Teller logic. The next level may then decompose the Hardware interfaces into the Keyboard driver, the Display driver, the Printer driver and the Beeper. At this level, these drivers may represent actual software modules.

An important point to remember is that in a design decomposition, only the lower level components are actually implemented. Higher level components represent a group of lower level components. This is illustrated in Fig. 6.2(a), where the Access control and the Alarm system components represent two groups of lower level components (Visitor identification, Door lock control etc.).

Design decomposition basically produces two types of system component: high level components and low level modules. Different software development standards use different terminology to identify the various levels of decomposition.

---

3. In large systems, subsystems often represent the first level decomposition of a system. This is further discussed in Section 6.3.

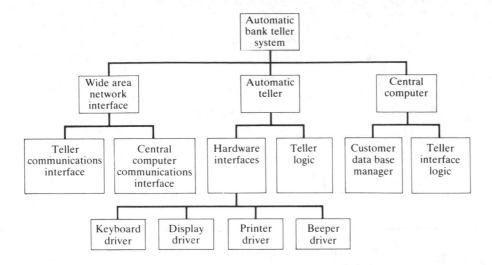

Figure 6.4 Automatic teller system – design decomposition diagram.

For example, the US DOD Standard 2167A (DOD 1988a) uses a somewhat cumbersome multilevel method of decomposition (see Fig. 9.4). It uses the term CSU (computer software unit) to identify the lowest level decomposition component. Intermediate level components are called CSCs (computer software components) and these may represent a group of CSUs and CSCs. High level CSCs are grouped into CSCIs (computer software configuration items), and these CSCIs are managed within the project as semi-independent development units. CSCIs are components that can be designed, documented and approved as separate entities within the overall software project. The DOD 2167A standard for software development is further discussed in Chapter 10.

A fully decomposed system, with all its low level components, is not always easy to grasp. This is especially true during the presentation of the system at a project review, when the system needs to be quickly understood by people who have not been involved in its design. On such occasions, the stepwise refinement technique is a convenient method for gradually presenting progressive detail by initially showing the first decomposition level, and then slowly revealing subsequent levels. This is demonstrated in Fig. 6.5. At a convenient intermediate decomposition step we can divide the design in two: the upper levels and the lower levels. This is used particularly when the design phase is implemented in two distinct stages: top level design and detailed design (see Fig. 6.5).

6.2 THE WORK BREAKDOWN STRUCTURE

So far we have discussed the division of a software *system* into either functional or design components. We will also consider the division of a software *project* into basic work components. The sum total of these work components covers all the tasks that need to be performed in order to complete the project successfully.

Large projects are difficult to manage. Without some basic order in the assignment of work tasks it is almost impossible to control the many people, materials and functions that are involved in the development process.

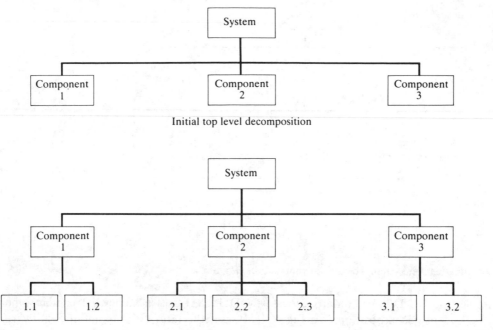

Initial top level decomposition

Intermediate level decomposition—top level design

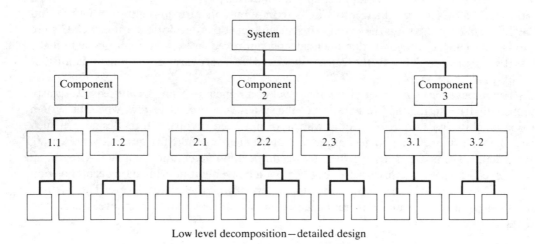

Low level decomposition—detailed design

Figure 6.5 Software decomposition by stepwise refinement.

6.2.1 Project decomposition

Just like any other large complex task, the development of a software project is more easily managed with the *divide and conquer* approach. Stepwise refinement, when applied to a software project, produces all the low level work tasks. This includes development tasks, managerial tasks, support tasks and administrative tasks. The decomposition of a software project into tasks is referred to as the *work breakdown structure*, or the *WBS*.

(a)

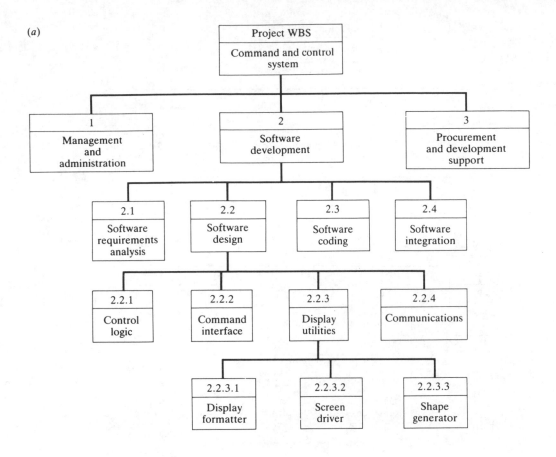

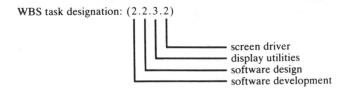

Figure 6.6 Work breakdown structure: (a) task designation.

Figure 6.6 presents an example of a work breakdown structure chart, and Table 6.1 presents the resulting work breakdown structure task list. The WBS task list contains all project work tasks, and can be used as a monitoring tool to monitor the status of assigned work tasks.

The initial WBS task list is often derived from the project schedule, which contains the project's activity list. The schedule activity list is similar to the WBS, though its purpose is different and it is usually less detailed. The schedule activity list is described in Chapter 10.

(b)

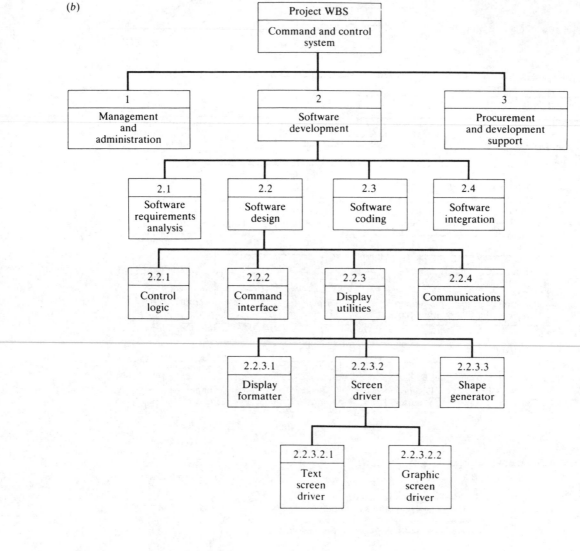

WBS task designation: (2. 2. 3. 2. 2)

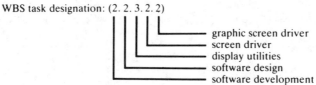

graphic screen driver
screen driver
display utilities
software design
software development

Figure 6.6 Work breakdown structure: (b) adding a task.

Table 6.1 Work breakdown structure task list

Task ID	Description	Status	Assigned to	Comments
1.	Management and administration			
2.	Software development			
2.1	Software requirement analysis			
2.2	Software design			
2.2.1	Control logic			
2.2.2	Command interface			
2.2.3	Display utilities			
2.2.3.1	Display formatter	Complete	J. Smith	
2.2.3.2	Screen driver	Started	F. Brown	
2.2.3.3	Shape generator	Started	A. Black	
2.2.4	Communications			
2.3	Software coding			
2.4	Software integration			
3.	Procurement and development support			
.	.			
.	.			
.	.			

It is sometimes helpful to include the higher level task groups in the WBS task list (e.g. tasks 1, 2, 3, 2.1, 2.2, etc. in Table 6.1). This provides a useful traceback for each low level task in order to identify the task groups from which it was derived. However, inclusion of high level task groups in the WBS task list can also cause confusion, as these items do not represent actual assigned tasks, and the *Status* and *Assigned to* attributes do not apply to them.

The WBS list of project tasks is derived from the project's *statement of work* (the *SOW*) that defines the scope of the project. The SOW is usually prepared before the official launching of the project (see Chapter 3), and is often part of the project contract between the customer and the developer. For internal projects, when an organization is funding its own development work, the SOW becomes synonymous with the Project definition specification or a similar document that defines the scope of work for the software project manager.

6.2.2 The WBS as a project management tool

The work breakdown structure defines all tasks to be performed during the development of the project. This will include tasks from such project categories as:

- Software development
- Installation
- Maintenance
- Management
- Training
- Procurement
- Documentation

These tasks are described in more detail in Table 6.2 (Section 6.3.4).

At all times, any work being performed by a member of the software project team must be part of a WBS task. No member of the team should ever perform any task that does not appear in the WBS list of tasks.

The WBS is a useful tool provided it is constantly updated. It should be updated periodically, together with the project development plan and the project schedule. It is reasonable to expect the WBS list to have tasks added, modified or even removed as project development progresses.

The WBS is essentially a management tool that provides the ability to assign well-defined tasks to members of the development team. It is through the WBS that progress is monitored as tasks are completed and potential problems are discovered. New tasks that were overlooked are identified, and estimates are revised based on the actual resources used for completed tasks.

The WBS is also a budgetary tool that provides a means of charging each development activity to the appropriate section in the project budget. This is one of the basic methods for planning and monitoring project expenditure.

There are many computerized utilities available to support the maintenance of the WBS. These utilities run both on small PC type computers and large mainframes. WBS utilities are often available as part of a manager's general planning utility, and provide other scheduling and monitoring features, such as PERT analysis and report generation.

Other methods have been developed for managing the many low level work tasks that comprise a large project. There are several variations and enhancements of the work breakdown structure technique,[4] some using sophisticated tracking tools, others using special symbols and techniques to analyze and monitor the work task list.

6.3 HANDLING LARGE PROJECTS

Clearly, small tasks are easier to handle than large tasks. As we have seen, this has been the reasoning behind the division of large projects into smaller components.

In a paper on the architecture of the space shuttle software system, Carlow (1984) remarked that '... tools and techniques alone cannot prevent or overcome the problems that will exist if a well-structured system architecture has not been established on the front end of the development process'. In his paper, Carlow describes the reasoning behind the structure and architecture of the complex software for one of the systems that was developed by the IBM Federal Systems Division for NASA's space shuttle. The point being made is that software architecture that is determined early in the development cycle plays a major role in establishing the quality of the final software product. Or, in short, major errors often start early.

The way in which a system is decomposed contributes significantly to the software architecture. There is usually no such thing as a single correct architecture or a single correct decomposition. Figure 6.7 presents two possible high level decompositions of a controlled access system. Both appear to be reasonable divisions of the system, but the architecture in Fig. 6.7(b) may require fewer interfaces between the main software components.

We will now consider some of the guidelines that should be followed when selecting a particular decomposition structure.

6.3.1 Subsystems

Large systems are often composed of major semi-independent components that may, themselves, be viewed as systems. An automatic bank teller system may be divided rather

---

4. Alternate methods include the Wilson and Sifer (1990) model that replaces the WBS with a structured planning technique based on a hierarchy of *work flow diagrams* (WFDs), a form of network of tasks that includes each task's input and output. The Wilson and Sifer method is a highly formal method and is considerably more complex than the classic WBS.

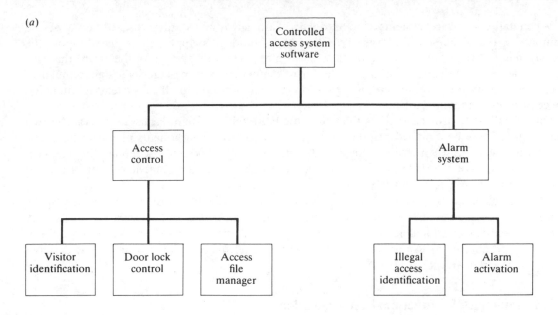

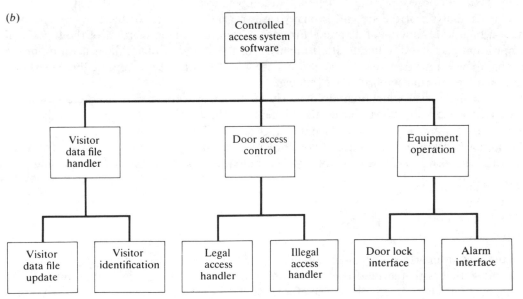

Figure 6.7 High level system decomposition – two approaches. Two different system architectures – (a) and (b).

naturally into two subsystems: the main computer subsystem and the automatic teller computer subsystem. Thus, a subsystem contains most of the characteristics of a system, except that a subsystem is not intended to function on its own.

When large software systems can be divided into subsystems, they discard some of the complexity that comes with largeness. The idea behind this approach is based upon the management of the development of each subsystem as a separate system, to the extent that this is possible. For each subsystem, a team leader or deputy project manager is assigned much of the responsibility for development, while responsibilities common to all subsystems are handled by central project management.

On a small-scale project, such as the automatic bank teller system discussed previously, two team leaders may be assigned responsibility for the two main components of the system. The project manager will then monitor the activities in each team, and will coordinate the technical and administrative interface activities between the teams. The assignment of software team leaders is further discussed in Chapter 5.

On a larger scale project, such as the development of the software for the NASA space shuttle, the project was so massive that it was, in fact, developed as several separate projects. A central office was responsible for the coordination and integration of all subsystems (both software and hardware). An insight into the magnitude of this complex project is provided in a paper by Madden and Rone (1984).

6.3.2 Guidelines for functional decomposition

As we have seen, the initial division of a software system is the functional decomposition, which corresponds to the structure of the software as it is perceived by the user. This division assists us in defining the requirements for the system and provides a method of identifying low level functions and attributing them to major system functions.

Many texts propose that the functional decomposition of a system should follow the requirements analysis of the system. In many cases a general outline of the requirements will produce a high level functional diagram. From that point on, the refinement of the functional decomposition goes hand in hand with the analysis of the system. In fact, the generation of the functional diagram is often an iterative process, in which the diagram is repeatedly revised and refined, as more information becomes available.

The basic high level functional decomposition of a software system is often based on preconceived ideas that evolve during the conception phase. These ideas may then dictate a specific division of the system from which the functional decomposition evolves.

This initial division of the system is not always the most logical and appropriate from the developer's perspective. A large inventory system could initially be perceived as comprising:

- A human interface
- A data base
- A report generator
- Update logic

But the human interface may span a number of different computers, and part of it may be heavily integrated with the report generator. Major features, such as reliability and backup features, may have been overlooked. Therefore a better division of the system might not define *human interface* as a high level function, preferring to include separate human interface low level functions within other major functions. Also, backup may be included in a high level *maintenance* function that would also cover data base compression and clean-up functions.

As a general guideline, no single functional decomposition should be selected just because it was conceived first.

As we have seen, a good functional decomposition is important, and may well determine the design and architecture of the system being developed. A sound strategy for defining a good software functional decomposition is to convene a meeting of the central people in the project at which a number of different divisions of the system are discussed. A functional decomposition should then be selected based on:

- Reason (e.g. different computers usually support separate functions)
- Ease of implementation (e.g. a good functional decomposition will usually foster a good design)
- Comprehensiveness (have all functions been covered?)

Ease of implementation is dependent on design criteria that are discussed next.

6.3.3 Guidelines for design decomposition

We have seen that the functional decomposition of a software system may be substantially different from the design decomposition of the system. However, a good functional decomposition will have taken into account design as the next development phase, and will often be a good starting point for the division of the system into high level design components.

The design decomposition of a system is only part of the full design of the software (there are many design methods – see, for example, Fairly (1985), or Pressman (1992)). However, from the project manager's perspective this is a crucial stage, as the design decomposition of a system determines the structure of the software as it will be built. The following is an overview of the basic design considerations that influence the method of system decomposition.

One of the early basic concepts of software engineering required a *structured* approach to the design and programming of software. The structured nature of the software is determined from the first stages of decomposition. In the late 1960s and early 1970s this approach was championed by Dijkstra (1972). The main objective was to move software development, (or simply *programming*, as it was then called) from immaturity to a fully developed engineering discipline. Many other structured design techniques have since been developed by Yourdon and Constantine (1978), Jackson (1975), DeMarco (1979) and Warnier and Orr (1977), to name but a few, but no single generally accepted standard has yet emerged.

As more experience was gained in the development of complex software projects, it became evident that the best design decomposition should strive to produce independent software components, or modules. Complex interfaces between modules were strongly discouraged, and such terms as low coupling, high cohesion and information hiding became the basic building blocks for good software modular design.

Simply stated, a good design decomposition produces small, simple, independent modules. Of course, in any system no two modules are truly independent, so the term independent here should be interpreted as meaning *as independent as possible* within the constraints of the project being developed.

On the lowest decomposition level, the degree of independence of modules is referred to as the extent of *coupling* that exists in the design. Coupling measures such interdependent features as data, control and module content (i.e. overlapping of module boundaries).

Probably one of the most fundamental principles in the design decomposition of software is centered around the concept of the *black box*. This principle, also referred to as *information hiding*, strives to produce modules that hide their design. Black boxes are only identified by their input and output, and not by the method that they use to generate the output from the input. Information hiding produces modules that hide their logic flow, and their data structures, from each other. Though the term *black box* preceded the evolution of software engineering as a discipline, the concept of information hiding in software design was first formulated by Parnas (1972).[5]

6.3.4 Guidelines for decomposition of work tasks

We have seen that the work required to complete a project can be divided into a group of simpler well-defined tasks represented by the *work breakdown structure* or the *WBS*. The WBS is not a decomposition of the software produced by the project; it is a decomposition of the project itself, and includes such activities as management, procurement, installation and, of course, software development.

The design structure of the system produces low level *development* work tasks. Each low level module is assigned three basic work tasks: module design, coding and unit testing. Additional development tasks such as prototyping, testing, and integration are derived from the other development phases.

Table 6.2 contains a typical list of high level WBS tasks to be included in the formal WBS task list (see Table 6.1). This is not an exhaustive list of all project development tasks, and not all projects will require all the tasks described. However, this table will be useful as a checklist to assist in locating tasks that may have been overlooked.

Non-development activities, such as high level management WBS tasks, are standard, to a large extent, and any variance is determined by either the magnitude of the project, or the introduction of a new management model. An example of a list of management WBS tasks appears in Table 6.3. This list contains many of the most important management tasks required for most software development projects. Those tasks that are mandatory for all projects are marked as such in the list.

Note that budget analysis and administration is not a mandatory management task, simply because not all projects administer their own budget. Some organizations have a financial officer responsible for the administration of project budgets.

Customer interface is also not a mandatory management task because not all projects have a customer. In the case of company internal projects, high level management, together with the designated users of the system being developed, play the role of customer. It is usually they who specify the initial project requirements, and it is to them that the project manager must come for final approval and for final system acceptance.

6.4 SUMMARY

Complex software projects can be divided into simpler components, and though the full project may be difficult to manage, each component will be easier to handle. The decomposition of software projects into smaller components is helpful in monitoring the activities assigned to the various development teams. The method of decomposition may differ, depending on the project manager's objective.

Stepwise refinement is an iterative method for the decomposition of a project into manageable components. Stepwise refinement is a useful tool for the definition of the functional, design and work decompositions of a software project. In a stepwise decomposition of a project, each component decomposes into the components directly below it. Each step of the decomposition describes the full system, but at a different level of detail.

---

5. A more detailed discussion of these design concepts can be found in the texts by Fairly (1985) and by Pressman (1992).

Table 6.2 High level work breakdown structure tasks

Software development
  Requirements analysis
  Prototype development
    Prototype specification
    Prototype design
    Prototype implementation
  Design
    Top level design
    Detailed design
  Implementation
    Coding
    Unit test
  Integration
    Software integration
    Hardware/software integration
  Testing
    Alpha testing
    Beta testing
    Acceptance
Installation
Maintenance
  Error correction
  Software enhancement
Management
  Planning
  Staffing
  Administration and services
  Budget administration
  Personnel management
  Quality assurance
  Configuration management
Training
Procurement
  Acquisition of development tools
  Acquisition of system components (off the shelf)
  Equipment selection
  Vendor selection
  Ordering procedure
  Inventory control
Documentation
  Technical writing
  Project publishing activities
  Development documentation
    Non-deliverable development documentation
    Deliverable development documentation
  Maintenance documentation
  User documentation

Table 6.3 Management and administration tasks

Mandatory	Management task
√	1. Planning
√	2. Preparation of estimates
√	3. Risk analysis and risk management
√	4. Scheduling
	5. Staffing
	6. Budget analysis and administration
√	7. Personnel management
√	8. Task assignment
√	9. Delegation of authority
√	10. Assignment of development resources
	11. Supervision of development equipment maintenance
√	12. Supervision and control of development
√	13. Organization of reviews and formal presentations
	14. Establishment of standards and methods
√	15. Quality assurance and control
√	16. Configuration management and control
	17. Supervision of subcontractors and vendors
√	18. Higher management interface and coordination
	19. Customer interface and coordination
√	20. Reporting
	21. Administration and services

The functional decomposition of a software project is a division of the system into its operational components; that is, those features that are seen by the user. The design decomposition of a software system is a division of the system into lower level components that coincide with the programming components of the system. The work breakdown structure (WBS) is the decomposition of a software project into low level work tasks.

Clearly, small tasks are easier to handle than large tasks, and this has been the reasoning behind the division of large projects into smaller components. Large systems are often composed of major semi-independent components, called subsystems, that may themselves be viewed as systems. When large software systems can be divided into subsystems, they discard some of the complexity that comes with largeness. The idea behind this approach is based upon the management of the development of each subsystem as a separate system to the extent possible.

The basic high level functional decomposition of a software system is often based on preconceived ideas that evolve during the conception phase. These ideas may then dictate a specific division of the system from which the functional decomposition then evolves. However, this initial division of the system is not always the most logical and appropriate from the developer's perspective. As a general guideline, no single functional decomposition should be selected just because it was conceived first.

The functional decomposition of a software system may be substantially different from the design decomposition of the system. However, a good functional decomposition will have taken into account design as the next development phase, and will often be a good starting point for the division of the system into high level design components. The high level design components are then further decomposed into successive lower levels that ultimately produce programming modules. A good modular design produces small, simple, independent modules.

The work breakdown structure is not a decomposition of the software produced by the project, but is a decomposition of the project itself, and includes such activities as management, procurement, installation and, of course, software development. Many of the WBS development tasks are derived from the development method that will be used, and from the design and architecture of the system.

EXERCISES

1. Software Systems Inc. (SSI) is developing a special purpose computer based on a common microprocessor. SSI have a cross compiler for the microprocessor that runs on their mainframe. The company has decided to develop a modest proprietary operating system for the new computer.

Consider a simple single-user operating system. Prepare a proposal for the functional decomposition of the operating system using stepwise refinement. Describe the functional decomposition chart for the first three levels.

2. For the operating system described in Exercise 1, and based on the functional decomposition, prepare a design decomposition. Describe the design decomposition chart for the first three levels. Choose a single high level component and describe the full decomposition down to the software module level.

Explain how you have taken into account the guidelines for independent modules. Explain how you have implemented the information hiding guidelines.

3. For the operating system described in Exercise 1, prepare a work breakdown structure chart for the first three levels and prepare a WBS tasks list.

Explain why some of the tasks in Table 6.2 are not applicable to this project.

4. Consider the software for a satellite project, including the launching and tracking of the satellite, and the operation of the satellite during and after launch.

Identify the main subsystems in the project and explain the advantage that is to be gained by defining them as subsystems.

Now consider a payroll system, including the staff file maintenance, issuance of payroll checks etc. Would there be any advantage in defining subsystems for this project? Explain.

SEVEN

SOFTWARE PROJECT MANAGEMENT IN A CLIENT/SERVER ENVIRONMENT

THE EVOLUTION OF A NAME

Are client/server software projects easier or more difficult to manage than other types of project? Well, firstly, it depends on whether you are developing *on* them or *for* them. In other words is your client/server system a development environment or is it a target environment?

Secondly, is your project well suited for this type of distributed environment or was it dictated by circumstance (i.e. you had no choice!)? Let us first understand how and why this distributed architecture evolved.

Some of the mainframes of just two decades ago would be easily shamed by the personal computers of today. The giant CDC 6000 series or the IBM 370 series would have a hard time competing today with many of the features of a 66 MHz 486 PC, not to mention Intel's Pentium or Motorola's Power PC.

One of the first challenges to mainframes came from minicomputers such as Digital Equipment's PDP and VAX. The minicomputers competed well in price and software, but in performance they could not compete with the sheer power of their bigger brothers. The small computer's lack of power was mostly evident in two areas: number crunching and the number of users. As computers became even smaller, cheaper and more versatile, the idea of connecting them together began to catch on. DEC had clusters, IBM had networks, and throughout the

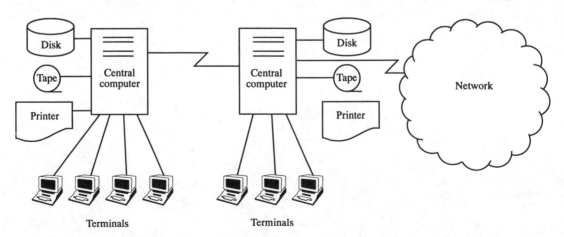

Figure 7.1 Distributed computer system.

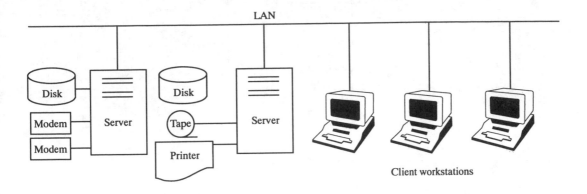

Figure 7.2 Client/server system.

industry the battle raged between the proponents of distributed processing and the proponents of centralized processing. When the battle smoke subsided, the supporters of distributed networked computers had won.

The distribution of computing power started the evolution toward client/server systems. For the software project manager this posed a new type of challenge. While the distributed system approach placed a computer in every department, the client/server approach placed a computer on every desk. Figure 7.1 presents a typical distributed system and Fig. 7.2 presents a client/server system.

The client/server concept places computing power in the hands of the end users, while allowing them to choose their own front-end computer. This new architecture provides both new challenges and opportunities for managing the development of a software project. This chapter discusses client/server environments from the *software project manager's* perspective. For a basic understanding of client/server systems in general, the reader is directed to any of several available texts on the subject.[1]

7.1 AN INTRODUCTION TO CLIENT/SERVER ENVIRONMENTS

The client/server concept can be applied to two basic models: the development environment model and the application environment model. In the development environment, a client server system is a development tool facilitating the development of a software project. In the application environment, a client/server system provides a specific service. From a more general perspective both models can be perceived as overlapping, as clearly a development tool also provides a specific service. The following examples illustrate the difference between the two models.

The network presented in Fig. 7.2 is a good example of a client/server development environment. In this example each software developer is provided with a client computer. The

1. See Sinha's excellent summary for a comprehensive technical overview of client/server computing (Sinha 1992), or Inmon's text on the development of client/server systems (Inmon 1993).

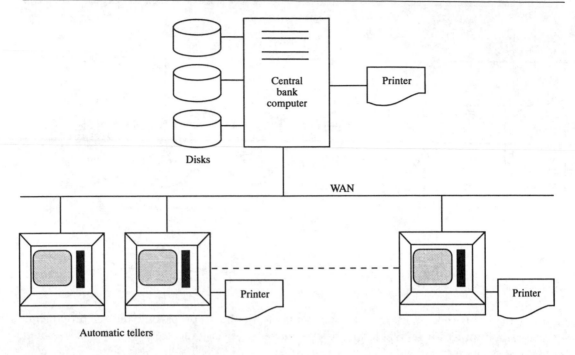

Figure 7.3 Automatic bank teller system.

developers communicate with each other through the network of servers and client computers, and share the resources (e.g. disk space or printers) connected to the servers.

A network of automatic bank tellers (see Fig. 7.3) is an example of an application client/ server environment where each client is a teller computer and each server is a regional (or central) computer. Here the *client/server* concept is applied to an architecture that existed before the *client/server* term was coined. Though this example includes the basic components of a client/server application system it does not include some of the added frills that come with modern client/server systems (such as direct communications between clients).

Another example of an application client/server environment is an inventory system where client computers are used for queries and transaction updates, and the server computers (there may be several) are used to provide access to the data base and to the printers.

7.1.1 Definitions and terminology

A client/server environment is a cooperative multiprocessing environment between processors (*clients*) and shared host processors (*servers*), where each user is given a dedicated system perception.

The key terms in this definition are (a) *cooperative*, emphasizing the need for well-defined communication protocols, (b) *shared*, indicating the basic aspect of a client/server environment, and (c) *dedicated*, implying that each user (client) is not aware of the resources being consumed by other users.

Ideally, the users are provided with a single system image (SSI) so that they believe that they have the whole system to themselves. This dedicated system perception, in most cases, remains only an ideal. In reality, only the objectives of cooperative environments and shared resources are totally achieved.

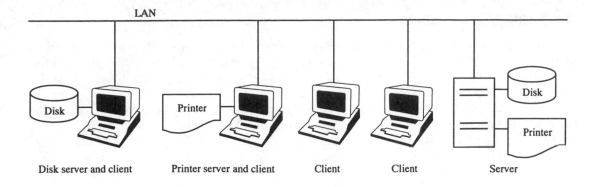

Figure 7.4 Clients also functioning as servers.

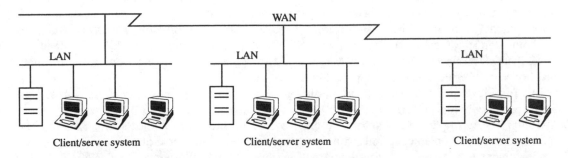

Figure 7.5 Client/server systems linked via a wide area network.

There are many variations of the client/server environment. Sun workstations are frequently used as client/server development environments, and PC networks (such as Novell) are often used as application environments.[2] These environments may have multiple servers (see Fig. 7.4) and occasionally servers may double as clients. In fact, in some client/server environments *any* client may also be configured as a server too.

Servers may communicate with each other either within a single client/server system or between separate client/server systems. In this wider context, client server systems may be hooked together via WANs (wide area networks) to logically form extremely large client/server systems (see Fig. 7.5). For example, consider a multinational corporation that has development centers in several countries. While each country may have its own client/server system, the whole corporation may be linked via an international WAN. Thus a client in, say, France, may be able to share a resource located in the United States. With the vast improvement in global communications and with the expansion of large international corporations, this type of development environment is now becoming prevalent.

2. These examples should not be perceived as restricting how client/server systems can be used. Clearly Sun workstations can also be used in application environments and Novell is equally applicable to development and application environments.

7.1.2 Client/server objectives

In a software development environment let us consider how a client/server system compares to a centralized system (minicomputers or mainframes) and to individual computers (e.g. desktop PCs). In the latter case several advantages are immediately apparent: the ability to share data files and to transfer information between users in real time.

Centralized computer systems do not necessarily provide a development environment inferior to a client/server environment. The centralized environment has such advantages as the low cost of adding a user (the cost of a dumb terminal[3]) and the relatively high power of the central processor. However, it is in the areas of versatility and low entry level cost that client/servers have the advantage. Ideally, the objective of a client/server development environment is to provide low cost development workstations with a high degree of integration. At an entry level, a client/server environment is inexpensive. The initial investment is low and the addition of more workstations is relatively inexpensive (though admittedly more than the cost of a dumb terminal). The environment can grow virtually limitlessly.

The degree of integration between development workstations depends on the type of client/ server system, the way it has been configured, the software packages being used, and the development standards being enforced. There are specific software packages (such as configuration management) that enforce a high degree of integration within a team of developers. However, ultimately it is the policy of the developing organization that determines just how tightly coupled the development activities will be.

In a non-development environment, application client/server systems have similar objectives. They provide a high degree of integration with a low cost entry level for small systems. Consider the example of the automatic teller system discussed previously. Small banks and large can equally implement similar automatic teller systems, and best of all, can communicate among themselves to enable cross-bank transactions. Clearly the network of tellers is highly integrated while the addition of a new teller machine is relatively simple and inexpensive.

7.1.3 Functions of the client

The client computer provides the interface between the system and the user. Modern client components will typically use a graphical user interface (GUI) such as that provided by MS-Windows, Windows NT, X-Windows or Motif. This type of interface provides the user with an intuitive form of communication with the system that is both easy to use and easy to master.

The client is the mediator between the user and the server and it requests services from the server. On the most elementary level the architecture looks like this:

$$\text{User} \longleftrightarrow \text{Client computer} \longleftrightarrow \text{Server computer}$$

One of the main differences between a simple terminal and a client is the client's ability to run its own software applications. The client usually hosts the presentation component of the overall system software and is therefore responsible for the reformatting and display of system outputs. The client also performs the initial manipulation and possibly also the initial processing of user inputs.

Different clients on the same client/server system may run different presentation software and they may use different GUIs. It is not uncommon to link an X-Station, a PC MS-Windows

---

3. However, every mainframe has a maximum number of terminals that it can support.

station and a Macintosh to the same client/server network. In fact, any front-end computer can function as a client as long as it adheres to the client/server interface standards (commonly referred to as APIs or application programming interfaces).

7.1.4 Functions of the server

One of the main functions of the server is to provide services to its clients. These services range from access to peripherals and networks to computing power on the server itself running remote applications. Ideally, the server will conceal the complexity of the client/server network from the client.

Another major function of the server is data access control. Servers commonly manage large data bases, which are accessed by clients or even other servers, in some cases, across large complex networks. The server in control of the data handles such functions as access control (e.g. password protection), data access contention (conflicting or competing requests primarily during data updates), and of course data base backup and recovery.

Within these large LANs and WANs (local area networks and wide area networks), the server functions as a gateway providing the client computers with access to the outside world. This important feature also provides access *from* the outside world to the client/server system from virtually anywhere. Access is provided either by permanently connecting to other linked networks or by dialling in (via modem) to other network nodes. Thus virtually any computer with a modem can function as a remote client.

Multiple servers do not necessarily mean multiple client/server systems. A single system may have more than one server. In a multi-server system, the servers function as a cooperative system dividing the tasks between them so that, for example, one server may handle the data base, another may handle communications, and a third may handle application processing. The complexity of this type of system is concealed by each server from the clients, making each client unaware of the existence of many servers.

Note that clients can also be servers. Any peripheral device connected to a client, or any other client resource, can be made available to other clients by setting up the client computer in the dual mode of client *and* server. Though not all client/server architectures support this dual mode feature, many do (such as IBM's PC network).

7.2 THE NETWORK

The network is the backbone of any client/server system supporting easy access and connectivity between nodes. This is provided through a layered network (see Table 7.1) concept referred to as an OSI architecture – open systems interconnection. The OSI architecture is designed to allow for the interconnection of different types of system. Though not exclusive to client/server systems, OSI provides one of its major strengths: the ability to easily link networks corporate-wide, nationwide, and even worldwide. The OSI architecture is common, though not essential, in client/server systems.

7.2.1 Network protocols

Network links, be they for linking clients and servers or for linking between networks, require protocols: the rules by which networks and network elements talk to each other. One of the most common communications protocols is the Transmission Control Protocol/Internet

Protocol, more commonly known as TCP/IP. TCP/IP is in fact a suite of protocols which supports LANs and WANs and which was originally developed for UNIX environments. For the client/server architecture there is the Client/Server Internetwork Protocol (IP) which works together with TCP/IP.

There are many other network communications protocols on various levels, such as SNA (Systems network architecture), which is widely used by IBM, Novell NetWare and Microsoft's LAN Manager. However, OSI, which was defined by the International Organization for Standardization (ISO), is particularly of interest in client/server environments because of its ability to connect heterogeneous systems.

There are seven OSI layers, which determine the different levels of network management, access and application. These layers[1] are described in Table 7.1

Table 7.1 The OSI layered model

Layer number	Layer name	Type of information	Layer description
7	Application	Messages	Provides application programming interface (API) to client/server application
6	Presentation	Messages	Translates data into user representation formats
5	Session	Messages	Provides services for communication between applications on different processors
4	Transport	Messages	Provides end to end control between nodes
3	Network	Packets	Switches and routes information across the network
2	Data link	Frames	Transfers units of information across the physical link
1	Physical	Bits	Transmits bit streams over a physical medium

OSI does not mean only *interconnection*; it also means *open*. Open networks provide easy access to any network element that abides by a set of basic rules or standards. These standards govern the way data is stored and accessed and the way network elements behave. The basic assumption of being *open* is that any network element that conforms to the behavior and access rules can gain access to all other network elements (assuming that there are no security restrictions). Thus OSI is considered to be an ideal architecture for a client/server network.

7.2.2 Network considerations

Easy interconnection is a significant benefit when managing a geographically distributed project; that is, when members of the development team are located at distant sites. Together with appropriate distributed development tools (e.g. configuration managers, error logs, access control, electronic mail) it can provide the environment needed to create a single cohesive team from many separate groups.

For the project manager, open networks also ease the restriction of development platforms having to be the same. An open network may have remote developers using Sun workstations, PC workstations or Macintoshes, and they may link Oracle or Informix data bases. This is by no means a recommendation for project managers to encourage different platforms amongst their developers, but it is an indication that it can be done.

In application environments, the network also provides an excellent infrastructure for many distributed target systems, such as:

---

1. See Sinha (1992) for a detailed description of the OSI layers.

- Information networks
  - professional literature searching
  - crime prevention
- Financial systems
  - banking
  - credit approval
- Access control
  - identification systems
  - immigration control

These are basically data driven systems where there is no single central data base. It is the network that links the many data storage locations and integrates them into a single access system. Client/server architectures are well suited to handling this type of network application.

7.3 PROJECT MANAGEMENT ADVANTAGES AND DISADVANTAGES OF A CLIENT/SERVER ENVIRONMENT

For the project manager, the client/server architecture, just like any other computer system architecture, has both advantages and disadvantages. These system qualities (or lack of) can impact the way a project is developed. They bear upon both the target environment and the development environment.

The advantages of a client/server architecture include:

- *Shared resources*
  Resources are more efficiently used due to the ability to share their use between users.
- *Reduced costs*
  The initial cost of a client/server system is less than most other types of multi-user system. Also, the cost of expanding the capacity of the system may be less.
- *Start small and grow*
  It is not necessary for the project manager to initially determine the size of the system; it can start small and expand as the need arises.
- *Smaller systems (downsizing)*
  It is relatively easy to reduce client/server systems in size with minimal impact on end-user performance.
- *No single point failure*
  The risk of bringing down the whole system due to a single failure is significantly less than in other types of systems, as the failure of one client computer does not usually effect others.
- *Distributed data access*
  The client/server architecture is an excellent way of providing distributed data access for large numbers of users[1] by making server data bases accessible over large networks.
- *Adding clients is simple*
  Client/server systems can be expanded easily and virtually limitlessly by linking additional client computers to the network.

---

1. See Microsoft (1992) for examples of client/server distributed data architectures.

- *Adding servers is relatively simple*
  There is no limit to the number of servers that can be linked to a client/server system thus providing additional processing power, peripherals, data access power and system management functions.

Unfortunately, the client/server architecture also has some disadvantages.

- *System administration*
  System administration rules can be difficult to enforce due to the large degree of freedom often available at the client station. For example, data may be stored locally on the client computer and not included in the system-wide backup.
- *Overloading a server*
  Though adding a server is relatively easy, this does not necessarily mean that servers are frequently added and removed. Thus, servers often become overloaded producing long resource queues when the capacity of the CPU is exceeded, or when the LAN or communications network is overloaded, or when disk space is exceeded. In general, response time during peak demand can become poor. Though these problems may occur in any system, they tend to be more serious in a client/server environment.
- *Limited number of users permitted to access packages*
  When clients share the use of an applications package (e.g. a graphics package or a CASE tool), they may be restricted by the number of computers licensed to use the package simultaneously. This means that an attempt to load an application package may occasionally be rejected.
- *Laborious maintenance*
  A large client/server system may include numerous computers, peripherals and other hardware components: servers, clients, printers, disks, routers etc. Hardware maintenance of such a plethora of components is often an extremely laborious task.
- *Difficult to manage*
  Management of a client/server development environment can be difficult, especially when the servers provide the developers with a large degree of system independence. This is especially true in a geographically distributed development environment.
- *Security*
  Security and access control can be difficult to control. There may be many data bases to secure at several different locations. Also, the large number of users with access to the system may be extremely difficult to track and control. It therefore takes more than one or two security measures to secure a client/server network completely (see Francis 1993).

The advantages and disadvantages of a business application client/server system from a business perspective are well summarized by Ullman (1993):

Client/server advantages

Feature	Benefit
Network webs of small powerful machines	If one machine goes down your business stays up.
Computer arrays with thousands of MIPS; clients aggregate MIPS beyond calculation	The system provides the power to get things done without monopolizing resources. End users are empowered to work locally.
Some workstations are as powerful as mainframes but cost one-tenth less	By giving you more power for less money, the system offers you the flexibility to make other purchases or to increase your profits.
Open systems	You can pick and choose hardware, software, and services from various vendors.
System grows easily	It's easy to modernize your system as needs change.
Individual client	You can mix and match computer platforms to suit the needs of individual departments and users.

Client/server disadvantages

Disadvantage	Significance
Maintenance nightmare	Parts don't always work together. There are several possible culprits when something goes wrong.
Support tools lacking	With the client/server architecture, you locate or build support tools yourself.
Retraining required	The software development philosophy for a Macintosh or for a Windows environment is different from that for Cobol or C.

7.4 SELECTING A CLIENT/SERVER ENVIRONMENT

As we have seen, client/server environments are appropriate for organizations that need to start small and grow. Other considerations include:

- Budget: how much can be invested in the system?
- Functionality: what is the system expected to accomplish?
- Current status: what exists today?
- Users: what type of people will be operating the system?
- Future: what level of growth is expected?

Providing answers to these questions is often a project in itself.

Budget is one of the primary considerations in selecting a client/server development environment. The initial investment is small, and the cost for adding additional users is usually moderate. It is, however, important to remember that there will always be expansion steps at points along the way where the investment will jump: the need for an additional server, an additional disk, additional communication ports, routers etc.

There are many considerations involved with the expansion of a client/server system, as few systems are totally independent. The current computing status is often *the* deciding factor, meaning that the need to interface with other systems becomes a primary consideration. There are several levels of interfacing:

1. *Total compatibility*

    On the highest system interface level, all major functions in the selected system must be identical to the existing system. The selected system must be capable of running the same software, it must have the same user interface and it must use the same communications interfaces.

    On this level, the system user can move from one client workstation to another without noticing any difference.

2. *Integrated*

    On an intermediate level, the selected system must be able to run similar functions (though not necessarily with the same software) and it must have similar communications interfaces.

    On this level, clients or workstations may work in the same way, but their user interfaces will not necessarily look the same.

3. *Connected*

    On the lowest interfacing level, the selected system must have similar communications interfaces.

    The only condition assured at this level is that the system elements will be able to exchange information; they may not run the same applications, and when they do, the applications may not look the same to the user.

The first level clearly dictates the type of hardware to be used; the server processors may need to be identical (or compatible) to be able to run the same software. Examples are networks of PCs or Sun workstations. However, it may not be necessary to require all PCs to have the same 486 or Pentium processors, or all Sun workstations to be of the Sparc family.

From the project management perspective, the totally compatible networked development architecture is the ideal environment for the distributed development of a project. When the development team is split into several groups located at different locations, totally compatible systems are helpful in enabling the groups to function as a single team.

On the integrated level, running similar functions may translate into similar data base software (e.g. either Oracle or Informix), but this software may run on different servers (e.g. HPs, Suns or PCs). This type of architecture is suitable for large organizations with separate semi-autonomous divisions within which different development activities occur.

As we have seen, the third level just means that the selected system has the ability to communicate with the existing system for the exchange of information. This architecture is common between large independent networks that exchange information but do not cooperate in development.

7.5 PROJECT MANAGEMENT

There are two very different perspectives to project management in a client/server environment depending on whether we are developing *on* it or *for* it.

● *The development perspective*

    Is a client/server system a suitable development environment for the project to be developed?

and

● *The target perspective*

    Is a client/server system an appropriate architecture for the support of the application to be developed?

Strictly speaking, the target perspective is a project design consideration, while the development perspective is much more of a project management issue. However, whether developing a software system *on* or *for* a client/server environment, there are several potential problems that need to be addressed.

7.5.1 Project control

As we have seen, client/server systems, due to their flexibility, can be both an advantage and a disadvantage to project management. Nowhere is this more evident than in the area of project control. Without adequate management tools, the project manager can easily lose control of the development activities.

So, if project control tools are required in all software projects, they are particularly required in client/server development environments. Some examples of these tools are:

- *Configuration management tools*
  As developers have their own workstations they have much more freedom in modifying project files (both text and code). A good distributed configuration management tool is needed to manage a central file library (usually located on one of the servers), and to monitor and control the check out and check in of project development files.
- *Time reporters*
  These types of tool report how much time has been devoted to various development activities. This is particularly important with a geographically distributed development team.
- *On-line task monitors*
  This tool reports the activities and progress of the development team and is also important for distributed development teams.
- *Information disseminators*
  It is imperative for the project manager to be able to announce and notify quickly and clearly. It is equally important for the developer to be able to do so. Electronic mail is a simple but most valuable tool that provides this capability.

For the project manager, the solution to the client/server control problem is to be aware of it from the start. Many of the potential pitfalls can be avoided just by assuring adequate development processes and methods and assuring that all developers abide by them.

7.5.2 Design decisions

As a general rule, the project manager's design decisions should not be influenced by the type of development environment but rather by the type of target environment. However, like all rules, this one too has its exceptions.

One such exception is the need for the project manager to match the design to the development team. Strange as this consideration may appear, it does have some justification. In a geographically distributed development environment it is important to decompose the project into well defined loosely coupled components or subsystems. This is a design decision. In a distributed development environment it is clearly much easier to manage a project that can be divided into independent components. If this cannot be done then a distributed client/server environment may not be a feasible development environment.

A typical example would be a project with several computers performing different functions, such as a security access control system. If we assume that this project is being developed by a team of six developers, one group of two developers within the project team may develop the algorithms for the recognition and permission functions, another two developers may develop the software for the alarm and sensor controls and a third group of two developers may be responsible for the permissions data base. Clearly, if these three function groups reside on separate computers or microprocessors then they can be developed and tested without the need for extensive interaction between the three groups within the development team.[1]

As stated earlier, most design decisions are related to the target environment. Client/server environments are usually selected as target environments for very specific design reasons. Some examples follow:

1. *More focus on the end user*

   A client/server target environment may be an ideal selection when the end user is the most important consideration, such as in commercial customer systems (e.g. automatic bank tellers). These types of system are usually real-time interactive applications.

   At the other extreme, batch applications (such as salary systems) or non-independent interactive applications (such as security systems) would not necessarily be well designed around a client/server system. These applications would not necessarily take advantage of the client/server benefits, such as the independence of the end user client computer. For example, if a secure building entrance is out of order we may want to declare the entire security system defective; however, if a single teller machine is out of order it would be helpful if we could design the system so that all other teller machines would work.

2. *Partitioning of application among processors*

   The ability to partition an application functionally is often a major design consideration. The automatic bank teller example demonstrates this concept well. Not only does the automatic teller system divide naturally into two separate major functions, it also partitions easily into separate platforms. Both these system qualities make a client/server design a natural choice.

3. *Segmentation of data*

   In distributed client/server systems the distribution of data is an important consideration. Many modern commercial data bases provide the means to distribute data between remote locations over a network. However, it is important to assure that this is transparent to the developer or end user. Data store and retrieve functions, searches and updates, as well as data base applications, must function as if the data base was located in a single location. One area that must especially be evaluated is performance: how would a decision to distribute a large data base impact data access time?

4. *General design guidelines*

   There are several general design principles that are often applicable to the management of a client/server-based project:

   - When merging several applications or functions into a single system, all client applications should be designed to have a similar *look and feel*; that is, a similar presentation, similar error handling and similar command interface.
   - Client/server systems are often best designed so that the main processing is performed on the server while the client provides the user interface functions.
   - The use of prototypes can be particularly helpful in the design of a client/server system. A prototype can be used to model the user interface on the client and simple simulators can be used to replace the functions of the server.

---

1. We can assume that project management, quality assurance, and configuration management will be performed from a single location.

This type of prototype is an ideal aid in the design of the client/server system.

- Object-oriented design approaches are often well suited for client/server systems. Being end-user oriented, these types of systems are often best designed by enabling the user to manipulate objects rather than the classic series of commands.
- Another design consideration of client/server systems, derived directly from their being end-user oriented, is the use of windows. Client user interfaces commonly use a multi-window presentation, well suited to object oriented designs, with pull down menus and iconized objects (e.g. X-Windows, Motif, MS-Windows).
- Another result of the end-user orientation in client/server systems is the increasing use of on line context sensitive help. Good designs are directed toward ease of use, which means intuitive operation of client/server interfaces and easy guidance without having to trudge through forests of reference manuals. A good help feature responds to user needs with minimal keystrokes and within minimal time.

7.5.3 Managing test and integration

Test and integration[1] is often the most difficult phase in the development of any software project. This is especially true in client/server development environments, due to the independence of each developer.

Configuration management and other project management support functions are vital for the successful test and integration of any software project, particularly for projects developed in a client/server environment. There are several project management guidelines that can make this phase easier:

- In a distributed development environment, subsystem testing can be performed independently at each development location, provided the previous guidelines on project partitioning were followed.
- Simulators are excellent tools for testing well-partitioned projects. For each subsystem, the simulators perform the basic interface functions of the other project subsystems. These tools should be defined at the beginning of the project and their development or deployment should be scheduled as a standard development task.
- On the local client/server level, it is perfectly acceptable for developers to perform independent unit testing on their client workstations. However, higher levels of testing and integration, including subsystem and system testing, cannot be independent and are best controlled using a good client/server configuration management tool.
- System level testing and integration requires the assignment of an integrator role. For large projects this is a dedicated assignment. In a client/server development environment, it is the responsibility of the integrator to assure that integration is performed as a centralized activity; in simple terms this means that developers cannot independently integrate system components on their workstation.
- For target client/server systems, the testing and integration strategy will almost always be to integrate and test the client and server separately and then to integrate the two.

To summarize, we can say that all the guidelines for the testing and integration of software system are especially applicable to client/server development environments; they must be more stringently followed when developers have more independent development facilities at their disposal.

---

1. Testing is further discussed in Chapters 4 and 8.

7.6 TIPS FOR MANAGING CLIENT/SERVER ENVIRONMENTS

The client/server environment is just one of many computer architectures. As we have seen it can be an excellent choice for distributed processing or development; it can also be a hindrance if either unsuitably selected or incorrectly employed. This section provides a few tips that may make life a little easier for the project manager, for both client/server development environments and target environments.

1. *Backups*

   Backups are important on any computerized data system. Backups have added importance on client/server systems due to the fact that data is neither stored nor controlled from a single location.

   A backup procedure must be implemented not only for every server disk and file system, but also for every client local disk.

2. *Response time*

   There is a feeling that applications, users and peripherals can always be added limitlessly. In theory this is true, but it is important to remember that at some point as the workload grows the system response time will degrade, unless the hardware grows too.

   Response time is also impacted by the amount of data handled by the client/server system and by the bursts (temporary high loads) of data at specific times.

   In a common client/server scenario the system performs well at the beginning and deteriorates as it becomes increasingly overloaded. Therefore system performance should be continuously monitored (many operating systems, such as UNIX, have real-time system performance monitors).

3. *Balancing between server and client*

   For many applications there are functions that can be performed by either the server or the client. Overloading of the system, or poor performance due to data traffic congestion, can often be alleviated by restructuring the division of work between clients and server, or between server and server.

4. *Plan for growth*

   The expansion of a client/server environment can be compared to a step function. There are points when the addition of clients is relatively simple and inexpensive and there are situations when expansion is difficult and expensive. This is true also when adding peripherals to the server.

   This step function is caused by the limited capacity of various system components, such as routers, backplane port sockets, disk space, memory and the number of servers.

   A common error is to assume that the addition of the next client station will be as easy as the addition of the last one. There should be a plan for growth which takes into account client/server system limitations and capacities, and application user restrictions (i.e. application vendors may have limited the number of permitted users). It is therefore important to assure that clients and servers are expandable (e.g. they are not restricted by a low limit on installable memory or disk space), and that applications do not have too low a limit on user capacity.

7.7 SUMMARY

A client/server environment is a cooperative multiprocessing environment between processors (clients) and shared host processors (servers), where each user is given a dedicated system perception. The client/server concept places computing power in the hands of the end users, while allowing them to choose their own front end computer.

Centralized computer systems do not necessarily provide a development environment inferior to a client/server environment. The centralized environment has such advantages as the low cost of adding a user (the cost of a dumb terminal) and the relatively high power of the central processor. However, it is in the areas of versatility and low entry level cost that client/servers have the advantage.

The client/server concept can be applied to two basic models: the development environment and the application environment. In the development environment a client/server system is a development tool facilitating the development of a software project. In the application environment a client/server system provides a specific service.

Ideally, the objective of a client/server development environment is to provide low cost development stations with a high degree of integration. At the entry level, a client/server environment is inexpensive. The initial investment is low and the addition of more workstations is relatively inexpensive (though admittedly more than the cost of a dumb terminal). The environment can grow virtually limitlessly.

The network is the backbone of any client/server system. Ideally, the network should support easy access and connectivity between nodes. This is referred to as an OSI network – open systems interconnection. The OSI network is based upon a layered architecture designed to allow for the interconnection of different types of system.

For the project manager there are both advantages and disadvantages in selecting the client/server architecture. The advantages of a client/server architecture include:

- The ability to share resources
- Reduced initial system costs
- The ability to start small and grow
- Smaller systems (downsizing)
- No single point failure
- Distributed data access
- Adding clients is simple
- Adding servers is relatively simple

On the negative side the disadvantages of a client/server architecture include:
- System administration is more complicated
- Servers are easily overloaded, degrading system performance
- Limited number of users permitted to access packages
- Maintenance of many different hardware components is a laborious task
- A distributed system can be difficult to control
- Security is more difficult

The client/server architecture can be a suitable development environment for software projects, most especially for when the development team is distributed in several locations. However, this type of development environment can be difficult to control effectively. For the project manager, the solution to the client/server control problem is to be aware of it from the start. Many of the potential pitfalls can be avoided just by assuring adequate development processes and methods and assuring that all developers abide by them. In short, the general principles for the management of software development need to be applied to client/server projects, only more stringently.

EXERCISES

1. The New York Municipal Library is replacing its information system. Until now, the library has operated using a central computer with terminals in each reading room and in each book check-out center. This old system is now being replaced by a client/server system.

Explain the advantages that will now be available to the library readers and librarians in moving from the old system to the new. Are there any disadvantages?

2. Suggest a design for the implementation of the New York Municipal Library's new client/ server system. What potential problems need to be avoided? What design considerations need to be considered?

Can you suggest more than one design? What are the differences between the various designs?

3. The New York Municipal Library has entered into agreements with the Municipal Library in Los Angeles, and with large libraries in London and in Paris. All libraries have agreed to implement similar client/server systems, but they will not necessarily be identical. What new potential problems need to be avoided?

Suggest a design for the overall network serving the four libraries.

4. All four libraries in New York, Los Angeles, London and Paris have agreed to jointly allocate a budget for the development of the new library system. However, both London and Paris have stipulated that parts of the system are to be developed in the UK and France as well as in the United States, with relative parts of the budget allocated to each country (e.g. half to the USA and a quarter each to the UK and France).

Because the largest team will be located in the USA, the project manager will also be located there. You have just been hired as the project manager. Explain how you plan to set up your development team.

How will you divide the project among the development groups? What potential problems are there and how do you intend to avoid them?

5. Class exercise: divide the class into three groups, representing the USA, UK and France. Elect a project manager from the USA group. The project manager is to allocate part of the project to each group to design.

Compare the three designs. Discuss the problems that arose due to the division of the team into three groups.

EIGHT

PROJECT SUPPORT FUNCTIONS

PROJECT MANAGEMENT SUPPORT

Software project management is the process of planning, organizing, staffing, monitoring, controlling and leading a software project.[1] Rarely can all these tasks be performed by the project manager; in fact, ideally they should not. Many control and monitoring activities can be assigned to project support groups. These support groups not only disburden the project manager and the development engineers from the support tasks; they also perform these tasks better by concentrating their efforts on specific support functions.

There are many types of project support function. Secretarial services, administrative support, document publication and procurement are examples of non-technical support functions; testing, configuration control, systems engineering, integration management and quality assurance are examples of technical support functions.

The larger and more complex a project the more support functions will be required. For example, a large project will often have its own quality control organization, while a small project may have to share this function with other projects. Similarly, many organizations maintain an independent test group whose role it is to test a software product before its release. In large projects, the independent test group is part of the project team, and is involved in testing and test planning throughout the development cycle.

This chapter describes the three major technical project support functions:

- Configuration control
- Software quality assurance
- Testing

These basic functions are required in every software development project. Configuration control manages the changes to the software product being developed, quality assurance monitors and controls the quality of the product, and testing verifies compliance with the product's requirements.

It is the project manager's responsibility to organize the project support groups and to document their planned activities in the project development plan (see Chapter 10). If these groups already exist within the organization, then their support needs to be coordinated and scheduled for the project. If the groups do not exist then they must be established within the project development team.

---

1. As defined in IEEE (1987a).

The size of a support group is clearly dependent on the size of the project; for example, a large project may require a group of two or three configuration control engineers, a medium size project may require one configuration control engineer, and a small project may assign this task part-time to a development engineer.

These decisions must be made by the project manager during the initial stages of the project. Project support functions that are well planned at the start of the project will contribute to effective project management throughout the project.

8.1 SOFTWARE CONFIGURATION CONTROL (SCC)

Configuration control is a management support function that supports the many different activities related to changes to the software product. This includes program code changes, requirements and design changes and version release changes. Configuration control is often regarded by developers as more of a hindrance than a benefit because it limits the freedom of the development team and places restrictions on what can and cannot be done. Configuration control does, however, provide an environment in which software can be developed in an orderly manner.

The term *configuration* is used here to describe the combination of software components to form an integrated system. When linked with the word *control*, the term is used to describe an efficient and orderly method by which this combination of components can be accomplished. Unfortunately, building software systems from low level components is no simple task. This is best illustrated by the following anecdote.

A large banking firm joined an international financial information exchange service. This service could provide the bank with on-line access to a central data base containing constantly updated information on world financial markets. In the modern world of fast electronic communications, this was an essential service for any modern banking institution. However, the bank's computer did not have the capability to interface with the financial service.

The bank assigned a project manager to develop the necessary software needed for the interface. After the integration phase began, one of the developers reported that a major milestone had been achieved: communications with the information service had been successfully established. The project manager reported this to his superiors and informed them that development was proceeding on schedule.

A week later members of top management visited the project and asked for a demonstration of communications with the information service. However, the project manager was unable to provide the demonstration. The developer who had reported the milestone could not repeat his earlier success. This was because additional features had been added to the communications software and these were not yet working. Even the previous features were no longer working.

Clearly, the developer should have kept a copy of the communications software without the new features. In a well organized project, the task of saving an earlier software version would have been performed by the configuration manager.

An interesting way of looking at configuration control is to regard it as a method of assuring that the project moves forward (or at least does not move backward). In the above related case, the project actually slipped backward.

Configuration control is essential for all developed items, including code, documentation and integration of components. Figure 8.1 describes the flow of configuration control for the development of a software module. A similar flow would apply to documents generated by the project. Configuration control is also necessary during the maintenance phase to assure that when a new system release is recalled due to severe defects it can be replaced by the previous release.

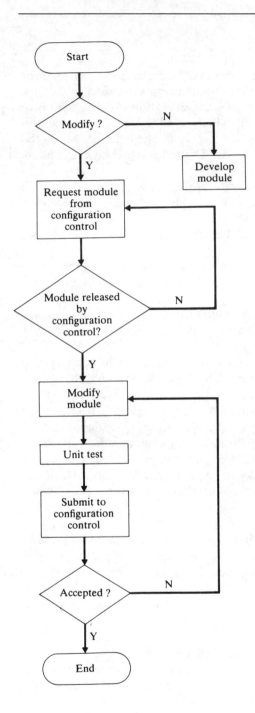

Figure 8.1 Software module configuration control flow.

8.1.1 Configuration control terminology

There are many terms used in relation to configuration control. Unfortunately, neither their usage nor their meanings have been standardized; several different terms are used to describe the same functions and ideas. One of the best attempts at standardization is contained in the IEEE's *Glossary of Software Engineering Terminology* (IEEE 1987b). However, even this glossary reflects the lack of common interpretation and usage of these terms, as several configuration control terms appear with multiple definitions. The following is an explanation, rather than an accurate definition, of some of the basic terminology.

A *software configuration control item* (SCCI) is a software project item that is considered a unit for the purposes of configuration control. This may include such things as software modules,[2] versions of software systems, or documents.

Change control is the process of controlling changes. This includes proposing the change, evaluating it, approving or rejecting it, scheduling and tracking it.

Version control, as applied to software development, is the process of controlling the release of software versions. This includes recording and saving each release, and documenting the differences between the releases.

Configuration control is the process of evaluating, approving or disapproving, and managing changes to configuration items. Configuration control also often includes version control functions.

Configuration management is the technical and administrative application of configuration control. This also includes the maintenance of a configuration control organization, change and version control standards, and configuration control facilities.

Other terms are the *configuration identification* designation used to identify configuration items, the *configuration control board* that approves or rejects engineering changes, and the *configuration audit*, which verifies compliance with configuration control standards.

The objective of configuration management is best defined not through the formal definitions of the IEEE glossary but rather through a more descriptive explanation as provided in the foreword to IEEE standard 828 (1987b) for software configuration management plans, which states:

> Software configuration management (SCM) is a formal engineering discipline which provides software developers and users with the methods and tools to identify the software developed, establish baselines, control changes to these baselines, record and track status, and audit the product.
>
> SCM is the means through which the integrity and continuity of the software product are recorded, communicated and controlled.

Some of the configuration management tasks overlap with the tasks of another support activity, software quality control (discussed later). In software projects where quality control and configuration control are performed by separate groups, a clear definition of the division of responsibility is necessary.

---

2 Many interpretations of the term *configuration item* do not include low level items such as software modules. The US DOD Std-2167 software development standard (DOD 1988a) applies the term to higher level components as defined in the DOD configuration control standard Std-480A. This interpretation refers to items that can be developed independently or repaired and maintained independently.

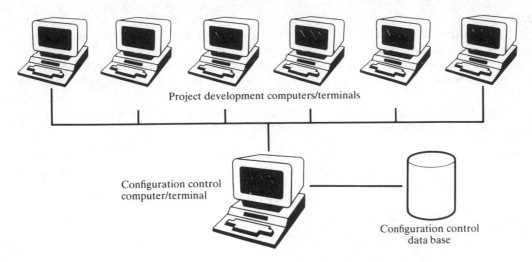

Figure 8.2 Networked configuration control.

8.1.2 Resources for configuration control

Configuration control is one of the first areas of software engineering that was recognized as a candidate for automation. Several configuration control activities, such as version control and change control, were automated in the early 1970s, with such tools as *make* and *SCCS* (see Rochkind 1975).[3] Some of these tools migrated from the UNIX operating system, where they were first used, to other environments, such as MS-DOS and Digital's VMS.

Many of the main configuration control activities are natural candidates for automated CASE (computer-aided software engineering) tools, as they are well defined, somewhat repetitive, and readily integrated into the development process. These tools can be easily interfaced with software code tools (e.g. editors and compilers) and word processors for the production of documents. Automated configuration control is best when used in a multi-user development environment such as a LAN. This way all controlled elements are stored in a central data base, and access by all developers is managed from a central configuration control system (see Fig. 8.2).

Effective configuration control requires effective and well-defined organization. Any configuration control method must be based on the following four concepts:

1. A clearly defined configuration management authority must be established.
2. Configuration control standards, procedures and guidelines must be produced and distributed to the developers.
3. Configuration control cannot be effective without the necessary tools and facilities.
4. A configuration management plan must be developed at the beginning of the project.

It is the project manager's responsibility to assign configuration management authority. This can range from a configuration control team in large projects to a part-time configuration control engineer in small projects. In either case, both the authority and the responsibility must

3. The evolution of configuration management is described in a paper by Ambriola *et al.* (1990), which also discusses the automation of the various configuration control activities.

be clearly defined. The configuration control engineer should be involved in all development activities, and must have the specific authority to approve or reject configuration items.

The development team members must be familiar with the configuration control standards, procedures and guidelines, which should be comprehensive and clear. This will reduce the number of rejections by configuration control due to non-compliance with unfamiliar standards.

The configuration management environment consists of the resources necessary for the implementation of the configuration control plan. This includes:

- Configuration control tools, including:
  - automatic version control and change control tools
  - monitoring, auditing and registration support utilities
- Storage facilities: a safe repository for all approved configuration items, including:
  - on-site storage for the day to day development process
  - off-site storage for catastrophe recovery

8.1.3 The software configuration management plan

The software configuration management plan (SCMP) is part of the project's software development plan. The SCMP may appear as a separate document or as a section within the project development plan. The SCMP documents the resources that are needed, how they are to be used, and which standards and procedures will be applied during the project. The SCMP then becomes the mandate for the configuration control group during project development. The issuance of this plan is the responsibility of the project manager, though in large projects it may be delegated to the configuration control manager.

Table 8.1 contains a list of the main subjects covered in the SCMP. When any of these subjects is covered elsewhere (e.g. in the software quality assurance plan), it can be omitted from the SCMP and replaced by a pointer to the document in which it is covered. Though most of the subjects in Table 8.1 are self-descriptive, the following are some guidelines:

- Configuration status accounting describes the way in which status information flows:
  - from the developers to the configuration management organization (audits and reviews)
  - from the configuration management organization to project management (status reporting procedures).
- Configuration identification describes the method for designating development items as SCCIs. This is part of the high level decomposition of the system into major development components (see Chapter 6).

The section on identification methods describes the way in which each component generated by the project is marked for unique identification.

- Security, restricted access and classification refer to the secure development of sensitive products (such as documents, software, patents, military classified information etc.). It is often convenient to assign many of these tasks to configuration control because of the need to be involved in the review and classification of documents and other related activities that are associated with security.
- Subcontractors, vendors and suppliers may or may not implement their own configuration management plan. It is the project manager's responsibility to assure either that subcontractors and external developers submit a CMP for review, or that the project's configuration manager assumes responsibility for their work.

Table 8.1 Example of the contents of a software configuration management plan

1. Software configuration management organization and resources
    Organization structure
    Personnel skill level and qualifications
    Resources

2. Standards, procedures, policies and guidelines

3. Configuration identification
    Method for defining SCCIs
    Description of the SCCIs for this project

4. Identification methods (naming and marking of documents, software components, revisions, releases, etc.)

5. Submission of configuration items
    Approval/rejection procedure

6. Change control
    Change control procedures (method of submission, review, approval and rejection)
    Reporting documentation (change requests, problem reports)
    Change review procedures and review board

7. Version control
    Preparation of software and documentation versions
    Release approval procedure

8. Storage, handling and delivery of project media
    Storage requirements
    Backups

9. Configuration control of subcontractors, vendors and suppliers

10. Additional control
    Miscellaneous control procedures
    Project specific control (security etc.)

11. Configuration status accounting
    Configuration audits and reviews
    Configuration status reporting procedures

12. Configuration management major milestones

13. Tools, techniques and methodologies

The SCMP may also include diagrams and flow charts to describe procedures for submitting change requests, or for reporting problems.[4]

Figure 8.3 presents an example of a general configuration control flow chart, suggested by the US DOD standard 2167A (DOD 1988a) (compare with the software module configuration control flow described in Fig. 8.1).

8.1.4 Some general guidelines

The list of activities covered by configuration control is far from standard. As a project management support function, the scope of configuration control covers many optional or elective activities. Therefore, as a basic guideline, it is perfectly acceptable to assign to configuration management, within a specific project, any related activity, such as allocating

---

4. For a more detailed description of the SCMP refer to IEEE (1987b).

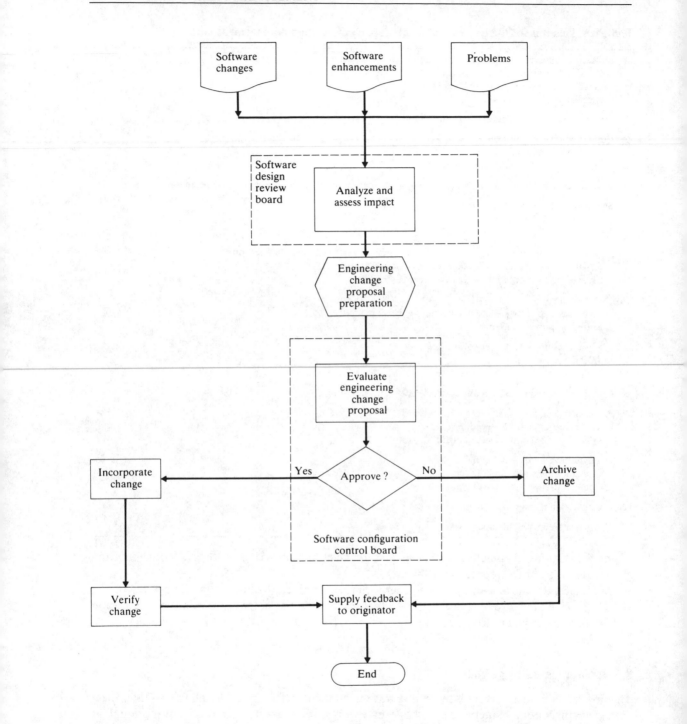

Figure 8.3 Example of a configuration control flow chart (from US DOD-Std-2167A).

SOFTWARE CHANGE REQUEST	SCR Number:	PAGE _____ OF _____

Name of originator:	Phone number:	Date:

Project:	System/Product:	Version/Release:

Reason for change:

Change description:

Reviewed by (name):	Signature:	Date:

Estimated person days:	Calendar time:	Schedule impact:

Estimates approved by (name):	Signature:	Date:

Change approval (YES/NO):	By (name):	Signature:	Date:

Figure 8.4 Example of a software change request form.

development resources, or arranging and staging customer demos. Both of these two examples utilize information available to the configuration manager: which product components are produced when, and by whom.

The keeping of records is important during all administrative project activities, but it is especially important in configuration control. The scourge of project management is the eternal dispute over misinterpreted or misunderstood verbal agreements. Poor change control is notorious for causing disputes between customer and developer. Similarly, poor version control can be catastrophic, especially when there are no records of the differences between versions.

Figure 8.4 contains an example of a change request form. This form records a software change from its initial submission, through its approval or rejection, and finally to its implementation and test (when approved). Note the need for signatures; these forms cannot be kept electronically – a signed hard copy must be maintained.

The following are some additional guidelines for effective configuration management. Some of these guidelines are equally applicable to other management support functions.

- Configuration management requires authority in order to be effective. This authority must be clearly delegated by the project manager to the responsible engineers. Any configuration management plan will become meaningless if the plan cannot be enforced.

  Blunt enforcement of any plan, policy or standard is best avoided, whenever possible. One of the qualities of a good manager is the ability to apply policy with minimal enforcement. Whenever policies and standards are readily accepted by the developers, they are more willingly followed and there are fewer rejections of submitted material. This leads to a more efficient development process.
- Configuration management should be implemented from the start of a software project. Many of the formal documents issued during the initial concept phase are crucial for the requirements and design phases, and must be placed under configuration control.

  The early application of configuration management is especially important in rapid prototyping, spiral models, or other iterative development methodologies. These development approaches initially produce several versions of each product. Many different versions can become an engineering nightmare without orderly configuration control.
- Occasionally some software configuration control activities may overlap with software quality assurance activities. In small projects, these two functions may be assigned to a single support engineer. Even in large projects, these two functions are sometimes performed by a single support group.

As a final general guideline, it should be noted that configuration management can be greatly exaggerated. The various configuration control activities are not an objective in themselves, they are a means. A typical example of the misapplication of configuration management (and misguided quality control), is a requirement to modify reused software to comply with current standards and procedures. Reused software is software developed previously in another project, and found suitable to be incorporated into the current project. In such cases it rarely makes sense to modify a complete and working product in order to make it comply with administrative standards intended to make it a complete and working product.

8.2 SOFTWARE QUALITY ASSURANCE (SQA)

Quality is difficult to define, especially when applied to a product development contract. Though not all software is developed under contract, quality still primarily remains a concern of the customer (and all projects ultimately have a customer). The British Standards Institution (1986) has stated that 'quality is in the eye of the beholder, a matter of the client's judgment'.

If it was difficult to find widely accepted definitions for configuration control terminology, it is doubly so for software quality assurance terminology. The IEEE's standard glossary of software engineering terminology (IEEE 1987b), contains no fewer than four separate definitions for software quality:[5]

1. The totality of features and characteristics of a software product that bear on its ability to satisfy given needs; for example, conform to specifications.
2. The degree to which software possesses a desired combination of attributes.
3. The degree to which a customer or user perceives that software meets his or her composite expectations.
4. The composite characteristics of software that determine the degree to which the software in use will meet the expectations of the customer.

The US DOD (1988b) defines software quality rather simply as:

5. The ability of a software product to satisfy its specified requirements.

Quality should be measured in terms of the customer's expectations. However, the customer's perspective is subjective. This section looks at quality control from the project manager's perspective, which must regard the achievement of quality control as an objective, systematic process.

8.2.1 Producing quality software

As we have seen, one of the main problems in producing quality software is the difficulty in determining the degree of quality within the software. As there is no single widely accepted definition for quality, and because different people perceive quality in different ways, both the developer and the customer must reach agreement on metrics for quality (this is discussed in more detail later). The method of measuring quality may differ for different projects.

This problem is discussed in a paper by Wesselius and Ververs (1990), in which they conclude that complete objectivity in quality assessment cannot be achieved. They identify three distinct components of quality:

● An objectively assessable component
● A subjectively assessable component
● A non-assessable component

The quality of a product is objectively assessable when the characteristics of the product, as stated in the requirements specification, can be identified.

The quality of a product is subjectively assessable when the characteristics of the product comply with the customer's expectations.

The quality of a product is non-assessable when it behaves according to our expectations in situations that have not been foreseen.

Wesselius and Ververs suggest that, for the quality of a software product to be assessable, as many characteristics as possible should be moved from the subjective and non-assessable

---

5. A detailed discussion of software development standards, including software quality control, appears in Chapter 9.

components to the assessable component. Essentially, this means that the requirements specification must describe as many measurable characteristics of the product as possible.

Experience supports Wesselius and Ververs' conclusions. Badly defined requirements are always a source of dispute between developer and customer. Well-defined, detailed and measurable requirements minimize disputes and disagreements when the development of the product is complete.

However, many development methods have a prolonged interval between the specification of requirements and the delivery of the product (refer to Chapter 4 for a discussion of the software development cycle). The determination of quality should not be postponed until development is complete. Effective software quality control requires frequent assessments throughout the development cycle. Thus, effective quality control coupled with a good requirements specification will clearly increase the quality of the final product.

The establishment of effective quality control frequently encounters various misconceptions and myths, the most common of which is related to the cost effectiveness of quality control. Cobb and Mills (1990) list several of these myths, and suggest methods of combating them. Two of the more prevalent myths identified by Cobb and Mills are described below.

Myth: Quality costs money This is one of the most common myths (not only in software development). In fact, quality in software usually saves money. Poor quality breeds failure. There is a positive correlation between failures and cost in that it is more expensive to remove execution failures designed into software than to design software to exclude execution failures.

Myth: Software failures are unavoidable This is one of the worst myths because the statement is partly true, and is therefore often used as an excuse to justify poor quality software. The claim that 'there is always another bug' should never be a parameter in the design or implementation of software.

As these myths lose ground in modern approaches to software development, the demand for suitable quality control standards and procedures increases. The IEEE issued their first standard for software quality assurance plans in 1984 (IEEE 1984), followed by a detailed guide to support the standard, issued in 1986. The US Department of Defense issued a separate standard 2168 for defense systems software quality programs (DOD 1988b), which forms a companion to the famous US DOD standard 2167A (DOD 1988a) for defense systems software development. The European ISO standard 9000-3, of 1990 (ISO 1990) gives a broader meaning to the term quality assurance and covers configuration control too.

8.2.2 Resources for quality control

When the SQA mandate includes configuration control activities, the required resources will also include those required for configuration control. Merging SQA and configuration control is not uncommon, and can eliminate some duplication of assignments and activities. Two alternative organizational charts are shown in Fig. 8.5. Note that for small projects, merging the two groups may mean simply assigning both responsibilities to the same person.

Though many tools are common to both quality control and configuration control, few tools are specifically designed for quality control. The following are some of the general support tools that can be useful in supporting SQA activities:

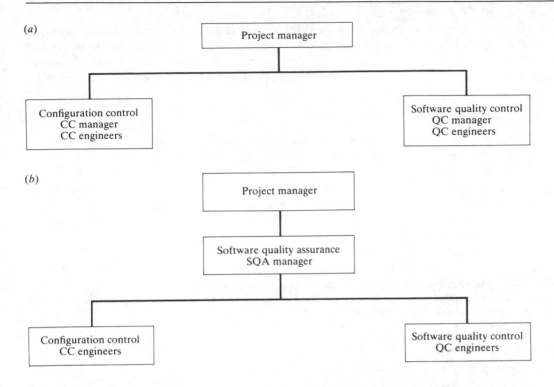

Figure 8.5 Configuration control and software quality control: (*a*) separate groups; (*b*) combined groups.

- Documentation utilities
- Software design tools
- Debugging aids
- Structured preprocessors
- File comparators
- Structure analyzers
- Standards auditors
- Simulators
- Execution analyzers
- Performance monitors
- Statistical analysis packages
- Integrated CASE tools
- Test drivers
- Test case generators

These tools support quality control in all phases of software development. Documentation aids can provide partially automatic document writers, spelling checkers and thesauruses etc. Structured preprocessors (such as the UNIX utility *lint*) are useful both to standardize code listings, and to provide additional compile-time warnings that compilers often overlook. Early warnings regarding possible execution time problems can be provided by simulators, execution time analyzers and performance monitors. Substantial software system testing can often be performed automatically by test suite generators and automatic test executors.

All SQA tools to be used during software development should be identified and described in the SQA plan. This plan includes a description of all required quality assurance resources and details of how they will be applied. Thus, at the start of the project SQA resources can be budgeted and procured as part of the required project development resources (see Chapter 10).

8.2.3 The software quality assurance plan

The software quality assurance plan (SQAP), like the software configuration plan, is also part of the overall software project development plan. The SQAP documents which resources are needed, how they should be used and which standards and procedures will be applied during the project. The SQAP then becomes the mandate for the quality assurance group during project development. The issuance of this plan is the responsibility of the project manager, though in large projects it will usually be delegated to the quality assurance manager. The SQAP may appear as a separate document or as a section within the project development plan, and may include the configuration management plan (if this has not been documented separately).

Table 8.2 Example of the contents of a software quality assurance plan

1. Software quality assurance organization and resources
     Organization structure
     Personnel skill level and qualifications
     Resources

2. SQA standards, procedures, policies and guidelines

3. SQA documentation requirements
     List of all documentation subject to quality control
     Description of method of evaluation and approval

4. SQA software requirements
     Evaluation and approval of software
     Description of method of evaluation
     Evaluation of the software development process
     Evaluation of reused software
     Evaluation of non-deliverable software

5. Evaluation of storage, handling and delivery
     Project documents
     Software
     Data files

6. Reviews and audits

7. Software configuration management (when not addressed in a separate document)

8. Problem reporting and corrective action

9. Evaluation of test procedures

10. Tools techniques and methodologies

11. Quality control of subcontractors, vendors and suppliers

12. Additional control
     Miscellaneous control procedures
     Project specific control

13. SQA reporting, records and documentation
     Status reporting procedures
     Maintenance
     Storage and security
     Retention period

Table 8.2 contains a list of the main subjects covered in the SQAP.[6] When any of these subjects is covered elsewhere, such as in the software configuration management plan (SCMP), it can be omitted from the SQAP and replaced by a pointer to the document in which it is covered. However, the SCMP and the SQAP are concerned with different aspects of the controlled items. The SCMP is primarily concerned with the format of controlled items while the SQAP is more involved with the contents of controlled items.

The SQAP must cover subcontractors, vendors and suppliers, irrespective of whether or not these external entities have their own quality assurance organization. In any project, the quality of external components is ultimately the concern of the project manager and the SQA organization. When a system fails, it usually makes little difference whether the failure is due to an externally developed component or an in-house developed component. The plans for supervising these external groups must be adapted to the type of external components being provided (off the shelf or new development) and the type of organization (do they have their own quality assurance organization?).

The SQAP, as part of the project development plan, should be reviewed and updated periodically and whenever any requirements, project development procedures, methodologies or other relevant activities are changed. The IEEE SQAP guide recommends periodic evaluation of two aspects of the plan: (1) the plan's content and (2) the plan's implementation.

The plan's content should be evaluated with regard to the specific SQAP standard used, to assure the plan's continuing compliance with the standard even when the characteristics of the software project change.

The plan's implementation should be evaluated in terms of the changing scope of the project, including the tasks and responsibilities referenced in the plan, and other new or changed characteristics of the project.

When updating the SQAP the following project activities and events should be considered:

- New or changed contractual requirements
- Additional standards and policies
- Additional project documents
- Changes in the project's organizational structure
- New tools and utilities
- Additional subcontractors and vendors

8.2.4 Software quality metrics

Much attention has been devoted to questions associated with the measurement of quality. How do we determine the extent to which a software product contains this vague attribute called quality? When is the quality of a software product high and when is it low?

One of the more recent developments in quality assurance (not only for software) is the realization that quality is not a binary attribute that either exists or does not exist. Kaposi and Myers (1990), in a paper on measurement-based quality assurance, have stated their belief that 'the quality assurance of products and processes of software engineering *must be based on measurement*'.[7] The earlier the measurement of quality begins, the earlier problems will be

---

6. Table 8.2 is a guideline and not the definition of a standard. Software development standards are discussed in Chapter 9.
7. Italics added by this author.

located. Cohen *et al.* (1986), in addressing the cost of removing errors during the early phases of software development, proclaim the existence of the famous *exponential law*.[8]

The quality of two products can be compared, and it is perfectly acceptable to claim that the quality of one product is greater than the quality of another. It is also acceptable to measure quality and deduce the extent of expected faults based on the measured result.

The set of measurable values associated with the quality of a product is referred to as the product's quality *metrics*. Software quality metrics can be used to determine the extent to which a software product meets its requirements. The use of quality metrics increases the objectivity of the evaluation of product quality. Human evaluation of quality is subjective, and is therefore a possible source of disagreement, particularly between customer and developer.

A number of methods for establishing software quality metrics are currently being developed, though no generally accepted standard has yet emerged. For example, an initial draft of IEEE Std-1061 (1990) includes a detailed discussion of software quality metrics in general, including a suggested methodology for applying metrics, and many examples and guidelines. Quality metrics, once defined, do indeed increase objectivity, but the definition itself is not necessarily objective and greatly depends upon the needs of the organization that produces the definition.

The basic approach for applying software quality metrics requires:

- The identification of all required software quality attributes. This is usually derived from the software requirements specification.
- Determination of measurable values to be associated with each quality attribute.
- A description of the method by which each measurable value will be measured.
- A procedure for documenting the results of measuring the quality of the software product.

A set of many values can be used to determine the overall quality of a software product. However, a single measure can be created to represent the overall quality of the software product. This requires:

- A weighted method for combining the measured quality attributes into a single measure of quality for the product.

Some examples of software metrics are:

Reliability   The percentage of time that the system is successfully operational (e.g. 23 out of 24 hours produces: $100 \times (23/24)$ percent)

Recoverability   The amount of time it takes for the system to recover after failure (e.g. 1 hour to reload from backups and 30 minutes to reinitialize the system)

User-friendliness   The amount of training time needed for a new user

The measurement of software quality should not be performed only at the end of a project. The degree of quality should be measured at regular intervals during development. Thus, any major reduction in the overall measure of quality should act as a warning for the project manager that corrective action is required. High quality at the end of the project is achieved by assuring high quality throughout the development of the project.

8.2.5 Some general guidelines

The basic software quality assurance activities cover the review and approval of the development methodology, the software and documentation, and the supervision and approval

---

8. The cost of error removal increases exponentially as software development proceeds along the development cycle.

of testing. Other SQA activities, such as the supervision of reviews, the selection and approval of development tools, or the administration of configuration control, depend on the way SQA is adapted to a specific project. The size of the project is usually the determining factor. The following guidelines discuss some of the parameters to be considered for different types of project when planning SQA.

- In small projects, many SQA activities can be performed by the project manager. This includes the organization and supervision of reviews and audits, the evaluation and selection of development tools, and the selection and application of standards.
- Test procedures and testing are always best when conducted by a separate independent team (discussed later). The decision on whether supervision of testing activities can be assigned to SQA depends on many factors, including the independence of the SQA team, the size of the project and the complexity of the project (see Chapter 6 for a discussion of the complexity of projects).

  When testing is performed by an independent test team, SQA's involvement will be minimal. In most other cases it will be the responsibility of the SQA team to plan and supervise the testing of the system.
- As a general guideline, it is usually undesirable for SQA to be performed by a member of the development team. However, small projects often cannot justify the cost of a dedicated SQA engineer. This problem can be solved by having a single SQA engineer responsible for two or three small projects (with each project funding its share of the SQA services).

One additional guideline is based on the conclusions of Wesselius and Ververs (1990) for the application of *effective* quality control:

- The ability to control software quality is directly linked to the quality of the software requirements specification. Quality control requires the unambiguous specification of as many of the required characteristics of the software product as possible.

8.3 SOFTWARE TESTING

The term *testing* has many meanings, but in its most common use the term is applied to the examination or evaluation of something in order to determine the existence of certain properties. In software testing, these properties are associated with the software's predefined requirements. Software testing is the process of determining the degree to which software satisfies specified requirements. Therefore software testing requires the existence of a software requirements specification *before* testing can be carried out.

In simpler words, we cannot meaningfully test software if we do not know what the software is expected to do.

Testing can be performed by the programmer, the integration engineer or by an independent test group. In most cases, software should never be tested by the programmer directly responsible for writing the code being tested. Programmers are rarely objective with respect to their own code, and their testing will not be effective. There are many ways to increase the objectivity of testing. The best way is to use an independent test group. Independent testers are engineers whose main assignment is to develop test plans and test cases and to test the system objectively and rigorously for compliance with the requirements specification.

8.3.1 Types of software testing

Testing is the last development activity of a software project. However, this does not mean that testing is conducted *only* at the end of a project. Software should be tested at each stage of its development.

The different types of software testing include:

- Unit testing
- Integration testing
- Subsystem testing
- System testing
- Regression testing
- Alpha testing
- Beta testing
- Acceptance testing

It is usually best to test software modules immediately after they are coded. This is one of the few cases where programmers test their own code. These initial module tests, called *unit tests*, are conducted by the programmer in order to determine whether they conform to a minimal set of requirements. They include such tests as:

- Entry and exit (no eternal loops) for a small basic set of input data.
- For given input, the output is reasonable.
- Subroutines are called in the correct sequence. This is tested by using *stubs* (empty subroutine shells).

After successful unit testing, the modules are submitted to configuration control. They are then released to integration, where they are assembled and tested as part of the integration test process. This includes the gradual assembly of the modules into a complete system by the integration team. As more modules are integrated into the system, all added functionality is tested. At this stage, previously tested functionality must be tested again to assure that no new module has corrupted the system. This is referred to as *regression testing*.

In large software systems, the modules may be first assembled and integrated with hardware into subsystems. After the subsystems have been tested separately, they are combined into a complete system.

After system integration is complete, final tests are conducted. This includes alpha and beta testing and acceptance tests. Alpha testing is conducted with the complete system, but without live data. Beta testing uses live data, but requires constant supervision by members of the development team. Once the system is stable, acceptance tests are run, and if they are successful the system is released (these stages are further discussed in Chapter 4).

The final stages of system testing are represented in the following example. An automatic bank teller system is being developed for a large bank. When the teller subsystem is complete it undergoes subsystem testing to assure that the automatic teller features function correctly. Then the central computer subsystem is tested with test data to assure that it processes the data correctly. Finally the communications subsystem is tested with a simulated teller on one end and a simulated central computer on the other.

The three subsystems are then integrated and full system testing is conducted to assure that the automatic teller and the central computer communicate and function correctly.

After system testing, the fully integrated automatic teller system is tested in an alpha test environment. The system is tested with realistic test data, and the operation of all features is examined and compared to the requirements of the system. This task is assigned to the independent test group.

After the automatic teller system passes alpha tests, it is deemed sufficiently reliable to be able to process real data. This is the beta test. However, only a single automatic teller station is connected to the bank's computer, and the operation of the system is constantly monitored by members of the development team. Any problems are immediately located and corrected, and beta testing continues until the teller system runs error and fault free for a predefined period of time (e.g. one month). The supervision of the beta phase is also assigned to the independent test group.

After successful completion of beta tests, the teller system then enters final acceptance tests. Representatives of the bank's technical staff supervise a predetermined set of tests, and confirm or reject the success of the acceptance tests.

The automatic bank teller system has thus gone through all major test phases. Not all of these phases are applicable to all projects. For example, alpha and beta testing may be applicable to commercial or user oriented systems, but not to the development of software for a communications satellite or for a military application. Another example is subsystem testing, which is obviously only applicable when the system is actually divided into subsystems.

In all cases, independent testing is highly recommended for the more advanced stages of testing (from system testing onward). Objective independent testing will often locate problems much earlier than subjective tests performed by the developers. This is of major benefit to the project, since the earlier problems are located the less costly they are to correct.

8.3.2 Formal testing procedures

There are many different testing approaches and procedures for each stage of software testing. It is important to select the appropriate approach for each stage. Several formal software testing standards[9] include guidelines on how the standard is to be applied at each stage.

The US DOD standard 2167A (DOD 1988a) refers to the following basic stages:

1. Computer software unit (CSU) testing.
2. Computer software component (CSC) testing. This refers to the testing of a related group of CSUs (see Fig. 9.4).
3. Computer software configuration item (CSCI) testing. This is an advanced stage of integration testing. In small systems, this corresponds to system testing, and in large systems that have many CSCIs this corresponds to subsystem testing.
4. System integration and testing. This corresponds to advanced system testing.

All DOD software testing stages are accompanied by an evaluation criteria table describing the test evaluation requirements. This includes such criteria as internal consistency, understandability, traceability and requirements coverage. These criteria are then attributed to the items to be evaluated, such as source code (and later updated source code), test procedures and test results.

The actual test procedures are documented as follows:

● The test plan documents the general testing policy for the project, the test methodology to be used and the required resources.

---

9. Software development standards are discussed in Chapter 9 and software development methodologies are discussed in Chapter 4.

- The test description contains details of:
    - the individual test procedures, describing what is to be tested, and which requirements are being verified.
    - the individual test cases, describing how each test is to be conducted, what the input will be, and what the expected output should be. This will also describe the pass/fail criterion for each test.
- The test reports, which document the execution of the tests and the results that were received.

Generally, all formal software testing procedures are based on four components: test planning, test description, test execution and test reporting. Most test standards support these elements, and differ in the amount of detail and documentation required.

The IEEE standard 829 (1987b) for software test documentation contains a much more detailed description of the recommended approach to software testing, including several examples and usage guidelines. The IEEE approach also includes the three basic components: test plan, test procedure specification (similar to the DOD test description) and the test incident report (similar to the DOD test report). Refer to Figs. 9.5 and 9.6 for an overview of all the formal test activities and documents recommended by the IEEE software development standards.

Testing procedures are not just determined by the standards that are adopted. The actual test methods and techniques must be adapted to the type of project being developed and the testing environment and tools that are available. In addition to test planning and reporting, it is the responsibility of the test engineer (or test group) to select the appropriate techniques to be used during the testing of the software system. Specific testing and integration techniques are discussed in Chapter 4.

8.3.3 Some general guidelines

In any software project there is a limit to what can and should be tested. Many test procedures are unreasonably complex and costly. It is important to suit the intensity of the testing to the cost of an undiscovered system defect. An inventory system need not be tested to the same degree as the software for a medical life support system.

Over-testing can also be misleading. Many test procedures require changes to the system being tested (e.g. on-line monitors, trace utilities), or the use of special test equipment. This may mean that the system being tested is not the system being delivered.

An interesting view of this problem was presented by Laplante (1990) in a paper linking Heisenberg's uncertainty principle (normally applied to physics) to software testing.[10] Laplante's theory states that the more closely a software system is examined, the more likely the examination process will affect the system being tested. This theory may have been suggested tongue in cheek, but it does bring home the basic message: over-testing can be detrimental to the system being tested.

Three of the basic requirements for good testing are:

- Well written requirements
- Good test procedures
- Efficient testers

---

10. Laplante suggests the following formula: $\Delta r \Delta s \approx H$ where Δr represents the uncertainty of the software code, Δs represents the uncertainty of the test specifications and H is some constant.

Good requirements are discussed in Chapters 4 and 9, but one of the basic conditions for a good requirement is that it must be testable. Therefore formal requirements should always be written with testing in mind. A required feature that cannot be tested cannot be shown to exist, and should therefore have no place in the formal requirements specification for the project.

Test procedures are intended to demonstrate the fulfillment of the requirements. Therefore they should be based on an approach called *negative testing*. This means that it is the test group's objective to prove that the developers did not do a good job. If the tests are conducted correctly, then when the testers fail, the project succeeds.[11] Testers should not be kind, because ultimately the users will not be kind either.

As we have seen, testing is best performed by an objective, independent test group. However, only large projects can support an independent test group. Small projects can share the services of independent test groups, and can even lend development engineers specifically for testing. Thus a development engineer in one project can become a part-time objective tester in another project.

Lastly, testing must be adequately documented. One of the worst types of test is a failed test that cannot be repeated. If a failure cannot be readily repeated, it often cannot be corrected. Therefore the test documentation must be sufficient to enable the developers to repeat the sequence of events that led to the failure of the test.

8.4 SUMMARY

Project support groups not only disburden the project manager and the development engineers from the support tasks, they also perform these tasks better by concentrating their efforts on specific support functions. There are many types of project support functions. Secretarial services, administrative support, document publication and procurement are examples of non-technical support functions; testing, configuration control, systems engineering, integration management and quality assurance are examples of technical support functions.

Three of the basic functions that are required in every software development project are:

● Configuration control; manages the changes to the software product being developed.
● Quality assurance; monitors and controls the quality of the product being developed.
● Testing; verifies compliance with the product's formal requirements specification.

The software configuration management plan (SCMP) and the software quality assurance plan (SQAP) document the resources that are needed for each support group, how they are to be used, and which standards and procedures will be applied during the project. The SCMP and the SQAP then become the mandate for the two groups during project development.

Software testing is the process of determining the degree to which software satisfies specified requirements. Test procedures are prepared in order to demonstrate the fulfillment (or lack of fulfillment) of the requirements. Therefore they should be based on an approach called *negative testing*. This means that it is the test group's objective to prove that the developers did not do a good job. If the tests are conducted correctly, then when the testers fail, the project succeeds.

Independent test groups are the preferred software system testers. Objective independent testing will often locate problems much earlier than subjective tests performed by the developers. As stated earlier, this is of major benefit to the project since the earlier problems are located the less costly they are to correct.

---

11. This emphasizes the point simplistically. Obviously, there are many other factors that also contribute to the success of a software project.

It is the project manager's responsibility to organize the project support groups, and to document their planned activities in the project development plan (which includes the SCMP and the SQAP). Project support functions that are well planned at the start of the project will contribute to effective project management throughout the project.

EXERCISES

1. You have been designated project manager for the development of an inventory system for a large manufacturing company. The inventory system to be developed is to be based on the sS *ordering method* (when the inventory level for any item drops below s then a quantity is ordered that will raise the level to S; each item has its own sS values).

Suggest four intermediate versions of the system to be released internally for system testing, alpha testing, beta testing and final release. What will be the functional difference between each version? Describe the version control procedures to be used, and suggest a version description form.

2. As project manager, define the configuration management and quality assurance organizations for the inventory system described in Exercise 1. How many people are required for these tasks, and what will the responsibilities of each person be? Explain your decisions.

3. As software quality assurance manager, write the reviews and audits chapter of the SQAP for the development of the inventory system described in Exercise 1. Which reviews and audits will be held, and when are they to be held? Describe the requirements for each review and audit and how each required item is to be approved. Describe the procedure for corrective action after each review and audit.

4. Plan the testing stages for the release of the inventory system described in Exercise 1. Which test stages do you suggest after the integration phase? Write the chapters in the test plan that describe each of these test stages. Which resources are required, and what test data is required? Assign the testers for each stage.

5. Define five major quality attributes of the inventory system described in Exercise 1, and define the quality metrics for these attributes. Explain the reasoning behind the metrics that you have defined.

6. Using the change request form described in Fig. 8.4, fill out all entries in the form for the following changes: (1) an order monitoring feature is added for items that fall below level s, (2) the sS level for each item is to be added to the inventory report, (3) the requirement for a 6 second response to an inventory query has been relaxed to 20 seconds, and (4) the required capacity of the data base has been increased from 2000 items to 5000 items. Explain the problems and considerations related to each form.

7. Class exercise: divide the class into four groups. Assign Exercise 6 to each group. Discuss the differences between the way each group filled out the change request forms (e.g. discuss the difference in estimates). Discuss the different problems identified by each group and the considerations that were taken into account.

SOFTWARE DEVELOPMENT STANDARDS

DEVELOPMENT STANDARDS: THE NECESSARY EVIL

For many software engineers, there is a contradiction between *software development* and *standards*. Standards limit much of the software developer's freedom, as of course, they are meant to do. Standards accompany the development cycle from beginning to end; there are design standards, documentation standards, coding standards, testing standards, and even standards for submitting and evaluating proposals (see Chapter 3).

Though standards can be regarded as a necessary evil, their application achieves a worthwhile result; it makes software development more manageable. This does not mean that only managers benefit from the use of standards. Standards promote a degree of tidiness and conformity which assists developers in understanding work produced by others and encourages them to produce work that is understandable by others.

One of the main challenges facing the project manager is the selection of the right standard. In many cases the development standards are specified as requirements, as is often the case with government projects. However, even when a specific standard is required, it must still be tailored to the needs of the project being developed. Certain parts of a standard may be 'tailored out' if they are not applicable, such as the omission of timing analysis from the design of a non-time-critical system or the relaxation of coding standards for program code that is being reused.

This chapter provides the project manager with basic information for the selection of a suitable set of software development standards. It discusses the various types of software standards and describes the merits of two of the most common: the IEEE software engineering standards, and the US Department of Defense standard 2167A.

9.1 AN OVERVIEW OF SOFTWARE DEVELOPMENT STANDARDS

The term *standard* has been broadly applied to various types of directive. Some standards may function as guidelines, suggesting or recommending development techniques or document formats. Other standards may function as a set of strict rules governing every aspect of the development activities. Figure 9.1 describes the principal software development standards, and the relationships between them.

One of the most comprehensive software development standards is the US DOD standard 2167 (DOD 1988a). The standard's introduction declares that it establishes uniform requirements for software development that are applicable throughout the system life cycle, and that

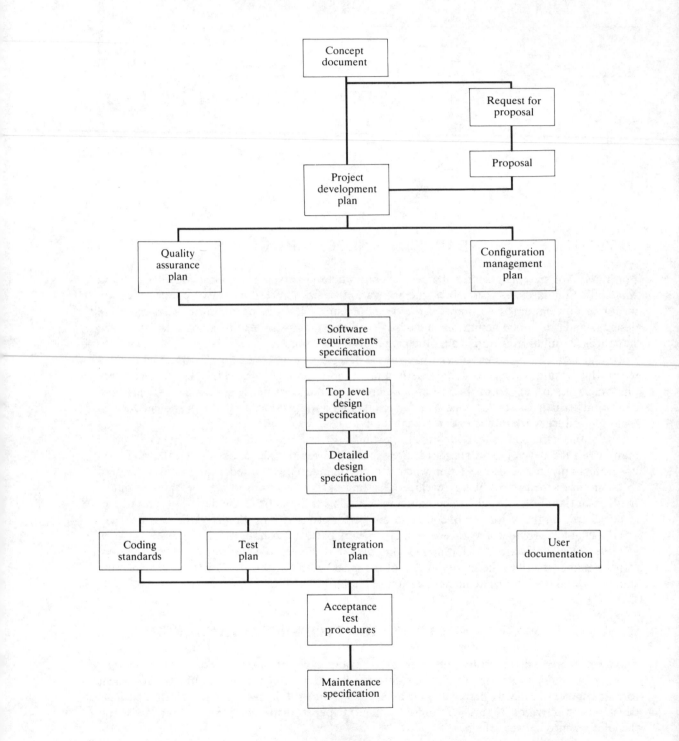

Figure 9.1 Principal software development standards.

the standard is not intended to specify or discourage the use of any particular software development method. Standard 2167 is, however, heavily inclined toward phased development methodologies, such as the Waterfall paradigm. Overmyer (1990), in an interesting analysis of the standard, reports that several researchers have successfully developed models that conform to the standard while introducing modern concepts of iterative requirements and design, though he concludes that 2167 was not developed with iterative design in mind.

For those seeking a less demanding standard than 2167, the IEEE software development standards offer a similar approach with much more flexibility. Many of the IEEE standards are more like guidelines than rigid standards.

Standards are easier to define and apply for the basic development activities (such as documentation and coding) than for development processes (such as design, testing and integration). Buckley, in his introduction to one of the earlier versions[1] of the IEEE software engineering standards, explains the IEEE's intention to go from product standard (e.g. a document) to process standard. In fact, the definition of standards for the process of software testing was one of the first processes to be tackled by the IEEE standards. This reflects the expansion of the scope of standards.

Buckley announced in 1984 that future standards would cover such new areas as software productivity metrics. But some things are easier to standardize than others, and the subject of productivity metrics is one of the more difficult. Zimmer (1991) states that 'with no standard definition of "productivity" it is very difficult to know what to measure, much less be able to measure it'. This led to the later introduction of three IEEE standards for *Measures to produce reliable software*, *Software productivity metrics*, and *Software quality metrics* (IEEE 1993).

Software testing is an area in which many standards have been produced. This is also true of software design, though much of the emphasis has been placed on the structure of design documentation. Software integration has fared less favorably, primarily because of the difficulty in standardizing such an intuition-ridden activity.

Testing is not the only area that has been widely standardized. It is surprising to find that the production of standards for one of the less definitive activities of software development has flourished in recent years, namely for software quality control. The difficulty in defining *software quality* is illustrated in the IEEE's standard glossary of software engineering terminology (IEEE 1987b), which contains no fewer than four separate definitions:

1. The totality of features and characteristics of a software product that bear on its ability to satisfy given needs; for example, conform to specifications.
2. The degree to which software possesses a desired combination of attributes.
3. The degree to which a customer or user perceives that software meets his or her composite expectations.
4. The composite characteristics of software that determine the degree to which the software in use will meet the expectations of the customer.

Software quality is defined by the US DOD (1988b) rather simply as:

5. The ability of a software product to satisfy its specified requirements.

While definitions 1 and 2 appear somewhat obscure, definitions 3, 4 and 5 are subjective, and seem to suggest that quality, like beauty, is in the eyes of the beholder. It is interesting to note

---

1. Buckley's introduction appears in the 1984 edition of the IEEE standards (IEEE 1984).

that in a later version of the IEEE glossary the controversial term *software quality* was removed entirely, leaving only a definition for the general term *quality*.

Software quality is not the only term with no single common definition; the same is true of such basic terms as *requirements*, *design* and *maintenance*. The way these terms are used in different standards also varies. This often causes confusion when the same terms mean different things to different people.

There are many reasons why standards are not standard, and subjectivity is just one of them. Software projects vary greatly, the needs of customers vary greatly, and the organizations that develop software vary greatly. It is therefore not surprising that the US Department of Defense, in recognizing that projects and needs vary, allowed for substantial tailoring of their software development standard 2167.

Many software development standards have been produced covering such activities as proposal evaluation (see Chapter 3), technical reviews and configuration control. Standards now exist for all the major project development activities.

Many of the prevalent software standards are satisfactory if they are applied correctly. Standards require discipline, which is not always easy to enforce in software engineering.

9.2 US DOD STANDARD 2167

Standard 2167 was produced by the US Department of Defense for the development of all mission critical defense software systems. After the release of various drafts and initial versions, the standard was issued in 1985, superseding the widely used Navy standard 1679A, and MIL standard 1644B. The intention was for 2167 to become the only official standard for the development of defense system software for the US military.

The first version of standard 2167 drew many comments from the DOD's software contractors and from within the Department itself. This led to the release of a modified DOD standard 2167A in 1988, with new accompanying standards 499 for engineering management and 2168 for software quality assurance.

9.2.1 Overview of Standard 2167

The stated objective of DOD standard 2167 (DOD 1988a) is to establish uniform requirements for software development that are applicable throughout the project life cycle. The standard includes the application of the following accompanying standards:

DOD–STD–480	Configuration control – Engineering changes and waivers
MIL–STD–490	Specification practices
MIL–STD–499	Engineering management
MIL–STD–1521	Technical reviews and audits for systems, equipment and computer software
DOD–STD–2168	Defense system software quality program
MIL–STD–881	Work breakdown structures for defense material items
DID	Data Item Descriptions (DID is pronounced to rhyme with *kid*)

The configuration control standard 480 enlarges upon the general configuration management directives and guidelines that appear within the body of the 2167 document.

Standards 490 and 499 cover general engineering directives for specification and management not specific to software development.

Standard 1521 describes the formal reviews and audits to be held during the development cycle.

Standard 881 describes the DOD requirements for the production and use of a work breakdown structure (WBS). In the 2167A release of the standard, 881 was no longer specified.

Standard 2168 (DOD 1988b) contains the requirements for the development, documentation and implementation of a software quality program. The software quality program includes planning for and conducting:

- Evaluations of the quality of software
- Associated documentation and related activities
- Follow-up activities necessary to assure timely and effective resolution of problems

The DIDs are a comprehensive set of documentation standards that cover all phases of software development, maintenance and the production of user reference manuals. The DIDs include a section called *preparation instructions* that provide a large degree of freedom by permitting tailoring of the document format and the use of alternate presentation styles. The full set of DIDs is described in Table 9.1.

Standard 2167 states that it is not intended to specify or discourage the use of any particular software development method (DOD 1988a). However, as mentioned previously, the standard is heavily inclined toward phased development methodologies, such as the Waterfall paradigm. The phased approach is inherent in the required development stages and reviews, requiring system design to be followed by software requirements, software design, implementation and testing. The standard includes a description of this approach, which is reproduced in Fig. 9.2.

Table 9.1 DOD Data Item Descriptions (DIDs)

Development documentation
    1. Software development plan
System documentation
    2. System/segment specification
    3. System/segment design document
Software design and requirements
    4. Software requirements specification
    5. Software design document
Interface design and requirements
    6. Interface requirements specification
    7. Interface design document
Version description
    8. Version description document
Test documentation
    9. Software test plan
    10. Software test description
    11. Test report
Release manuals
    12. Computer system operator's manual
    13. Software user's manual
    14. Software programmer's manual
    15. Firmware support manual
Maintenance documentation and source code
    16. Computer resources integrated support document
    17. Software product specification

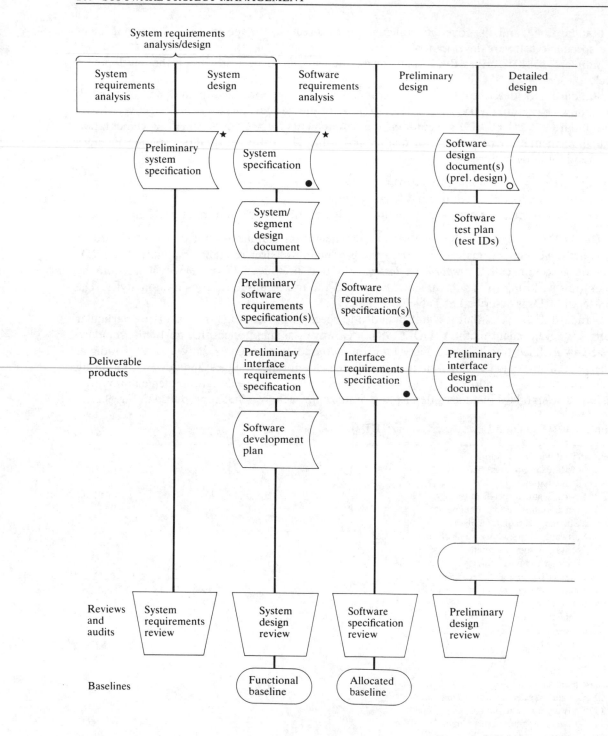

Figure 9.2 The DOD 2167A software development approach (from DOD-Std-2167A).

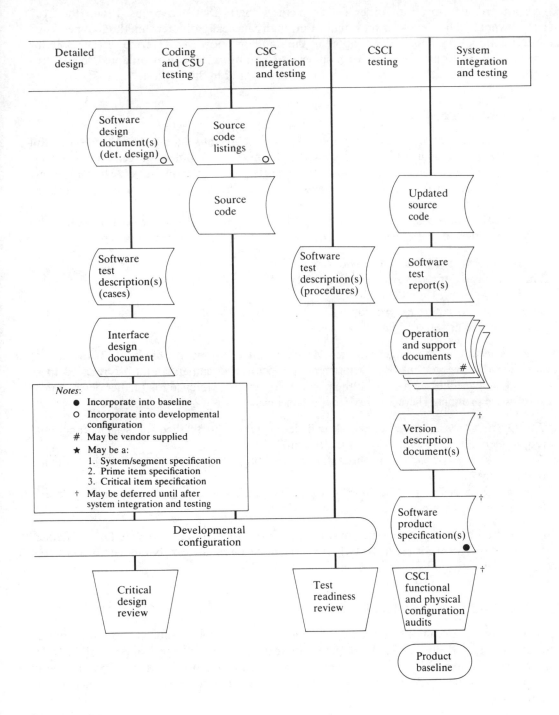

Figure 9.2 (continued)

The standard also mentions other design methodologies that can be used with the 2167 general concept, such as rapid prototyping. But, many basically different methodologies, such as the spiral model,[2] are not easily adapted to the standard. However, Overmeyer (1990), in his discussion of 2167, concludes that, with sufficient tailoring, 2167 can be adapted to iterative development methods. The tailoring of 2167 is discussed later in this section.

9.2.2 Reviews and audits

Reviews and audits are one of the major control tools built into standard 2167. A successful review is often a prerequisite for proceeding to the next development stage. Thus a review formally affirms the customer's approval of the preceding development work. A formal review is also often accompanied by a major payment milestone. This makes it a critical event both for the customer and for the contractor.

The main software project reviews and the relationships between them are shown in Fig. 9.3.

The formal review proceedings are described in MIL standard 1521, which covers:

- The documents and items to be reviewed
- The designation of the chairperson for the review
- The items to be presented and discussed
- The approval/disapproval procedure
- The corrective action procedure

Project reviews are where major project development decisions are finalized. These critical decisions are documented in the development specification documents, and are referred to as *baselines*.[3] The baselines then become the primary sources of reference for further development of the software product. There are three major baselines:

- *The functional baseline*; set at the system design review to finalize the system functional requirements (i.e. the user's view of the system).
- *The allocated baseline*; set at the software specification review to finalize the software requirements.
- *The product baseline*; this baseline is set at the conclusion of the development cycle and finalizes the development of the software product.

An additional intermediate baseline may be set at the critical design review (CDR) to finalize the design of the software product. Other intermediate baselines can be added to define the conclusion of important development activities.

9.2.3 The Data Item Descriptions (DIDs)

The Data Item Descriptions define the formal documentation standards for all required documents generated during the development of software according to standard 2167. DIDs apply to the development of one or more computer system configuration items (CSCIs), a term used throughout the 2167 standard to identify high level decomposition components of a computer system.

---

2. The spiral model, described by Boehm (1988), is an iterative converging model that is clearly difficult to adapt to the 2167 standard. It is a useful model for projects that are initially not sufficiently defined.
3. Baselines are further discussed in Chapter 10.

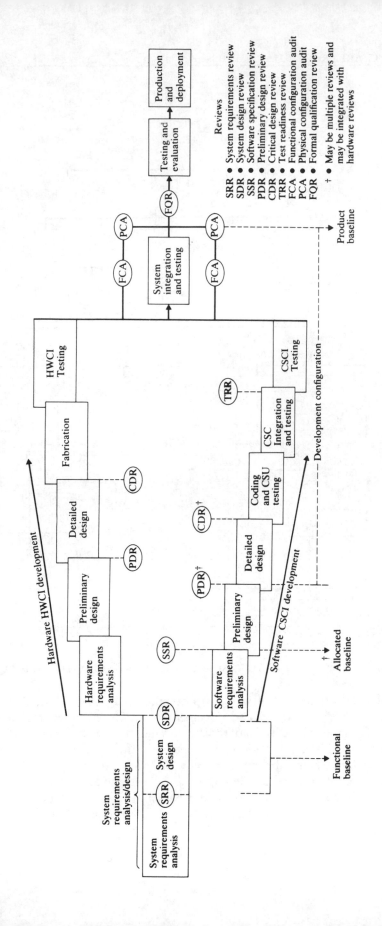

Figure 9.3 An example of DOD 2167 reviews and audits (from DOD-Std-2167A).

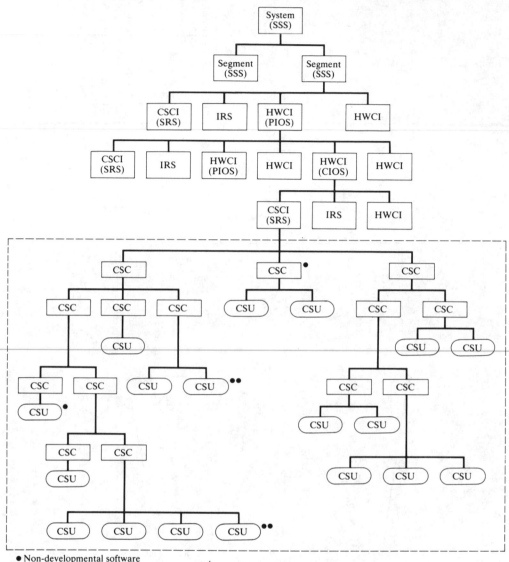

● Non-developmental software
●● Same CSU used by different CSCs

Figure 9.4 An example of DOD 2167 system decomposition (from DOD-Std-2167A).

A CSCI, as applied to software, is a component of the system that can be individually controlled, configured, tested and documented. CSCIs are often reviewed and approved as separate development items, and though a single review or audit can consider more than one CSCI, each is usually addressed separately during the review process. There are no clear-cut guidelines for the division of a software system into CSCIs as the division is essentially one of convenience, but generally the methods used are similar to the high level decomposition techniques described in Chapter 6. Figure 9.4 presents as an example the decomposition of a system into CSCIs and lower level CSUs, according to the 2167A standard.

Table 9.2 DOD Data Item Description standards

Data requirements title	Acronym
1. System segment design document	SSDD
2. Software development plan	SDP
3. Software requirements specification	SRS
4. Interface requirements specification	IRS
5. Interface design document	IDD
6. Software design document	SDD
7. Software product specification	SPS
8. Version description document	VDD
9. Software test plan	STP
10. Software test description	STD
11. Software test report	STR
12. Computer system operator's manual	CSOM
13. Software user's manual	SUM
14. Software programmer's manual	SPM
15. Firmware support manual	FSM
16. Computer resources integrated support document	CRISD
17. Engineering change proposal	ECP
18. Specification change notice	SCN

Table 9.2 contains a list of the DIDs referenced by standard 2167A. The software quality DID is referenced separately in the DOD software quality program standard 2168.

All DID document formats follow a similar pattern. Several of the sections are common to most, if not all of the documents, such as:

- Title page format
- Table of contents
- Scope (including identification, overview, references etc.)
- Other applicable documents
- Notes and appendices

In addition, the page format, page numbering scheme, section numbering scheme and various other preparation instructions are common. This clearly suggests the use of an automatic tool to assist in the preparation of the documents, a practice greatly encouraged by the 2167 standard. Many such tools have been developed to support 2167, and Polack, in a paper analyzing the use of CASE tools for DOD projects (Polack 1990), concludes that these tools do indeed save time, and result in a higher quality software system.[4]

Each DID describes the requirements for the preparation of a specific document, but the main emphasis is on the required content and not on the required format. This is specifically addressed in the preparation instructions accompanying each DID, which state that other presentation styles, including charts, tables or matrices, are acceptable (e.g. Hatley and Pirbhai (1988) or Ward and Mellor (1986)). There is also substantial flexibility in the requirements regarding the content of the documents. The standard provides for considerable tailoring to adapt the standard to the type of project being developed.

---

4. An example of a CASE tool that supports the 2167 standard is *Teamwork* by Cadre.

9.2.4 Tailoring the standard

Tailoring of standard 2167 is not only encouraged, it is required. The foreword to 2167 states that the standard must be appropriately tailored by the program manager to ensure that only cost-effective requirements are cited in defense solicitations and contracts.

The DOD has issued a guide for tailoring that can be used as a reference source for adapting the standards to the type of project being developed.[5] Two basic principles apply to tailoring:

- The tailoring process is the *deletion* of non-applicable requirements.
- Tailoring of the standard should be carried out by the contracting agency.

The first principle means that these modifications can only include the deletion of requirements from the standard (and not changes to the requirements in the standard). The second principle means that the contractor (i.e. the developer) cannot tailor the standard without receiving permission from the contracting agency (i.e. the DOD).

Tailoring of the 2167 standard must be completed as early as possible. This is best performed either during contract negotiations or as one of the initial activities as soon as the project begins. The following is a description of the basic procedure for tailoring standard 2167:

1. Review all standard 2167 requirements, including:
   - reviews and audits
   - documentation
   - testing activities
   - quality assurance activities
   - configuration control activities
   - other required development activities.
2. Identify the requirements that are not applicable, justifiable or reasonable for the project being developed. For example, the Firmware Support Manual will not be required if no firmware is being developed, or two design reviews (PDR and CDR) may not be necessary for a small project.
3. Prepare a list of requests for deletions from the standard. This may include:
   - exclusion of documents
   - exclusion of sections in documents
   - exclusion of activities
   - exclusion of parts of activities.
4. Prepare a written description of the justifications for each item that is requested to be tailored out.
5. Submit the tailoring request, together with the justification, as early as possible (preferably before the project begins).

In order to be able to differentiate between forgotten items and tailored items, all tailored items must be clearly referenced. When submitting a list of documents for a formal review or milestone, all documents tailored out should be listed together with a statement to that effect. Within a document, when a paragraph is tailored out a statement to that effect will appear directly after the paragraph number. If a paragraph and all of its subparagraphs are tailored out, only the highest level paragraph number need be included.

---

5. Tailoring guidelines can be found in DOD-HDBK-248 *Guide for application and tailoring of requirements for defense material acquisition.*

The list of the DIDs together with the list of tailoring approvals are an integral part of the project deliverables. Until tailoring approval has been granted, the developer is obligated to provide the full list of DIDs, with all their inclusions. This is the reason why tailoring should be concluded as early as possible.

9.2.5 Advantages and disadvantages of standard 2167

One of the most frequent complaints about 2167 is that it creates projects whose main product is paper and not software. In other words a massive amount of time and effort is devoted to the generation of documentation. Subsequently, additional time needs to be devoted to keeping these documents constantly updated.

Other criticisms of the standard (see Polack 1990) include complaints that it prevents the application of modern software development practices such as rapid prototyping and software reuse. As we have seen, these methods can be applied to 2167 though they may not fit naturally into the standard's general approach (see Overmyer 1990).

The standard is not easily applied to very small projects, as it requires substantial tailoring in order to reduce the overhead to a reasonable level. On the other hand, very large projects can benefit greatly from the standard, as it makes the projects more manageable and the development activities more visible.

Standard 2167 provides the customer with significant visibility during all major stages of development. This can increase the probability of customer satisfaction with the final product. However, all this is at a price. Control, documentation and reporting require the assignment of substantial resources, and these resources increase the cost of the development effort.

One of the main advantages of 2167 is that it does an excellent job of standardizing. It is one of the most comprehensive sets of standards in existence for software development, and it provides clear specific requirements for the control of most of the software development activities.

It is not a developer's choice, as few developers would voluntarily choose 2167. It is a customer's choice, and it supports the control of the development process from the customer's perspective. From a developer's perspective, 2167 provides a clear set of requirements that remove many of the ambiguities and obscurities that lead to customer–developer conflicts.

9.3 THE IEEE SOFTWARE ENGINEERING STANDARDS

In 1984, the Institute of Electrical and Electronics Engineers (IEEE) published their first set of software engineering standards (IEEE 1984). This set included four development standards that covered requirements, quality assurance, testing and configuration management, and a fifth, long awaited, standard glossary of software engineering terms.

The first set of standards, though far from complete, formalized a trend toward flexibility. The standards were more like guidelines and included many examples and suggestions.

Later editions of the standards covered other areas of software engineering, such as design, verification and validation (V&V), and a standard specific to software development in Ada. As the number of standards began to grow, the IEEE also issued a standard about software standards, to be used as a method for planning the development and the evaluation of standards.

In 1993, the IEEE issued their landmark collection of standards, including 22 software engineering standards: the results of over a decade of work. This volume, for the first time, comprehensively covered all phases of software development and many of its associated activities. Leonard Trip, in his introduction to the volume (IEEE 1993), explained the two basic themes that drove this immense work: consensus and timeliness. The standards averaged about three years each to produce, and they averaged an approval rate of 90 percent based on a ballot return of 85 percent. The 1993 collection was indeed a major milestone in software development's effort to become an engineering discipline.

9.3.1 Overview of the IEEE standards

The 1993 collection of software engineering standards includes:

1. IEEE Std 610.12–1990 (Formerly 729-1983)
   Standard glossary of software engineering terminology
2. IEEE Std 730–1989
   Standard for software quality assurance plans
3. IEEE Std 828–1990
   Standard for software configuration management plans
4. IEEE Std 829–1983
   Standard for software test documentation
5. IEEE Std 830–1984
   Guide to software requirements specifications
6. IEEE Std 982.1–1988
   Standard dictionary for measures to produce reliable software
7. IEEE Std 982.2–1988
   Guide for the use of standard dictionary for measures to produce reliable software
8. IEEE Std 990–1986
   Recommended practice for Ada as a program design language
9. IEEE Std 1002–1987
   Standard taxonomy for software engineering standards
10. IEEE 1008-1987
    Standard for software unit testing
11. IEEE Std 1012–1986
    Standard for software verification and validation plans
12. IEEE Std 1016–1987
    Recommended practice for software design descriptions
13. IEEE Std 1028–1988
    Standard for software reviews and audits
14. IEEE Std 1042–1987
    Guide to software configuration management
15. IEEE Std 1045–1992
    Standard for software productivity metrics
16. IEEE Std 1058.1–1987
    Standard for software project management plans
17. IEEE Std 1061–1992
    Standard for software quality metrics methodology
18. IEEE Std 1063–1987
    Standard for software user documentation
19. IEEE Std 1074–1991
    Standard for developing software life cycle processes

20. IEEE Std 1209–1992
    Recommended practice for the evaluation and selection of CASE tools
21. IEEE Std 1219–1992
    Standard for software maintenance
22. IEEE STd 1298–1992
    Software quality management system, part 1: Requirements

Three of the 1987 standards, 990, 1002 and 1012, were later reaffirmed in 1992.

In 1986 the IEEE also produced ANSI/IEEE Std 983-1986, *Guide for software quality assurance planning*, which was not included in their 1993 standards collection. This standard was produced as a guide for using standard 730.

It is also noteworthy that, in a rare departure from its customary practice, the IEEE adopted an Australian standard, 1298, defining the requirements for a software quality management system.

The stated intention of the IEEE standards is to leave the development methodology up to the developer. The standards fit easily into the phased Waterfall approach, though they can also be adapted to other methods, such as rapid prototyping and the Spiral model.

The software requirements standard 830 is an excellent example of a document that goes well beyond the basic function of a standard. It states that its intention is to guide the user toward the development of a 'good software requirements specification'. For example, it lists the basic characteristics of a good SRS as:

- Unambiguous
- Complete
- Verifiable
- Consistent
- Modifiable
- Traceable
- Usable during the operations and maintenance phase

This list can then be used as a checklist,[6] to evaluate the requirements specifications in the following manner:

1. Is each requirement clear and does it have the same interpretation to all who read it? (unambiguous)
2. Are all requirements documented, have we assured that no 'verbal' understandings remain? (complete)
3. Can we prove in a reasonable manner, and at a reasonable expense, that each requirement has been met? (verifiable)
4. Does any requirement conflict with another requirement? (consistent)
5. Is the requirements specification documented in a way that will enable it to be easily corrected or changed later? (modifiable)
6. Are the origins of each requirement clear (backward traceability), and can the testing and design documents be later traced to requirements? (forward traceability)
7. Has the requirement specification been written so that it can be understood not only by the organization writing it, but also by the software maintenance organization? (usable)

---

6. A rather obvious eighth characteristic is *implementable*, which implies that it must be possible to implement each requirement within the constraints of the project. Unimplementable requirements may refer to unattainable levels of reliability and performance or impossible interfacing between incompatible components.

The other IEEE standards also include many guidelines and examples. The software design standard is described as a set of recommended practices for design descriptions. The standard includes a sample outline for a design specification document, as well as recommendations on the content of each paragraph.

Testing has received considerable attention in the IEEE standards. Standard 829 covers the preparation of test documentation, standard 1008 covers the software unit testing, and standard 1012 covers verification and validation throughout the development cycle. Standard 1012 includes an excellent description that covers all project development testing activities. This is reproduced in Figs. 9.5 and 9.6.

The 990 standard is an unusual departure from generality and deals with a specific programming language, Ada. For those familiar with Ada the reasoning behind this will be clear, as Ada is much more than a programming language. The Ada language phenomenon is discussed in Section 9.4.

The taxonomy for software engineering standards is an unusual and interesting phenomenon too, and warrants special attention.

9.3.2 The IEEE taxonomy for software engineering standards

Standard 1002, taxonomy for software engineering standards, is an interesting phenomenon in that it attempts to provide a standard for selecting, classifying and comparing other software standards. Its purpose is also to assist in identifying the need for standards where none exist, or where none suitable exist. The standard also contains a list of definitions that includes the many types of software development standard, and the terminology to be used in identifying them.[7]

The taxonomy is an excellent reference for a comprehensive understanding of the various software development standards, and the relationship between them. The taxonomy provides a division (or *partition*, according to the standard) of software standards by type, and a division of software engineering by function and life cycle. To complete the taxonomy, a framework describes the relationship between the two partitions.

Figures 9.7(*a*) and (*b*) describe the partition of standards by type and the partition of software engineering by function and life cycle. Figure 9.8 is an example of the type of table used to define the basic taxonomy framework.

Standard 1002 can be helpful in organizations that are considering the move to formal software development, or when the suitability of existing formal practices is being reevaluated. The standard is not dependent on other IEEE standards, and can be applied to any formal software development standard.

9.3.3 A synopsis of the IEEE standards

The following synopsis of the IEEE software standards is reproduced from the IEEE 1993 standards collection.

Synopsies of the Standards

The main motivation behind the creation of these IEEE Standards has been to provide recommendations reflecting the state-of-practice in development and maintenance of software.

---

7. IEEE Standard 1002 includes the definition of the term *taxonomy* as 'A scheme that partitions a body of knowledge and defines the relationships among the pieces. It is used for classifying and understanding the body of knowledge'.

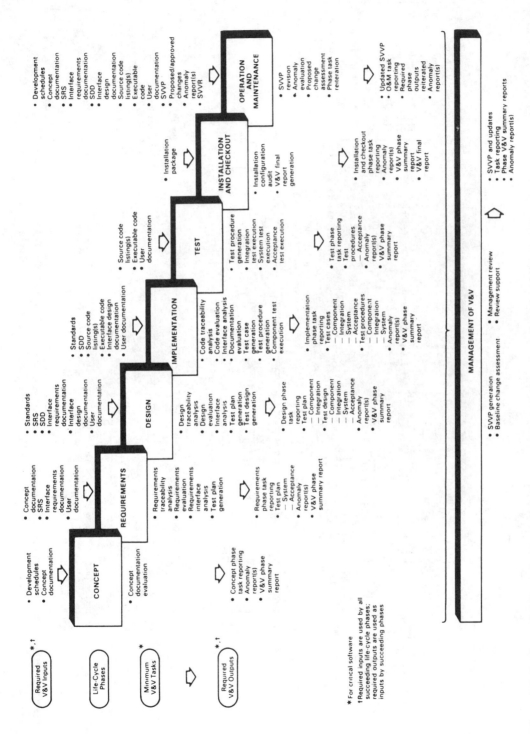

Figure 9.5 Testing activities: software verification and validation plan overview. (Reproduced from IEEE Std 1012–1986, *IEEE Standard for Software Verification and Validation Plans*, © by the Institute of Electrical Engineers, Inc., with the permission of the IEEE.)

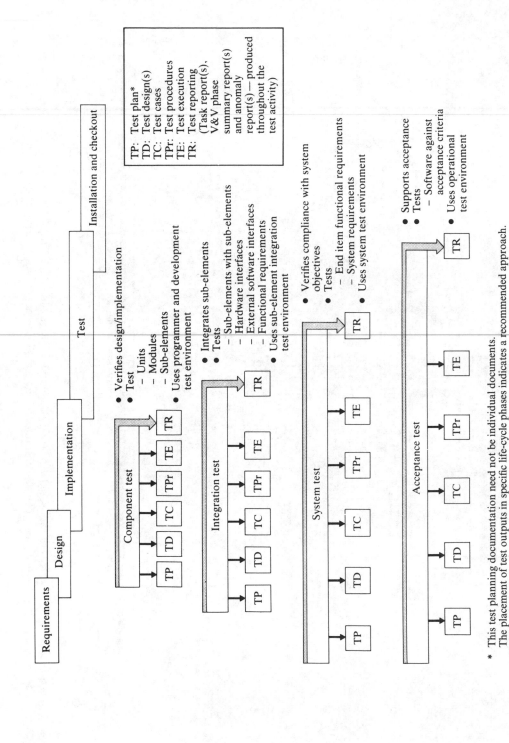

Figure 9.6 Testing activities: test tasks and documentation. (Reproduced from IEEE Std 1012–1986, *IEEE Standard for Software Verification and Validation Plans*, © by the Institute of Electrical Engineers, Inc., with the permission of the IEEE.)

156

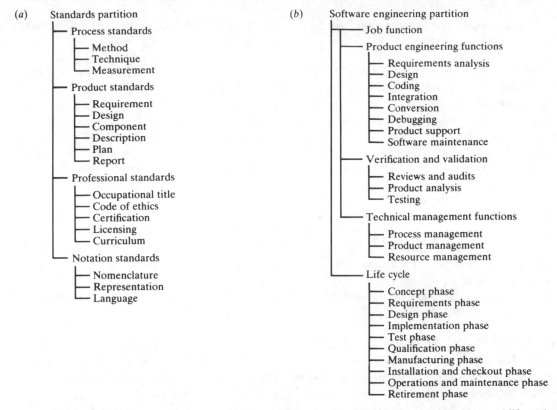

Figure 9.7 (*a*) Partition of standards by type; (*b*) partition of software engineering by function and life cycle. (Reproduced from IEEE Std 1002–1987, *IEE Standard Taxonomy for Software Engineering Standards*, © by the Institute of Electrical and Electronic Engineers, Inc., with the permission of the IEEE.)

For those who are new to software engineering, these standards are an invaluable source of carefully considered advice, brewed in the cauldron of a consensus process of professional discussion and debate. For those who are on the cutting edge of the field, these standards serve as a baseline against which advances can be communicated and evaluated.

The following are synopses of the standards included in this volume:

IEEE Std 610.12. IEEE Std 610.12 is a revision and redesignation of IEEE Std 729. This standard contains definitions for more than 1000 terms, establishing the basic vocabulary of software engineering. Building on a foundation of American National Standards Institute (ANSI) and International Organization for Standardization (ISO) terms, it promotes clarity and consistency in the vocabulary of software engineering and associated fields.

IEEE Std 730. This standard has legal liability as its basic rationale. It is directed toward the development and maintenance of critical software, that is, where failure could impact safety or cause large financial or social losses. The orientation is toward delineating all of the planned and systematic actions on a particular project that would provide adequate confidence that the software product conforms to established technical requirement.

The standard establishes a required format and a set of minimum contents for software quality assurance plans.

IEEE Std 828. This standard is similar in format to IEEE Std 730, but deals with the more limited subject of software configuration management. The standard identifies requirements for configuration identification, configuration control, configuration status accounting and reporting, and configuration audits and reviews. The implementation of those requirements provides a means by which the evolution of the software product items are recorded, communicated, and controlled. This provides assurance of the integrity and continuity of the software product items as they evolve through the software development and maintenance life cycle.

IEEE Std 829. This standard defines the content and format of eight documents that cover the entire testing process. The test plan prescribes the scope, approach, resources, and schedule of the testing activities. It identifies the items to be tested, the testing tasks to be performed, the personnel responsible for each task, and the risks associated with the plan. Test specification is covered by three document types, while test reporting is covered by four document types. The standard shows the relationships of these documents to one another as they are developed, and to the test process they document.

IEEE Std 830. This guide describes alternate approaches to good practice in the specification of software requirements. To enable the reader to make knowledgeable choices, extensive tutorial material is provided. This guide covers the attributes of a good software requirements specification, as well as specification methodologies and associated formats.

IEEE Std 982.1. This standard provides definitions of selected measures. The measures are intended for use throughout the software development life cycle in order to produce reliable software. The standard does not specify or require the use of any of the measures. Its intent is to describe the individual measures and their use.

IEEE Std 982.2. IEEE Std 982.2 is a companion to IEEE Std 982.1 and provides guidance in the use of the measures in IEEE Std 982.1. It provides information needed by industry to make the best use of IEEE Std 982.1.

IEEE Std 990. This recommended practice provides recommendations reflecting state-of-the-art and alternate approaches to good practice for characteristics of Program Design Languages (PDLs) based on the syntax and semantics of the Ada Programming Language. In this document, these are referred to as Ada PDLs.

IEEE Std 1002. This standard describes the form and content of a software engineering standards taxonomy. It explains the various types of software engineering standards, their functional and external relationships, and the role of various functions participating in the software life cycle. The taxonomy may be used as a method for planning the development or evaluation of standards for an organization. It could also serve as a basis for classifying a set of standards or for organizing a standards manual.

IEEE Std 1008. Software unit testing is a process that includes the performance of test planning, the development of a test set, and the measurement of a test unit against its requirement. Measuring entails the use of sample data to exercise the unit and the comparison of the unit's actual behavior with its required behavior as specified in the units' requirement documentation.

This standard defines an integrated approach to systematic and documented unit testing. The approach uses unit design and unit implementation information, in addition to unit requirements, to determine the completeness of the testing. The standard describes a testing process composed of a hierarchy of phases, activities, and tasks. Further, it defines a minimum set of tasks for each activity, although additional tasks may be added to any activity.

IEEE Std 1012. This standard has a threefold purpose:

a) To provide, for both critical and noncritical software, uniform and minimum requirements for the format and content of Software Verification and Validation Plans (SVVPs).

b) To define, for critical software, specific minimum Verification and Validation (V&V) tasks and their required inputs and outputs that shall be included in SVVPs.

c) To suggest optional V&V tasks to be used to tailor SVVPs as appropriate for the particular V&V effort.

IEEE Std 1016. A software design description is a representation of a software system. It is used as a medium for communicating software design information. This recommended practice describes that documentation of software designs. It specifies the necessary information content and the recommended organization for a software design description.

IEEE Std 1028. Software reviews and audits are a basic part of the ongoing evaluation of software products as they pass along the software development life cycle. This standard provides direction to the reviewer or auditor on the conduct of evaluations. Included are processes applicable to both critical and noncritical software and the procedures required for the execution of reviews and audits.

IEEE Std 1042. The purpose of this guide is to provide guidance in planning Software Configuration Management (SCM) practices that are compatible with IEEE Std 828. The guide focuses on the process of SCM planning and provides a broad perspective for the understanding of software configuration management.

IEEE Std 1045. This standard defines a framework for measuring and reporting productivity of the software process. It focuses on definitions of how to measure software process productivity and what to report when giving productivity results. It is meant for those who want to measure the productivity of the software process for creating code and documentation products.

IEEE Std 1058.1. This standard specifies the format and contents of software project management plans. It does not specify the procedures or techniques to be used in the development of project management plans, nor does it provide examples of project management plans, instead the standard sets a foundation for an organization to build its own set of practices and procedures for developing project management plans.

Draft IEEE Std 1061. This standard provides a methodology for establishing quality requirements and identifying, implementing, analyzing, and validating the process and product of software quality metrics. This standard does not prescribe specific metrics. It does include examples of metrics together with a complete example of the standard's use.

IEEE Std 1063. This standard provides minimum requirements on the structure and information content of user documentation. It applies primarily to technical substance rather than to style. Users of this standard may develop their own style manual for use within their organizations to implement the requirements of this standard.

IEEE Std 1074. This standard defines the set of activities that constitute the processes that are mandatory for the development and maintenance of software. The management and support processes that continue throughout the entire life cycle, as well as all aspects of the software life cycle from concept exploration through retirement, are covered. Associated input and output information is also provided. Utilization of the processes and their component activities maximizes the benefits to the user when the use of this standard is initiated early in the software life cycle. This standard requires definition of a user's software life cycle and shows its mapping into typical software life cycles. It is not intended to define or imply a software life cycle of its own.

Draft IEEE Std 1209. This recommended practice provides individuals and organizations with a process for the evaluation and selection of computer-aided software engineering (CASE) tools. The recommended practice addresses the evaluation and selection of tools supporting software engineering processes including project management processes, development processes, and integral processes.

Draft IEEE Std 1219. This standard defines the process for performing the maintenance of software. It prescribes requirements for process, control, and management of the planning, execution, and documentation of the software maintenance activities.

IEEE Std 1298. This is Australian standard AS 3563.1-1991. This standard establishes requirements for a software developer's quality management system. It identifies each of the elements of a quality management system to be designed, developed, and maintained by the developer with the objective of ensuring that the software will meet the requirements of a contract, purchase order, or other agreement.

9.3.4 Advantages and disadvantages of the IEEE standards

The IEEE software engineering standards are a flexible set of standards, guidelines and recommendations that can be applied to various software development methodologies. The standards are relatively easy to use, and they include many examples that demonstrate the way in which they are intended to be used.

Though all IEEE software engineering standards are compatible, they have been developed so that each standard can be used individually. This means that each IEEE standard can be used without the need to use any other standard.

However, many of the standards' advantages can also be perceived as disadvantages. They leave a great deal of freedom to the implementor, so that, in the interest of standardization, each organization must define the way they are to be implemented.

			Type of standard			
			Process standard	Product standard	Professional standard	Notation standard
Job function	Verification and validation	Reviews and audits				
		Product analysis				
		Testing				
	Technical management	Process management				
		Product management				
		Resource management				
Software life cycle		Concept				
		Requirement				
		Design				
		Implementation				
		Test				
		Manufacturing				
		Operation and maintenance				
		Retirement				

Figure 9.8 Basic taxonomy framework table. (Reproduced from IEEE Std 1002–1987, *IEEE Standard Taxonomy for Software Engineering Standards*, © by the Institute of Electrical and Electronic Engineers, Inc., with the permission of the IEEE.)

9.3.5 A comparison of the IEEE and DOD standards

The IEEE and DOD standards are based upon a similar interpretation of software engineering in so far as much of the terminology is similar and the general approach is similar. The objective, though, is not similar. The DOD 2167 standard was developed to support the interests of the customer (the DOD), while the IEEE standards were developed with the interests of the customer and developer equally in mind.

The following is a summary of the main differences between the two standards:

1. The DOD standard is mostly a set of directives, while many of the IEEE standards are primarily guidelines and recommendations.
2. The DOD standard provides a single overall set of directives while the IEEE is a set of individual standards.
3. The IEEE standards are more flexible and provide a much wider degree of freedom than the DOD standards.
4. Both the DOD and the IEEE standards can be tailored to the needs of a specific project. But the IEEE standards go further, as the adoption of an individual standard does not require the adoption of any other.
5. Both the IEEE and the DOD standards are inclined toward the phased approach to software engineering. Though they can both support other development methodologies, IEEE is more easily adapted to iterative approaches.

9.4 EUROPEAN SOFTWARE STANDARDS

The International Organization for Standardization (ISO) is probably the most influential organization of its type in Europe. Though several European countries have developed their own software development standards, many of these standards are variations or adaptations of the ISO standards. Recently, the ISO standards have started gaining wide international acceptance.

9.4.1 The ISO 9000 standards

The International Organization for Standardization, based in Switzerland, is a worldwide federation of national standards bodies, with branches and affiliations in many countries. One of the areas in which ISO has been active for many years is the definition of standards for quality. These standards have been designated as the ISO 9000 series, and have been developed for various areas of technology.

The ISO 9000 standard for software defines its objective as follows (ISO 1990):

This [software] part of ISO 9000 is intended to provide guidance where a contract between two parties requires the demonstration of a supplier's capabilities to develop, supply and maintain software products.

The guidelines in this part of ISO 9000 are intended to describe the suggested controls and methods for producing software which meet a purchaser's requirements. This is done primarily by preventing nonconfirmity at all stages from development through to maintenance.

As the above description states, the ISO standards are excellent for use between organizations (customer and developer) where software development contracts are needed. The standard is much more stringent than its IEEE counterpart, though less demanding than 2167.

Not surprisingly, many of the areas covered by the ISO 9000 standard are similar to those covered by the corresponding IEEE and DOD standards. The following overview covers the ISO 9000 software processes and addresses some ISO specific issues.

1. *Management responsibility*
   This includes the definition and documentation of quality objectives and policy. It covers such areas as the organizational structure and management reviews.
2. *Quality system*
   This activity covers the process by which quality is built in to the software product during development, rather than it being discovered at the end of the process.
3. *Internal quality system audits*
   Internal quality audits are carried out according to a predefined audit plan in order to verify whether quality activities comply with the quality plan and in order to determine their effectiveness.
4. *Corrective action*
   This activity investigates the cause of non-conformance in a software product and defines the actions needed to correct the problem and to prevent recurrence.
5. *Contract review*
   This process defines the requirements of a contract between supplier and purchaser. It covers such areas as contingencies and risks, discrepancies between tender and contract, subcontracting and terminology.
6. *Purchaser's requirements specification*
   This process is similar to the corresponding IEEE and DOD standards.
7. *Development planning*
   This process is similar to the corresponding IEEE and DOD standards.
8. *Quality planning*
   This process defines the content of the quality plan, including measurable quality objectives, test activities and quality responsibilities for configuration management.
9. *Design and implementation*
   This process is similar to the corresponding IEEE and DOD standards..
10. *Testing and validation*
    This process is similar to the corresponding IEEE and DOD standards.
11. *Acceptance*
    This process refers to the acceptance tests (or criteria) for the delivery of a validated software product.
12. *Replication, delivery and installation*
    Replication covers the copying of the software product: the number of copies, the storage media, documentation etc.
13. *Maintenance*
    This process is similar to the corresponding IEEE and DOD standards.
14. *Configuration management*
    This process is similar to the corresponding IEEE and DOD standards.
15. *Document control*
    This process covers the determination of documents to be controlled, approval and issuance procedures, and change and withdrawal procedures.
16. *Quality records*
    The quality records process covers the procedures for the identification, collection,

indexing, filing, storage, maintenance and disposition of quality records. These records are used to demonstrate the achievement of the required quality level.

17. *Measurement*

    This process covers the collection and reporting of quality measurements according to specific improvement goals. It also addresses the need for remedial action if metric levels grow worse or exceed established target levels.

18. *Rules, practices and convention*

    This set of processes covers a general area in which the supplier is required to set rules, practices and conventions in order to make the ISO 9000 quality standard effective.

19. *Tools and techniques*

    This is also a very general process that covers the need to provide adequate tools, facilities and techniques to make the ISO 9000 quality system effective.

20. *Purchasing*

    This process covers the acquisition of software and hardware products for the development of, or for inclusion in, the final product. The process also covers the assessment of subcontractors.

21. *Included software product*

    When existing products, either from the purchaser or from a third party, are required to be included in the supplier's system, this process addresses procedures covering how this is to be implemented. Areas addressed include validation and protection of the included product, as well as support for the included product after the final system is delivered.

22. *Training*

    This process addresses the preparation of a training plan for the operation of the new system. It covers not only training in using the system being developed, but also training to acquire related skills that may be needed to use the system.

The ISO software standards cover several areas not directly addressed by the IEEE and DOD standards (such as contract review). They require significant expansion and interpretation for use within an organization, as many activities are not defined in detail.

The ISO organization provides accreditation to organizations that conform to its 9000 standard. This accreditation is often a prerequisite for participation in many European (and sometimes non-European) tenders or requests for proposals (RFPs).

9.4.2 The British standards

The British Standards Institution (BSI) produces standards for various areas of engineering.

The British standard relevant to software development is designated BS 5750. It covers:

- A guide to selection and use
- A guide to quality management and quality system elements
- The specification for design/development, production, installation and servicing
- A specification for production and installation
- A specification for final inspection and test
- Guides for the use and application of BS 5750

In several other areas, BS 5750 is virtually identical with the corresponding ISO 9000 software standards (see BSI 1991).

9.5 THE ADA STANDARDS

Ada is a programming language, but it is a unique programming language. It is championed by one of the largest consumers of software development services in the world; the US Department of Defense. Ada is a US military standard, designated ANSI/MIL-STD-1815A. Ada also comes with a distinct European flavor, and in fact it was adopted in the early 1980s as the common implementation language by the European Economic Community. The European Community also participated actively in the language design and reviews of Ada, and many large European projects have subsequently been developed in Ada.

Ada is mandated today for all software developed for the US DOD unless a waiver has been granted. The success of Ada is still being debated, and the many waivers that have been granted by the DOD are an indication of the difficulties the language is experiencing in gaining acceptance. Like the 2167A standard, Ada is the customer's choice, not the developer's choice. There are many developers who would swear by Ada, but there are many more who would swear at Ada.

The language was initially used for non-real-time applications because of slow task switching problems with the first Ada compilers. These problems disappeared as more sophisticated Ada compilers became available, and Ada is now used for data processing, system development and real-time applications.

9.5.1 The Ada environment

Ada is also used as a design tool. Ada was regarded from the start as much more than a new language, and the structure of the language makes it suitable for use as a program design language (PDL). This characteristic of Ada was no accident, as the DOD set the development of Ada support environments as a target that went hand in hand with the development of the language itself. The requirements for the Ada language were defined in the Steelman document,[8] and a second document, the Stoneman document, defined the requirements for support environments.

Many Ada compilers are today provided as an integral part of an Ada development environment. Apart from the compiler itself, this includes CASE tools for generation of documentation, software design, debugging and integration, and testing.[9]

9.5.2 The IEEE standard for Ada PDLs

The IEEE has singled out Ada as a software design tool warranting special attention. The IEEE issued standard 990 in 1987, defining a set of recommended practices for the use of Ada as a PDL.

Standard 990 refers to the characteristics of an Ada PDL, not the use of Ada as a PDL. This is due to the attempt by the standard to generalize by addressing any PDL based on the syntax and semantics of Ada (the standard thus coins the term *Ada PDL*).

IEEE Standard 990 formalizes a practice that evolved naturally with the users of Ada. The standard describes the required characteristics of an Ada PDL, most of which can be readily applied to any good PDL. These required characteristics include the support of many design methodologies and certain good design practices such as modularity, information hiding and

---

8. The DOD issued the Stoneman document in 1976, defining the 'Requirements for Ada Programming Support Environments', and the 'Steelman' document in 1978, defining the 'Requirements for High Order Computer Programming Languages', which laid the foundations for the Ada language (named after Augusta Ada Byron, presumed to be the first computer programmer, and the daughter of the British poet Lord Byron).
9. Tahvanainen and Smolander (1990) is a useful source of information about tools for design, simulation, coding and other areas of software development.

connectivity. The standard can be used as a checklist to evaluate PDLs, and more specifically it can be helpful in understanding how Ada can best be used as a PDL.

The IEEE Ada PDL standard documents a phenomenon that was developed naturally by users of Ada as a programming language. Ada as a PDL is easily adapted to the design phase of software development, and when so used it provides an obvious additional advantage. After design is complete, a substantial amount of the code has already been written. This has led to the development of a number of Ada CASE tools that produce Ada code.

9.6 OTHER SOFTWARE DEVELOPMENT STANDARDS

One of the early standards for software documentation was issued in 1976 by the US National Bureau of Standards. The standard, called *Guidelines for Documentation of Computer Programs and Automated Data Systems*, was issued as a Federal Information Processing Standards Publication. The publication of the standard coincided with the humble beginnings of the evolution of software as an engineering discipline.

The Bureau of Standards followed with five more software standards between 1979 and 1984, which included:

- Guidelines for documentation of the initiation phase
- A guideline for evaluating software development tools
- Guidelines for verification, validation and testing of software
- Guidelines for the management of software documentation
- A guideline for software maintenance

As an initial attempt to provide a national standard these standards were a major step forward. Other early standards were issued by ANSI in 1974 and by various branches of the US military during the early 1970s.

In Europe, the British Standard BS 6224 was issued in the early 1980s, and the ISO issued software standards in the late 1980s.

Several standards champion a specific tool or technique. BS 6224 includes an interesting design technique which is referred to as the design structure diagram (BS 6224 DSD). The DSD is a graphical representation of a software design (like a flow chart) that encourages a structured approach to the design process. The basic DSD technique is excellently described in the standard document itself.[10]

Many techniques have not been universally adopted. This has resulted in a profusion of methods, standards and techniques. For example, software quality assurance has received much attention both in the IEEE and in the DOD standards. The ISO standard 9000-3 of 1990 (ISO 1990) presents a somewhat different basic approach. The European standard gives a broader meaning to the term quality assurance, and covers:

- Management responsibility
- Audits and reviews
- Testing
- Configuration control
- Training

---

10. A discussion of the DSD technique is provided by Macro and Buxon (1987).

Several other standards have been produced both in Europe and in the United States. Selecting a suitable standard is, in itself, a major project activity. The error of using no software development standard is almost as great as attempting to apply the full DOD Std-2167A to a small data processing project.

Probably the most important point to remember when selecting a suitable standard for a software project is that the development standard is a means, not an end. The standard must support the achievement of the objective: the successful development of quality software. If the standard interferes with the achievement of this objective, then it is most probably either the wrong standard or is being applied incorrectly.

Standards are most successful when they flow with the current. Whenever possible, a standard should provide a formal framework for good practices already in existence. When existing practices are inefficient, the standard should support their replacement with practices that can easily be implemented. It will always be difficult to introduce a standard that meets with the resistance of developers.

9.6 SUMMARY

Standards can be regarded as a necessary evil, and their application achieves a worthwhile result: it makes software development more manageable. One of the main challenges facing the project manager is the selection of the right set of standards. This chapter provides the basic information necessary to assist the project manager in making that selection.

The types and variations of software development standards are many, and there is no indication that standards are becoming standard. Many of the prevalent software standards are satisfactory provided they are applied correctly. Standards require discipline, and discipline is not always easy to enforce in software engineering.

The US Department of Defense standard 2167 solves the discipline problem by requiring the application of the standard as part of the project contract. The intention was for 2167 to become the only official standard for the development of defense system software for the US military.

A less rigid set of standards than 2167 was produced by the IEEE. The IEEE software engineering standards are a flexible set of standards, guidelines and recommendations that can be applied to various types of software development methodologies. The standards are relatively easy to use, including many examples to demonstrate the way they are intended to be used.

Both the IEEE and the DOD standards are based upon a similar interpretation of software engineering in so far as much of the terminology is similar and the general approach is similar. The objective, though, is not similar. The DOD 2167 standard was developed to support the interests of the customer (the DOD), while the IEEE standards were developed with the interests of the customer and developer equally in mind.

The International Organization for Standardization (ISO), based in Switzerland, is a world-wide federation of national standards. One of the ISO's main areas of activity is the development of standards for quality. These standards have been designated as the ISO 9000 series, and have been developed for various areas of technology. The ISO standards are excellent for use between organizations (customer and developer) where software development contracts are needed.

The ISO software standards are much more stringent than their IEEE counterpart, though less demanding than 2167.

An abundance of standards has been produced both in Europe and in the United States, making the selection of a suitable standard, in itself, a major project activity.

A software development standard is a means, not an end. The standard must support the achievement of a basic objective: the successful development of quality software. If the standard interferes with the achievement of this objective, then it is most probably either the wrong standard or is being applied incorrectly.

EXERCISES

1. The US DOD has contracted you to develop the software for an inventory optimization utility. The system will receive information on specific military items, the number required of each, the locations, and the expected consumption rate of each item. The system will then output recommended levels of inventory for each item, along with the location for each inventory stock.

The system is to be developed according to standard 2167A. Prepare a list of 10 major tailoring requests for the standard and explain the justification for each request.

2. Compare the IEEE and DOD standards in relation to the project described in Exercise 1. Explain which standard you think is more suitable. Is there any area covered by the ISO 9000 standard that would make it preferable?

3. Prepare an outline of a requirements specification for the project described in Exercise 1. Based on the IEEE guideline for a good requirements specification, give examples for each of the seven characteristics described.

4. Describe the framework that links the DOD standards to software engineering. Use the table defined in the IEEE software engineering taxonomy standard 1002.

Define the framework also for the IEEE standards.

Compare the IEEE and DOD frameworks to the ISO 9000 standards.

5. Consider the suitability of a high level programming language that you are familiar with to be used as a program design language. Discuss the advantages and the disadvantages of the language you have chosen as a PDL.

PROJECT SCHEDULING

SCHEDULING: THE PROBLEM

Any project can be completed, given an infinite amount of time and resources. Realistically, the amount of time available for project development is always finite. In fact, in most cases it is less than the project manager considers sufficient. Few projects are completed ahead of time; many projects overrun their schedule.

The following case history underscores some of the main elements of scheduling.

In the late 1970s, a large California-based defense contractor was developing a complex air defense system for the military. After the integration phase began, and for the following period of about six months, all efforts were directed toward the first major system test, to be conducted together with an east coast subcontractor.

The subcontractor was to send up a plane that would communicate with the subcontractor's computer system on the east coast, and that system in turn would communicate with the main contractor's test site in California. Many of the basic system functions were to be tried out during this costly system test. As the time approached for the test, every member of the team was under extreme pressure to assure that the test would be successful.

On the designated day for the test, all project personnel arrived at work early in the morning to assure that the equipment was functioning correctly. The east coast subcontractor sent up the plane, and the system was activated.

The test failed. Not only did it fail, in fact it never began. The reason was that no one had remembered to order dedicated communication lines from the phone company between the east coast subcontractor's site and the California test site. All attempts by management to have the phone company urgently install the lines on the day of the test failed because there just wasn't enough time. The total failure of the system test cost the contractor dearly, and probably cost some managers their jobs.

This anecdote underscores many of the problems of project planning and scheduling. Such errors may occur because of pressure of time due to unrealistic schedules, or because of poor assignment of personnel within the project organization.

Projects are almost always developed under pressure of time. There is pressure to 'get going', and pressure to 'show us something that works', and of course there is pressure to get the system installed and working. Probably the most common time related pressure is 'get that darned bug fixed quickly'! This kind of pressure can cause havoc with the project development plan, tempting the project manager to seek the *quick and dirty fix* or the short cut. And it is short cuts that lead to the kind of costly errors described above.

This chapter discusses methods for preparing a realistic schedule that project managers and the development team can reasonably commit to. Of course, preparing a realistic schedule is not the only objective; getting the schedule approved is just as important. Gaining approval for a reasonable schedule, and other related problems, will also be discussed.

No matter how well the project schedule is prepared, the schedule is useless unless it is adhered to. It is the project manager's responsibility to withstand pressure and to assure that the project is developed in an orderly fashion, according to the schedule. Whenever circumstances change, the project schedule should then be updated to reflect the new situation.

The project schedule is one of the most important parts of the project development plan. The plan includes not only the scheduling of development activities, but also the scheduling of project resources, particularly people. This chapter discusses scheduling within the context of the project development plan.

10.1 THE PROJECT DEVELOPMENT PLAN

The project development plan is one of the first formal documents produced by the project. Within this document, the project manager describes in detail:

- How the project will be developed
- What resources will be required
- How these resources will be used

The project development plan assures that the development of the project is well charted before the main development activities begin. In addition to the basic development schedule, the plan addresses such issues as:

- The timely provision of equipment and tools so that they are available to developers when needed
- The availability of staff to perform the development tasks in accordance with the schedule
- Provision of contingency plans in the event that project risks materialize
- The designation of duties within the development team, and the assignment of these duties to the team members

The contents of the project development plan may be adapted to the size of the project; it may be a large document or just a few pages. Table 10.1 presents an outline of some of the subjects covered in the project development plan.

Not all subjects in Table 10.1 are applicable to all projects. For example, many projects do not administer their own budget. Some organizations have a financial officer responsible for the administration of project budgets. The interface with external sources is another area not applicable to all projects. The term *external sources* covers such activities as interfacing with subcontractors, vendors and representatives of the customer.

Many standards have been produced for the project development plan. The formal structure of the project development plan document differs, depending on the actual documentation standard used. For example, the US DOD standard 2167 provides the option of describing the testing, configuration management and quality assurance plans in three separate documents. For large projects, this option can become a requirement.

The IEEE standard 1058.1 describes what is referred to as the software project management plan, which is essentially the same as the project development plan. This standard is largely compatible with the 2167 project development plan, although it is significantly less detailed.

Table 10.1 Software project development plan items

1. System overview

2. Software development management
   Project organization and resources
   Development facilities
   Project organizational structure
   Personnel

3. Schedule and milestones
   Scheduled activities
   Milestones and baselines
   Activity network diagrams
   System component source
   Budget administration
      Milestone payments
      Major budgetary expenditures
      Expenditure authorization procedure

4. Risk analysis

5. Security

6. Interface with external sources

7. Procedure for formal reviews

8. Corrective action process

9. Problem change report

10. Software engineering
    Standards and procedures
    Development methodology
    Development resources
    Personnel – qualifications and function

11. Testing procedure

12. Software configuration management

13. Software quality assurance

This standard, too, provides the option of including configuration management and quality assurance plans, or of describing them in separate documents.

The project development plan should be prepared as a standalone document, in the sense that it should be read and understood without the need to refer to other documents. A general overview of the project is therefore usually included in the first section of the document. References for additional detail, of course, should always be provided, including pointers to such documents as the project contract, the concept document or the market research analysis.

The software development management section, which describes the organization and resources that will be used to develop the product, should always be included. The management section discusses how the facilities will be organized to support the development effort. This is one of the sections that provide much of the detail needed to prepare the heart of the development plan, namely the development schedule. The schedule provides answers to two basic planning questions: *what* and *when*, while much of the remaining sections discuss *how*.

The discussion in the *how* sections provides information on how the project will be organized, how risks will be handled, how reviews will be conducted, how standards will be applied, what development methodologies will be used, and how the product will be tested.

It is usually best to leave the completion of the schedule section (Section 3 in Table 10.1) for last. The schedule, being dependent on most of the other sections, is the most sensitive part of the development plan. After a first draft of the development plan is ready, an initial development schedule can then be prepared. As we shall see, the schedule will then be further refined as the development plan goes through progressive iterations.

10.2 SCHEDULED ACTIVITIES AND MILESTONES

A project development schedule is a list of activities and their anticipated time of implementation. There are many ways of representing a schedule: lists of activities, diagrams, graphs etc. The most common methods of schedule representation are PERT network diagrams, Gantt charts and lists of milestones (these methods are described later).

All methods of schedule representation should essentially provide the same basic information: activities and time of implementation. Therefore the first step in preparing a schedule is the determination of the project activities.

As we have seen, the project development schedule is one of the most important elements of the project development plan, and this plan is required at the initial stages of the project. Unfortunately, a full list of activities is usually not available until well into the design phase.

Therefore an initial version of the project schedule usually starts with a list of high level activities, and this initial schedule is repeatedly refined as more information becomes available. A full discussion of methods of refining the list of work activities appears in Chapter 6.

An initial schedule may contain only the basic phases of the software development cycle (requirements specification, design, implementation etc.). This first version of the schedule is often produced together with the initial project estimates before the project is officially launched. As more detail becomes available, better estimates are produced and the schedule becomes more refined and more reliable. Project estimates are discussed in detail in Chapter 11.

10.2.1 The scheduled activity list

As we have seen, scheduling first requires a list of project activities. This list is often developed in conjunction with the work breakdown structure (WBS) table. The WBS breaks down all project activities to a much lower level, called work tasks. The WBS provides a method for monitoring actual work being performed by the development team and is especially useful for assigning low level work tasks to project personnel. The WBS is further discussed in Chapter 6.

Table 10.2 contains an example of part of a project schedule list of activities. The table refers to two major activities: integration and testing.

A schedule list of activities contains the following information:

1. *Activity ID*. This is a meaningful decimal identification, similar to the WBS task designation, and provides a method of identifying each activity according to the various work assignment classifications (see Fig. 6.6).
2. *Activity name*. This is similar to numerical identification, and is used as a convenient activity reference.
3. *Description*. This is a short description of the activity.
4. *Start date*. This refers to the date the activity is scheduled to begin.

Table 10.2 Sample activity list

Activity ID	Activity name	Description	Start date	End date	Dependencies	Assignment responsibility
5	Integration	System software and hardware integration				
5.1	Equipment	Procurement of integration equipment	10 Jan	31 Jan	5.3	J. Smith
5.2	Installation	Set up installation site	20 Jan	20 Feb	5.1	H. Baker
5.3	Integration plan	Prepare integration plan	1 Jan	28 Jan		R. Brown
5.4	Phase 1	Initial S/W integration phase	22 Feb	20 Mar	5.1	L. King
5.5	Demo 1	Initial integration milestone	21 Mar	22 Mar	5.4	L. King
5.6	Phase 2	S/W–H/W integration phase	15 Mar	30 Apr	5.4	L. King & J. Black
5.7	Demo 2	S/W–H/W integration milestone	1 May	2 May	5.6, 5.5	L. King & J. Black
5.8	Phase 3	Full system integration	20 Apr	31 May	5.6	L. King
5.9	Demo 3	Full system integration milestone	1 Jun	2 Jun	5.8, 5.7	L. King
6	Testing	System alpha, beta and acceptance testing				
6.1	Test team	Establish test team	15 Apr	30 Apr		R. Brown
6.2	Test cases	Prepare testing procedures and test cases	1 May	31 May	6.1	R. Brown & B. Knight
6.3	Alpha equipment	Alpha site equipment procurement	1 Apr	30 Apr		J. Smith
6.4	Alpha installation	Install alpha site system	1 May	15 May	6.3	H. Baker
6.5	Alpha testing	Full functional system test at alpha site	15 May	30 Jun	6.2, 6.4	B. Knight & L. King
6.6	Beta installation	Install alpha equipment at beta site	1 Jul	5 Jul	6.5	H. Baker
6.7	Beta testing	Live system run in at beta site	6 Jul	31 Jul	6.6	B. Knight & L. King
6.8	TRR	Test readiness review for acceptance test	30 Jul	31 Jul	6.7	L. King
6.9	ATP	Acceptance test procedure to complete system development	1 Aug	4 Aug	6.8	L. King & R. Brown
6.10	Test report	Prepare ATP test reports	5 Aug	8 Aug	6.9	J. White

5. *Completion date*. This refers to the date the activity is scheduled to be completed.
6. *Dependencies*. This refers to other activities on which this activity is dependent. This activity cannot be completed until the dependency activities are completed.
7. *Assignment/responsibility*. This identifies the person who has been assigned responsibility for this activity.

All scheduled project activities are listed together with the above information. At this stage it is important to assure that activities do not overlap; this means that no two high level activities include the same low level activity. Finally, the schedule list is sorted according to the start date of the activities. This procedure provides the most basic form of a project schedule.

10.2.2 Major milestones and baselines

Clearly, not all activities are of equal importance. Some activities signify major events in the project development cycle. The completion of the requirements specification is a major milestone, as is the completion of the design specification. Other major events may include the completion of a prototype or the installation of the first beta test system. Of course, the most important project event is the conclusion of the project, often signified by the successful completion of the acceptance tests. These important events warrant special attention, and are recorded in a separate list of major project milestones.

Major project milestones often gain added importance due to their linkage to other events, such as development budget payments. Fixed price project payments are often linked by the customer to the successful completion of certain agreed milestones. This produces significant pressure on the project manager to complete the milestone on time (which undoubtedly was the customer's intention). However, schedules, just like any other part of the development plan, need to be updated periodically, and it is often in the project's best interest to modify the milestone completion dates. This is not always recognized by customers, a fact that occasionally causes customers to act contrary to their own best interests.

These problems are not necessarily applicable for in-house projects when the customer and the development team are part of the same organization. In such cases, the *customer* may be the marketing department, or a group of users within the company. Budgetary modifications are then authorized by a common management authority that may be sensitive to the needs of both the in-house customer and the project development team.

Milestones are used not only as points of payment, but also for the measurement of progress on the project and for determining baselines.

If milestones have been described as major project events, then baselines can be described as major milestones. The IEEE definition for the term *baseline* includes the phrase 'a formally agreed specification that then serves as the basis for further development'. Baselines have important significance in the US DOD 2167 standard for software development, where they refer to critical points during software development when major decisions are finalized. As such, 2167 devotes considerable effort to the approval procedures for software project baselines.

Often the first project baseline is the approved system requirements specification document, called the *functional baseline*. This document is the basis for all design and implementation, and in particular it is the basis for system testing and acceptance. Therefore it is usually regarded as the most important project baseline. Examples of other project baselines are the system design and often the system prototype if it is approved as a basis for further project development (see Section 9.2.2).

10.3 GANTT CHARTS

Long before the advent of computers, Henry L. Gantt lent his name to a simple and very useful graphical representation of a project development schedule. The Gantt chart shows almost all of the information contained in the schedule activity list, but in a much more digestible way. The schedule information is more easily grasped and understood, and the activities can be easily compared. The Gantt chart enables us to see, at any given time, which activities should be occurring in the project.

Figure 10.1 is a typical example of a Gantt chart. The symbols used in the chart are widely accepted, though not standardized. The inverted triangle, for example, is commonly used to represent a significant event, such as a major milestone.

The Gantt chart in Fig. 10.1 demonstrates the ease with which important schedule information can be quickly perceived. We can immediately see that, except for the maintenance phase, all phases overlap, and that from November to mid-December 1992 three high level activities overlap.

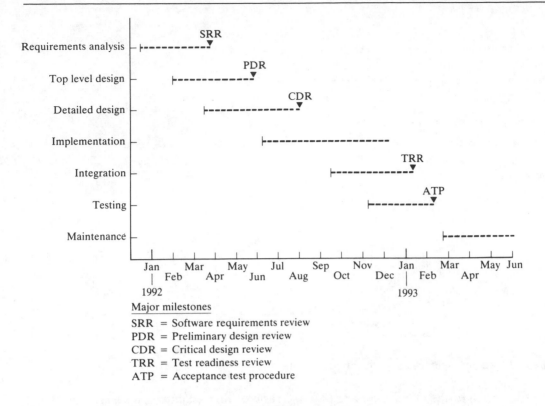

Major milestones

SRR = Software requirements review
PDR = Preliminary design review
CDR = Critical design review
TRR = Test readiness review
ATP = Acceptance test procedure

Figure 10.1 High level Gantt chart – project development schedule.

More detailed charts can also include the names of the engineers assigned to each activity, and the equipment that will be needed for each activity. This information can be added next to the activity time lines in the graph, or as an inserted reference table (similar to the list of major milestones in Fig. 10.1). Some variations of the Gantt chart do include this type of information on the chart, but this can cause clutter, which is contrary to the main objective of the chart; to enable important schedule information to be grasped quickly.

It is also important to understand what Gantt charts do not provide. In a Gantt chart, it is difficult to provide information on the amount of resources required to complete each activity. A common mistake is to conclude that if five engineers are assigned to integration, and the integration activity starts in mid-September 1992 and ends in mid-January 1993 (four months), then integration requires 20 work months. In fact, integration may start with only one engineer, with one more joining during the second month, and the remaining three engineers joining during the third month. The integration team may then be reduced to three engineers during the fourth integration month.

Figure 10.1 includes only seven activities. As more detail becomes available, more lower level activities can be included on the chart. When the chart has more activities than it can reasonably carry (a subjective decision), additional charts may be added. For example, the design activity can be presented on a separate Gantt chart (see Fig. 10.2).

Figure 10.2 presents both high and low level activities. For example, 'Integrate phase I model' contains three low level activities: 'Integrate executive', 'Integrate operating system' and 'Integrate user interface'. This provides the continuity link between the detailed Gantt chart (Fig. 10.2) and the higher level chart (Fig. 10.1).

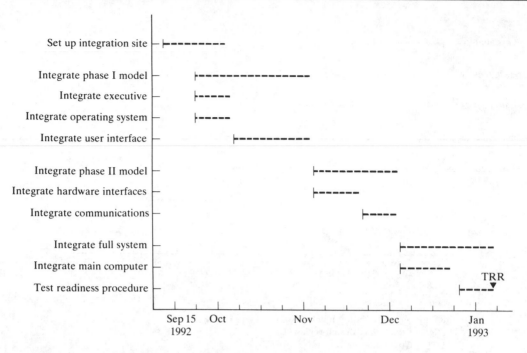

Figure 10.2 Detailed Gantt chart – integration schedule.

Note that each period of one month in Fig. 10.2 has been divided into four weeks. Though not completely accurate, this is a common approximation, used also in estimation (see Chapter 11), and apart from being convenient, it also provides some slack for minor scheduling adjustments.

Similar detailed Gantt charts can be prepared for each of the major project development phases. Non-development activities will also appear on the Gantt chart, such as 'Procurement of development tools', or 'Market research'. This is particularly useful when certain development activities are dependent on other non-development activities, such as the procurement of development tools (e.g. a compiler) that need to be completed before the implementation activities can begin. In cases where such dependent relationships may have been overlooked, they will often emerge from a review of the Gantt chart. This type of dependence between activities is best presented in another type of chart, called a *Network precedence chart* or a *PERT chart*.

10.4 PERT CHARTS AND THE CRITICAL PATH

The air defense anecdote related at the beginning of this chapter provides an excellent example of the dependence between scheduled activities. Dependence exists when one activity cannot be completed unless another activity is completed. A graphical technique called *precedence network charts* can provide answers to two of the problems related in the anecdote: the need to identify dependencies, and the need to assure that responsibility for each activity has been assigned.

The program evaluation and review technique (PERT)[1] uses a precedence network to plan

---

1. A concise and detailed description of the PERT technique appears in Gillett (1976).

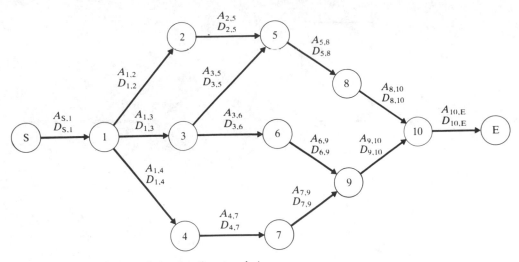

$A_{i,j}$ = Activity starting at node i and ending at node j
$D_{i,j}$ = Duration of activity $A_{i,j}$

Figure 10.3 A typical PERT chart.

project activities and to monitor their performance effectively. Like Gantt charts, there are many variations of PERT. The basic conventional PERT technique describes a network with nodes as events and activities as connections.

Each activity is associated with two related events, its *start* and its *end*. The end node of an activity can coincide with the beginning node of a second activity when the completion of the second is dependent on the completion of the first. This means that an activity can only be completed when all other activities ending in its start node have been completed.

Figure 10.3 presents an example of a PERT network chart representing the flow of project activities from start to end. Each event is represented by a numbered circle. The network begins with the start event, called the source node, and concludes with the end event, called the sink node. Each connecting line represents a project activity. Activity $A_{i,j}$ describes the activity that begins at event i and ends at event j. Attribute $D_{i,j}$ represents the amount of time that is scheduled to elapse between the beginning and end of activity $A_{i,j}$.

An important aspect of the PERT chart method is the concept of parallel activities. Each event node branches into a number of activities that can be performed in parallel. In Fig. 10.3, activities $A_{1,2}$, $A_{1,3}$ and $A_{1,4}$ can be performed in parallel. However, each of activities $A_{S,1}$ and $A_{10,E}$ cannot be performed in parallel with any other activity. We can also see from the chart that activity $A_{3,6}$ can be performed in parallel with either activity $A_{5,8}$ or activity $A_{8,10}$, but not both. Similarly, at any given time activity $A_{3,6}$ can be performed in parallel with only one of the following three activities: $A_{1,4}$, $A_{4,7}$ and $A_{7,9}$.

Figure 10.4 is an example of a PERT chart that includes numerical duration attributes. We can see from the chart that activity $A_{S,1}$ is scheduled to continue for five units of time (possibly weeks). When schedules need to be shortened, these duration values can be most helpful to the project manager. The duration values can assist in locating areas where additional effort is best directed.

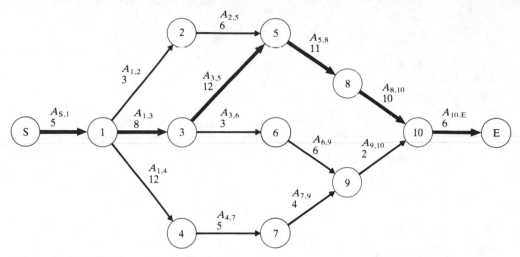

Figure 10.4 PERT chart showing the critical path.

10.4.1 The critical path

Criticism of project development schedules is common, and should be expected by project managers. Large projects have many interested parties involved in scheduling, such as corporate management, the customer, subcontractors, vendors, users, the marketing department etc. One of the most frequent criticisms refers to the need to shorten the schedule. A common error on the part of the project manager is to assume that wherever additional effort is directed, it will shorten the schedule. However, in some cases, shortening activities will have absolutely no impact on the overall schedule duration.

In order to examine this phenomenon, we must first understand that in all non-trivial networks there are many ways of moving from the source node to the sink node. For example, in Fig. 10.4 a possible path runs from node S to 1 to 3 to 6 to 9 to 10 to E. Another possible path runs from node S to 1 to 2 to 5 to 8 to 10 to E. Each path can be characterized by a number that represents the total duration of the path, calculated by summing the durations for all activities along the path.

Table 10.3 contains a list of all possible paths from node S to node E in the PERT chart in Fig. 10.4, together with the length of each path. Path 2 is the longest, 52 weeks. The longest path is referred to as the *critical path*, and it determines the duration of the project.

By shortening the duration of an activity along the critical path we can usually shorten the duration of the whole project. There are a few extreme cases where this will not occur, notably when there are two critical paths. However, one thing is certain; shortening an activity that is not on the critical path will not shorten the length of the whole project.

Table 10.3 All possible paths from S to E (based on Fig. 10.4)

Path	Length	Critical path
1. S,1,2,5,8,10,E	41	
2. S,1,3,5,8,10,E	52	√
3. S,1,3,6,9,10,E	30	
4. S,1,4,7,9,10,E	34	

10.4.2 PERT packages and enhancements

Some enhanced versions of the PERT chart support additional planning activities, such as personnel assignment, resource allocation and cost analysis. The chart can then draw attention to situations where personnel are assigned more responsibilities than they can handle, or where allocation of resources conflicts.

An interesting adaptation of PERT, called flowgraph representation, which was developed by Riggs and Jones (1990), uses precedence networks to perform project life cycle cost analysis. The flowgraph technique analyzes project costs based on relationships between quantities, unit cost, time variables, staffing costs and learning etc., all of which are represented on the PERT-like chart.

The flowgraph representation technique places a significant amount of information on the network graph. This information, just like the basic PERT information, must be kept constantly updated. A small change to a large PERT chart can require the complete redrawing of the chart and the recalculation of the critical path. The resulting tedium does not promote much enthusiasm for keeping the chart updated. For this reason, many computerized PERT utilities have been developed.

PERT software packages have been available for many years, but it is only during the past few years that good professional PERT packages have become available on PCs and other small computers. These packages take much of the tedium out of the preparation of PERT charts, and also come with additional features such as various planning analyzers for activity assignment, 'what if' scenarios and resource allocation. Computer utilities have been developed to perform flowgraph representation analysis which produces scheduled costs for major project activities.[2] These utilities have proven invaluable for project managers and release managers from laborious desk work, providing them with more time to actively manage the project.

10.5 SCHEDULING PERSONNEL

This section deals with the *scheduling* side of staffing and personnel management. The motivation and management of people is discussed in Chapter 5.

Essentially, the development team is a resource, just as development equipment is a resource. However, scheduling people is not the same as scheduling equipment. The project manager's most important project resource is the development team, and therefore special attention must be given to the scheduling of the activities of team members. As the number of project activities varies, so the size of the development team varies throughout the project development life cycle. The team's organizational structure becomes more important as the size of the team grows.

10.5.1 The development team size

The size of the development team is influenced not only by the number of activities, but also by the intensity of the activities. Some activities are intense at the beginning of the project and decline toward the end, and vice versa. For example, planning requires more human resources

---

2. Riggs and Jones (1990) in their paper on project cost analysis describe the graphical economic cost analysis technique (GECAT) computer program. Other computer packages are discussed in Tahvanainen and Smolander (1990).

at the beginning of the project and fewer at the end, while configuration control requires fewer at the beginning and more at the end.

Figure 10.5 demonstrates this relationship between planning and control. As the intensity of planning decreases, fewer people will be required for this activity. Similarly, as the intensity of control increases more people will be required for such activities as testing, quality assurance and configuration management.

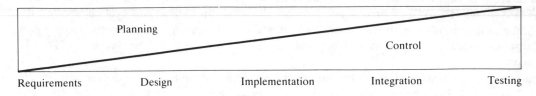

Figure 10.5 The relationship between planning and control.

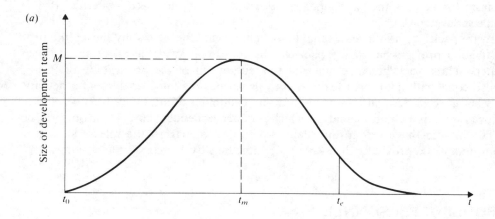

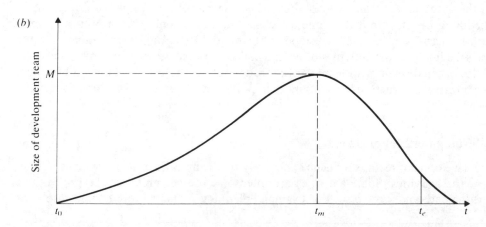

Figure 10.6 Distribution of development team size: (a) normal distribution; (b) skewed distribution. $M =$ maximum size of development team, $t_0 =$ start of project, $t_m =$ maximum staffing point, $t_e =$ end of project.

The team size often varies according to the familiar bell shaped normal distribution. This is demonstrated in Fig. 10.6(a), which describes a small development team at the start of the project, a large development team during the mid-project phases, and then again a small team at the end of the project.

At either end of the development cycle, when the team size is small, many of the organizational functions are unnecessary. In many cases, team structures only become necessary toward the end of the requirements phase. As the project nears completion, teams may be disbanded, and one or two team members may assume responsibility for the development work of a whole team.

In some cases, Fig. 10.6(a) may not represent the scheduling of the development team with sufficient accuracy. Figure 10.6(b) presents an asymmetric skewed curve similar to the normal distribution which describes a slower staffing rate at the start of the project and a more rapidly decreasing staff size toward the end. This is often typical of complex projects when the integration and test phases require a considerable effort. In fact, the skewed curve is generally more representative of staff scheduling than the normal curve, though the degree of inclination of the curve varies.

The way in which the maintenance phase is regarded also impacts the staffing curve. The staffing curve will look different if the maintenance phase is considered part of the development cycle. The resulting curve, shown in Fig. 10.7, has a lingering descending edge that continues throughout the maintenance phase.

Figure 10.8 describes a possible team size distribution function in a medium size project with a maximum team size of 18. Initially, with a team size of three, configuration control and quality assurance will be handled by the project manager. As the team grows to eight these responsibilities will be assigned to a team member, who may also fulfill other responsibilities.[3] As the team grows to 12, a configuration control engineer and a quality assurance engineer will be required, at least part-time. When the team reaches its peak size, these two engineers will probably be required full-time.

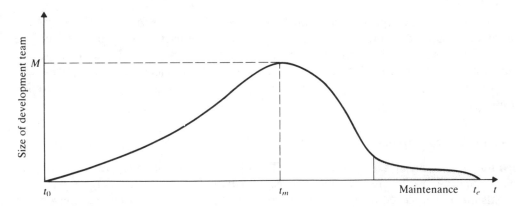

Figure 10.7 Distribution of team size, including maintenance. M = maximum size of development team, t_0 = start of project, t_m = maximum staffing point, t_e = end of project.

---

3. It is not always possible to assign configuration control and quality assurance activities to other development team members, as these activities often require specific skills and knowledge. For example, ANSI/IEEE standard 730 recommends a substantial quality assurance program for software projects. Similarly, ANSI/IEEE standard 828 defines a considerable configuration management program.

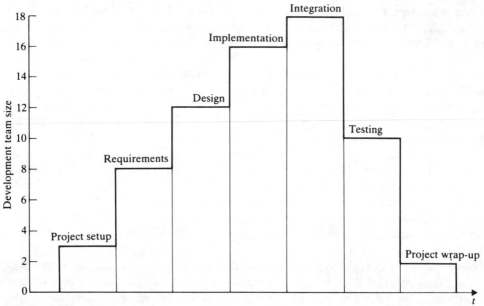

Figure 10.8 Example of development team size.

The team size is determined by the total number of people assigned to the project. However, in scheduling the team size, the allocation of two people, each for half of a full-time assignment, does not necessarily equal the assignment of one person full-time. It is difficult to deal with the allocation of half a person to an assignment. In such cases, such as quality assurance or configuration control, the expense to the project of assigning these activities can be reduced by sharing these functions with other projects. This is especially true for small projects.

Testing is another example of personnel resource sharing between projects. Many organizations have an independent test team that is not directly part of the project team. The independent test team becomes involved in the project mainly toward the end of the development cycle (although some test activities do start much earlier). Such teams can then move from one project to another provided the test activities have been scheduled appropriately.

10.5.2 Skills and experience

The scheduling of personnel is not just a case of allocating a number of people for each stage of the project. Specific skills are required for each activity and appropriately experienced professionals must be assigned the responsibility for these activities. Table 10.4 presents a list of some of the classes of personnel required for each project development stage. Not all projects require all classes of personnel, such as in the case of small projects, where two or more of the project positions can be filled by one person.

Although Table 10.4 refers to different professional positions that require different qualifications, it is always an advantage when team members' qualifications are versatile. It is then possible to reassign team members within the project, thus saving much of the learning curve overhead that usually needs to be scheduled for new team members.

Table 10.4 Classification of software project positions

Classification	Project positions
Managers	Project manager, Team leaders, System engineers
Administrators	Secretaries, Administrative assistants
Configuration control	Configuration manager, Configuration controller
Quality assurance	Quality management, Quality assurance engineer
Analysis and design	Systems analysts, Design engineers
Coders	Programmers
Technical writers	Documentation writers, Editors
Testers	Independent test team, Test case developers

Learning curve activities are often overlooked. Project familiarization for new team members is not the only case where learning curve overhead exists. Training is also an important factor that must be scheduled. However, not all training needs can be known during the initial stages of the project. Training requirements become evident as decisions are taken regarding the development environment (such as programming language, development computers etc.), and as the individual team members are selected and their skills and experience become known.

There are many problems related to the scheduling of people. Experience and skills of team members are not reliable measures of expected performance. The scheduling of engineers based on supposedly measurable qualities has long been a controversial subject. The substantial variation in software programmer performance was reported by Sackman *et al.* as early as 1968, and is further discussed in Chapters 5 and 11.

10.5.3 The infamous man month

Another common source of error, when scheduling people, is the difference in the way the term *man month* (or, as it is now called, *work month*) is used. If a project manager calculates that a specific scheduled activity requires six work months to complete, does that mean that if a suitable engineer is assigned for six months then the activity can be completed in six months?

Well, the answer is . . . maybe! In many cases the activity cannot be completed in six months, because a person seldom provides six months of work during a six month calendar period. People take vacations, they celebrate holidays, and they are occasionally sick. Generally, people provide between eight and ten months work during a twelve month period. This must be taken into consideration when preparing a schedule.

When project managers inform their superiors that a project will require an investment of six years, they must be clear about the type of years they are talking about. Is it six calendar years, which means the project can only be completed six years from the starting date? Or is it six work years, which means that there are 72 months of work to be performed, which can be divided between a number of people? Or is it really 48 work months, with additional vacation, holidays, and sick leave?

Also, there is a maximum number of people that can be assigned to a project. Three hundred and sixty-five engineers cannot complete a one year project in one day! And just as nine women cannot have a baby in one month, some projects take a specific amount of time, no matter how many people are assigned. Therefore the significance of the duration of the project as well as the duration of each major activity must be clearly understood and presented as part of the schedule. The schedule should take into account absenteeism, overhead (discussions, meetings and just plain talking) and it should explain which activities cannot be shortened and which can.

Reducing the duration of an activity has its price. Adding more people to a project generates more overhead. If five people can develop a project in two years it does not follow that ten people can develop the project in one year. This is due to the additional communications between the team members; more meetings are necessary, more coordination is required and more management and administration is required. And of course one cannot continue to reduce the duration of an activity by assigning more and more people to it. The law of diminishing returns is valid when assigning people to a project, and at some point people begin getting in each other's way. Zero and even negative contribution can be reached rather quickly when a project is well into development, and the learning curve becomes long and costly.

10.6 SCHEDULING RESOURCES

The previous section discussed the scheduling of the project's most important resource – the development team. But without the necessary tools, the development team cannot be expected to do a good job. If the project's target computer is not available when the integration phase is scheduled to begin, then the integration phase may very well not begin. We therefore see that a form of the *critical path* principle is also applicable to the availability of development resources. This means that if the availability of a critical scheduled resource is delayed it will delay the completion of the project.

There are ways of dealing with availability problems for critical resources, such as *risk analysis*. The objective is to provide contingency plans in the event that critical resources are not available according to schedule. Risk analysis is further discussed in Chapter 2.

10.6.1 Scheduling work space

At the outset of the project, work space, particularly office space, is usually one of the first major resources required. The project area should be preassigned and well defined. As the project progresses, the required work area will increase.

The need for adequate work space is often overlooked when scheduling development facilities. A well-defined and separate work area is an important factor in forming a development team. When project team members are dispersed throughout a large area and mixed with other project teams many problems arise. Communication between team members is more difficult, management becomes more complicated and a dedicated team spirit does not develop.

Scheduling office and work space is one of the first steps in scheduling resources. Space requirements are a function of the estimated personnel requirements, the equipment requirements and the project staffing schedule.

Table 10.5 contains a checklist of some of the items to be considered when scheduling work space. Of course, not all topics are applicable to all projects. Naturally, the actual space requirements depend on the size and type of each project. Many defense and security projects require special restricted access areas, referred to in the checklist as a *secure area*. Another item, *storage and inventory rooms*, would be required only for projects that include large amounts of hardware and equipment.

Table 10.5 Workspace items – checklist

1. Management office space
2. Secretarial administrative office space
3. Meeting rooms
4. Development team rooms and desk space
5. Computer room
6. Laboratory
7. Test and integration areas
8. Lunch and recreation area
9. Storage and inventory room
10. Secure area

10.6.2 Scheduling equipment

With the right tools, the job can always be done better. But as we have seen, having the right tools is not enough: the tools must also be available at the right time. The objective of the scheduling of equipment is to assure that adequate development tools are available in sufficient quantity, when needed.

In the early years of software development the basic tools included a programmer, a compiler and a computer to run the code. Modern development tools today include much more than a compiler and a computer. Software utilities ranging from integrated design tools to sophisticated test and debugging tools are now available. In fact, the computer has been harnessed as an aid to the developer to assist in specific development activities, producing the term *computer-aided software engineering* or *CASE*.

Clearly, not all computer projects are purely software projects. Many computer systems require the development of both software and hardware. This includes such projects as communications systems, military systems, robotics and various industrial systems. In such cases special purpose equipment is required for the test and integration phases. A central project office must then coordinate the planning and scheduling of software and hardware development to assure the timely availability of the development equipment.

Assuring the availability of adequate development equipment is an important part of good planning. Bad scheduling can lead to situations where members of the development team are left idle or partly idle waiting for the delivery of equipment. Even if team members can be reassigned temporarily, their efficiency and effectiveness as developers will be significantly reduced.

10.6.3 Vendors and subcontractors

Not all scheduled activities are directly dependent on the project manager and the development team. Frequently, outside parties are also involved in project development. As we have seen, the timely delivery of equipment is crucial to the development schedule, and this often requires procurement from outside parties.

It is not uncommon, especially in large or complex projects, to subcontract certain parts of the project to companies who have specific expertise in relevant areas. This means that direct control of development may be delegated to the subcontractor.

It is difficult to schedule resources and activities over which the project manager does not have full control. In such situations the project manager has two alternatives:

1. Leave the scheduling to the subcontractor or vendor
2. Retain control over the subcontractor or vendor

In the first case, when scheduling is left to the outside party, the project manager is at the mercy of a party over which he has no control. If the other party slips the delivery schedule, it may cause a schedule slippage for the whole project. This is best handled by:

1. Motivating the outside party to deliver on time (e.g. penalizing the party for late delivery)
2. Identifying late delivery as a project risk, and preparing contingency plans to handle the situation should it occur

In the second case, when the project manager retains control over the outside party, many of the benefits of subcontracting are lost. For large projects, a position must be created for a supervisor of subcontractors and vendors. It is the responsibility of the supervisor to be constantly aware of the work being performed by outside parties, through:

- Visits to subcontractor and vendor sites
- Reviews and milestone evaluations
- Periodic reports from subcontractors and vendors

In addition, it is important for the supervisor to be able to motivate the outside party by linking payments to successfully completed milestones, and by imposing penalties for late delivery.

10.7 MONITORING AND UPDATING THE SCHEDULE

The schedule is not a static document, and is subject to constant change. An outdated schedule has little (if any) value. The schedule, as part of the project development plan, must be periodically updated. In order to enable the project manager to maintain an updated schedule, current information must flow regularly from the development team. This is achieved through periodic reports, reviews and other monitoring activities.

10.7.1 Periodic reports

Periodic reporting is one of the formal methods of assuring a regular flow of information from the development team to the project manager. The recommended practice for preparing and submitting reports is described in Section 5.3.1.

Team members should submit their periodic reports to their team leader, who then summarizes the reports and submits the summary together with a copy of the individual reports to the project manager.

The project manager then summarizes the reports from the team leaders, together with reports from other project personnel, such as the head of the test group. The resulting document, which includes the project manager's report, forms the project progress report, and is an official project document which is submitted to top management. The distribution list for the project progress report may also include the individual development team members, the customer, and the project subcontractors.

The periodic reports are the basic channels of information used to evaluate and update the project development plan and, specifically, the project schedule. However, periodic reports should never be the only source of information for these activities. It is the responsibility of the project manager to verify the completeness and accuracy of the information reported.

The frequency of reporting is an issue to be decided by the project manager. Usually, a bi-weekly report is adequate for internal project needs, and a monthly report is adequate for external project needs. However, during critical phases of the project more frequent reports may be necessary.

10.7.2 Other schedule monitoring activities

One of the elements of good management is the establishment of personal contact between managers and staff. Personal contact supports many management goals, one of which is the verification of progress reports.

The main problems with periodic reports are those of objectivity, interpretation and accuracy. The project schedule is not always interpreted or perceived in the same way by management as it is by the developers. The famous 90/50 syndrome discussed in Chapter 5 is illustrative of this situation. This, we may recall, states that 'it takes 50 percent of the time to complete 90 percent of the work, and an additional 50 percent of the time to complete the remaining 10 percent of the work'.

This means that when team members begin reporting that they have *almost completed* a task, it may well require a substantial amount of time to really finish the task. This is because it is often relatively easy to get something going, but the tedious drudgery required to wrap up a task requires a significant amount of work. And of course, this is in addition to the natural optimism of the developer in expecting that nothing will go wrong.

There are many methods for monitoring progress that involve personal contact between the project manager and the development team. Weekly project and team meetings are good opportunities to discuss progress, and informal reviews of specific activities enable the project manager to see and evaluate the actual work that has been produced.

When a schedule is not being achieved, it is sometimes a sign that the team member entrusted with a specific activity does not support the schedule. Such situations underscore the importance of having the development team involved in the preparation of the schedule. It is usually easier to have a developer commit to a schedule when he or she was involved in its preparation.

10.7.3 Updating the schedule

As we have seen, the project development plan must be reviewed periodically. The schedule should be updated whenever the periodic review justifies it or whenever a significant event occurs. For example, if the review shows that many activities are behind (or ahead of) schedule, or that several new activities need to be added to the activity list, then a new schedule should be produced. Also, if the development of part of the project is replaced by purchasing a similar off the shelf component then the schedule should be modified to reflect a smaller development effort.

Table 10.6 contains a checklist of scheduled items that should be reviewed (and possibly updated) periodically, or whenever a significant project event occurs.

The first item in Table 10.6 refers to updating the activity list. This task, in effect, is derived from other items in the checklist, such as reviewing the approved requirements and design changes or updating the list of project risks. After all items have been reviewed and, if necessary, updated, then the schedule representation medium should be updated (Gantt chart, PERT chart etc.). As in the preparation of the initial schedule, it is always good practice to have members of the development team review the new schedule before its release. Scheduling errors, omissions and conflicts can thus be identified and corrected before the schedule is distributed.

Table 10.6 Schedule update checklist

1. Activity list
2. Personnel assignments
3. Risk list and risk analysis
4. Resource allocation
5. Third party status (subcontractors, vendors, suppliers)
6. Schedule chart (Gantt)
7. Precedence network (PERT)
8. Approved requirements and design changes

10.8 SOME GENERAL GUIDELINES FOR SCHEDULING AND PLANNING

Planning begins with the start of the project, and in some cases even before. As we have seen in Section 10.1, *all* project activity should be planned. The lack of planning is frequently the principal reason for failure. A good first step in planning a project is to prepare a project development plan outline, as described in Table 10.1, and gradually begin to fill in the sections.

10.8.1 Refining the initial activity list

As we have seen, the initial list of activities, together with the projected dates to accomplish the activities, produces an initial schedule. The refinement of the activity list is an iterative process that will eventually produce the detailed project development schedule.

As the schedule progresses and becomes more detailed, the activity list will contain low level activities that will be assigned to specific team members. It is therefore most important for the project manager to include the relevant team members in this phase. It is always preferable to have engineers propose a schedule for their area of responsibility rather than to dictate the schedule to them. Generally, team members feel much more committed to a schedule that they prepared than to one prepared for them.

A common technique is to hand detailed activity lists to the members of the development team and have them submit a proposal for the completion dates. The project manager should then call a meeting with the various development groups in order to resolve any disagreements and problems. This process should then be iterated until an acceptable and agreed schedule is produced. Only if agreement cannot be reached should the project manager exercise his or her authority and set the parts of the schedule that remain in discord.

Table 10.7 summarizes some of the basic guidelines for the production and maintenance of a detailed development schedule.

10.8.2 Gaining approval for the schedule

Preparing a realistic schedule is not the project manager's only objective; getting the schedule approved is just as important. Too often, a realistic schedule is painstakingly prepared by the project manager and submitted to corporate management, only to have it rejected for business reasons. This underscores the importance of project managers being aware of the broader corporate picture, and not just restricting themselves to the narrow technical perspective.

When preparing the overall project development plan, the project manager should naturally expect pressure in two basic areas: (1) the completion date and (2) development costs. Other pressures may also be brought to bear, but these two basic areas are universal.

Table 10.7 Schedule guidelines

1. Promote team involvement
2. Iterate from high level to detailed schedule
3. Be aware of needs of customer, management, users and marketing
4. Schedule not only activities, but resources and personnel too
5. Resist pressure to commit to an unreasonable schedule
6. Use computerized scheduling tools
7. Schedule contingency plans for risks
8. Update the schedule periodically or after major project events

For the project manager, the best way to respond to such pressure is to attempt to view the project from other non-technical perspectives.

If pressure is brought to bear by the customer, the project manager should try to understand the customer's concerns and attempt to address these concerns within a realistic schedule. Will the customer accept an early delivery of a partial system? Is there an off the shelf solution that will suffice for a while until the full system is completed?

If pressure originates from higher management, the project manager should try to discover the reason for the pressure. Has the project become far too large for the available budget? If so, can the project be implemented in phases, with many of the sophistications delayed until more financing is available?

Wishful thinking and self delusion is usually the worst policy. It is always best to stick to a reasonably achievable schedule. The best approach for the project manager is to be honest. Never promise anything you do not expect to be able to deliver!

A proven and effective approach is always to present a problem together with a solution. This means that when the schedule cannot support the expectations of the customer or of higher management, the problem should be presented and explained, and an alternative schedule should be suggested together with a modified set of objectives. The following example will demonstrate this approach.

ACO, a well-established company, has been involved in retail support services for many years. They recently decided to develop a new networked computerized system that would interface with the existing cash register systems in order to provide a wide variety of services to the stores and their customers. Two things were clear from the outset: firstly, there was a definite demand for these services, and secondly, this company was not the only one aware of this demand.

BCO, the company that was offered the development contract, realized that the system was far from trivial. Realizing that ACO wanted to beat the market, BCO submitted the shortest realistic schedule that they felt they could commit to. However, the schedule was rejected by ACO.

After further investigation by BCO, it became evident that ACO had already committed to delivery dates for the system to some of their customers. ACO also felt that there was a *perishable opportunity* in the market, and they would lose their customers if they could not deliver on time.

BCO proposed an intermediate system that would not be networked between stores and which would have reduced functionality. This intermediate system would run on the same hardware, and all functions would be compatible with the final fully functional system. This intermediate system would be delivered to ACOs customers earlier, and would be replaced later by the full system. This was acceptable to ACO.

BCO resisted the temptation of promising an impossible delivery date in order to assure that they would be awarded the contract. They explained the problem to ACO and suggested a solution that addressed ACOs problems with their customers. By choosing this course, BCO also gained the confidence of ACO, which proved to be helpful throughout the project.

No one, be they customer or management, can justifiably expect the impossible. Therefore, in order to gain approval for the project development schedule, the recommended course of action is:

1. Do not present the schedule in a vacuum. The schedule must be part of an overall project development plan.
2. Learn the perspective of your audience, including the customer, top management and sales and marketing. Study their viewpoints and understand their concerns.
3. Assure that the schedule is reasonable, and well prepared. Be ready to justify all milestones.
4. Seek support from other experts and professional reference sources in order to substantiate any problems that you present.
5. Always present a problem together with a solution.
6. Be confident yourself that you are right. If you doubt your own assertions then you are not ready to present the schedule.

A realistic schedule approved by management (or by the customer) is a major step toward the successful development of a project. When a schedule is unrealistic, it is often camouflaged with such terms as tight, aggressive or challenging. However, tight, aggressive and challenging schedules are rarely conducive to successful projects.

10.8.3 The relationship between schedule, resources, quality and functionality

As we have seen, the project development plan charts a course from the current situation to the project objective. The plan describes the resources necessary to achieve the objective within a specified schedule. The required resources and the schedule can both be calculated (or estimated) based on the declared objective of the project.

The project objectives, being the functionality described in the requirements specification, are not necessarily the only requirements of the project. A specific schedule may also be required (e.g. to develop the project within one year). If the required schedule is too short, then this additional requirement may be an unfeasible requirement. However, if the required schedule is not too short, then, together with the functionality, it will determine the required resources.

The resources may also be a requirement (a maximum development team size, or a specific development computer). If the resources are unsuitable, then this additional requirement may be an unfeasible requirement. When the required resources are suitable, then, together with the functionality, they will determine the schedule.

The question that remains is what happens if both the resources and the schedule are required? Usually this means that the extent of the functionality is then determined by the schedule and the resources. This means that within a given schedule, and with given resources, the amount of functionality is limited.

Another way of looking at this triangle of dependent project attributes (functionality, schedule and resources) is to introduce a fourth attribute: quality. This means that if all of the previous three attributes are predetermined, then the quality of the software product is also determined. However, the project manager enters dangerous ground when all four attributes are predetermined (see Fig. 10.9).

The determination of at least one (preferably two) attributes must be left to the project manager. It is perfectly valid for the customer or for higher management to ask what functionality can be provided with a given budget and given resources and at a given quality level.

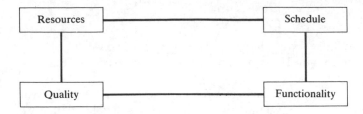

Figure 10.9 The four attributes of a development project (any three determine the fourth).

Similarly, the project manager can be asked what resources are needed in order to develop given functionality within 18 months at a given quality level.

10.9 SUMMARY

The project schedule is one of the most important parts of the project development plan. This plan is often the first formal document generated within the project, and includes not only the scheduling of development activities but also the scheduling of project resources, particularly people.

The project development plan describes in detail how the project manager plans to develop the project, what resources will be required and how these resources will be applied.

A schedule is a list of activities and their anticipated time of implementation. There are many ways of representing a schedule: lists of activities, diagrams, graphs etc. The most common methods of schedule representation are precedence network diagrams (such as PERT), Gantt charts and lists of milestones.

It is a common error to assume that wherever additional effort is directed, it will shorten the schedule. Shortening activities will have absolutely no impact on the overall schedule duration if these activities are not on the project's critical path. The critical path is the longest path through the network precedence chart, from the start node to the end node.

Scheduling resources is just as important as scheduling activities. Development resources include facilities, work space, equipment and human resources.

The project manager's most important project resource is the development team. As the number of project activities varies, so the size of the development team varies throughout the project development life cycle. The team's organizational structure becomes more important as the size of the team grows.

An outdated schedule has little value. The schedule, as part of the overall project development plan, must be periodically updated. In order to enable the project manager to maintain an updated schedule, current information must flow regularly from the development team. This is achieved through periodic reports, reviews and other monitoring activities.

A realistic schedule approved by management (or by the customer) is a major step toward the successful development of a project. When a schedule is unrealistic, it is often camouflaged with such terms as tight, aggressive or challenging. However, tight, aggressive and challenging schedules are rarely conducive to successful projects.

EXERCISES

1. You have been designated project manager for a large truck delivery company's dispatching and routing system. Each truck will be equipped with a digital communications device that will communicate with a central computer.

Your project will develop the software to communicate with the trucks and dispatch them according to optimum routing algorithms. The system will also maintain a detailed data base that will include information regarding the company's trucks, their current location, their drivers and the delivery routes. The system will also provide on-line query and update capabilities, as well as report generators.

Prepare an activity list for this project. Identify the major milestones and define the project's baselines.

2. Prepare a high level Gantt chart for the project described in Exercise 1. Prepare a detailed Gantt chart for two of the high level activities. Explain any overlap between activities.

3. Prepare a high level PERT chart for the project described in Exercise 1. Include all development and non-development activities. Locate all paths through the network and identify the critical path.

Demonstrate how the critical path can change when a single duration attribute changes. Explain the dependencies as they are represented in the chart.

4. Prepare a staffing schedule for the project described in Exercise 1. Describe how many team members will be needed at each stage, what their skills should be and what their assignments will be within the project.

5. Prepare a resource schedule for the project described in Exercise 1. Describe each development resource and explain why and when it will be required.

Discuss the implications for the project development effort of not being able to obtain each resource.

6. Consider which elements of the project in Exercise 1 may be dependent on outside parties. Discuss which development activities can be considered for subcontracting and which components can possibly be purchased off the shelf.

7. Consider the problems that may be expected during the integration phase of the project described in Exercise 1. Prepare a sample project progress report that is being submitted two weeks after integration begins.

ELEVEN

THE PREPARATION OF ESTIMATES: METHODS AND TECHNIQUES

ESTIMATION: THE PROBLEM

Estimation is concerned with the prediction of uncertainties. It is more dignified than fortune-telling, though not always more accurate. This can best be illustrated by the following anecdote.

In the early 1980s, a major American defense contractor was awarded a US Department of Defense software development contract. The company had been divided into small 'profit centers', and each such center was required to justify its existence by being profitable. On being informed of the contract award, engineers from the profit center, after initial celebration, set about planning the launch of the project. Only then did they discover that the expected development cost used in their proposal was based on their original estimate of 80 work years, while their new calculations produced an estimate of 120 work years. This would potentially cause a budget overrun of 50 percent!

The additional 40 work years would cost the company about four million dollars, and while this amount would not break a major corporation, it was a significant amount for the profit center and could cost a number of senior managers their jobs.

The profit center management sent a letter to the Department of Defense stating that they had miscalculated the cost of developing the project, and requested that they be permitted to resubmit a corrected proposal. If their request was rejected, they stated, they would be willing to withdraw and permit the contract to be awarded to the company that had submitted the next best proposal. The answer they received stated that not only would they not be permitted to resubmit their proposal, but should they try to withdraw, the Department of Defense would take legal action against the company that would cost them well in excess of their anticipated loss.

At this stage, the managers of the profit center were probably preparing to clean out their desks when a suggestion was put forward by one of the engineers. He suggested that a super-team of developers be established that would be composed of the best engineers in the profit center. These engineers would be pulled out of other projects that were well under way and where their contribution was no longer essential. Then the super-team would be assigned to the new project in an attempt to complete the project with as small an overrun of the original estimate as possible.

The plan was approved, and the best possible development team was assembled. The super-team members were requested to make every effort to complete the project in less than the 120 work year estimate, with the objective of reducing the 80 work year estimate overrun to the extent possible.

So the project was developed over a three year period by the best team the profit center could put together, and the outcome was that the project was developed in 60 work years!

This short anecdote highlights the basic questions related to the preparation of estimates.

How are professional estimates prepared? What was the correct estimate in this case; 80, 120, or 60 work years?

What good is an estimate in *work* years if it is so heavily dependent on the identity of the person doing the work?

Is the motivation of the developers a factor in estimating the resources necessary for the development of a project?

And lastly, how can a manager budget a project if professional estimates can be off by as much as 100 percent?

This chapter will address these and other related questions, and will provide tools that enable such concerns to be taken into account in the preparation of project development estimates.

11.1 PROJECT ESTIMATES

Any unknown quantity can be estimated, while known quantities do not need to be estimated. For the software project manager, there are many unknown quantities that must be estimated. These are associated with such areas as:

1. Project development costs
2. Project development schedule
3. The size of the project development team
4. The amount of software to be developed
5. The required hardware resources

How to estimate these quantities is not the only problem that needs to be addressed; the units used to measure these quantities must also be considered.

Project development costs are best measured in monetary units, such as dollars or pounds. However, it is acceptable for an initial estimate to be prepared in an intermediate measure that is later converted into monetary units. A common intermediate unit for project development costs is *work months* (or *man months* or *engineer months* etc.). This can later be converted into monetary terms by estimating the cost of a single work month (more about this in Section 11.4).

A project development schedule is obviously estimated in units of time such as days, weeks, months or years. The schedule, like most plans, must have a beginning and an end. Often, when a project is being planned, the formal beginning is not known, and hence the end is also unknown. In such cases the acronym ARO (After Receipt of Order) is commonly used, and the schedule is constructed using such designations as: *End of top level design – 4 months ARO*. A more detailed discussion of software project development schedules appears in Chapter 9.

Estimates of the development personnel required for the project are clearly in units of people. However, the development personnel should be grouped according to some common classification, such as software engineers, programmers and support staff, and each group should be estimated separately. The time on the project of each person should also be estimated by identifying their entry into the project and their exit from the project. This will commonly produce a *normal distribution curve*[1] with a small development staff at the start and end of the project and a maximum staff size close to the middle[2] (see Fig. 10.6(*a*)).

The amount of software to be developed is commonly estimated in either of two measures: by

---

1. The normal distribution curve is further discussed in Section 11.5.
2. The distribution of the development team size is further discussed in Section 10.5.1.

lines of code or by Kbytes of memory. Both methods have their advantages and their disadvantages. The number of lines of code is a more representative measure of the degree of development effort, but it is also heavily language dependent in that a hundred lines of high level language code does not require the same degree of effort as a hundred lines of assembler code. 'Kbytes of memory' is representative of the amount of software and may be relatively independent of the source programming language, but a single high level READ instruction can generate much more machine code than a complex mathematical algorithm.

The amount of hardware resources is measured in various units depending on the particular resource being considered. This is discussed in more detail in Section 11.6.

11.2 STEPWISE ESTIMATION

The 'divide and conquer' approach is often applied in many different areas of software engineering (see Chapter 6). This method, which divides a large problem into numerous smaller problems, is also used in most estimating techniques. The basic approach is to decompose the project into well defined components, and then to iterate step by step until only small units remain, which can then be more easily estimated.

The first step in project decomposition is the division of the project into the following four categories (see Fig. 11.1):

1. *Off the shelf* components
2. *Full experience* components
3. *Partial experience* components
4. *New development*

Each category represents a class of development activities that can be estimated separately, using different methods of estimation. As we shall see, each category is also associated with the degree of *risk* involved in the development of the software.

For the purpose of this discussion, we will consider only components of actual software development, and not their related activities, such as management, configuration control or quality assurance, which are discussed later.

11.2.1 Off the shelf components

Off the shelf components are elements of the project that have been previously developed as part of other projects. Examples of off the shelf components are mathematical subroutine

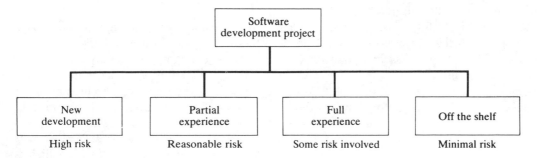

Figure 11.1 Software project development categories by degree of risk.

libraries, software test cases (test suites), hardware peripheral drivers, various algorithms, and even major project components such as the user interface. An off the shelf component is any piece of existing software that can be incorporated into the current project with little or no modification.

The risk involved in using off the shelf components is minimal. Incorporating this category of components into the project potentially lowers the development cost of the project. This practice is greatly encouraged in the DOD standard 2167 (see Chapter 9) where it is referred to as 'reusable software'.

Minimal risk is still different from no risk, and a price is paid for using off the shelf components. The price is in often having to make do with less functionality or suitability than would be provided by redeveloping the components specifically for the project. This is similar to the inexpensive off the rack ready-made suit compared to the much more expensive tailor-made suit. Sometimes the ready-made suit may be a perfect fit, but usually some compromises must be made.

Off the shelf components often require, to some extent, adapting the project to the component rather than adapting the component to the project.

11.2.2 Full experience components

Full experience components are the essence of what companies are really all about. Companies usually specialize, meaning that Boeing makes planes and not televisions and IBM makes computers and not planes. But both develop software.

There is always a tendency to develop expertise in specific areas, but the advancement of technology would be much slower if development groups did not widen these areas of expertise from time to time. This too is true of software development. Most projects contain components that are similar to components in previously developed projects. Examples of full experience components in which companies specialize would be the development of compilers, professional packages (accountancy systems or inventory systems) and even major subsystems such as communication networks.

A full experience component is any part of the software project about which we can say 'We have done something similar in the past'. However, it is most important to emphasize that the term full experience is valid *only if the experience has been retained*. That means that some of the developers who were involved in the previous similar projects are still available (they have not left the company) and the information regarding the previous projects exists and is documented. The fact that a company has previously developed a Pascal compiler is not in itself sufficient grounds to classify the development of a C compiler as a full experience activity, particularly if the members of the compiler development team have resigned from the company and have left no development documentation behind.

There is relatively little risk in the development of full experience components. There is a basic assumption that if we have done it before we can do it again. This is not always so. The main risk is in errors of classification. This refers to cases where components only *look* similar, but are in fact quite different. An example would be the classification of the development of a telecommunications system as being full experience based on the previous development of a local area network (LAN). Both involve the development of a communications system, and include such tasks as protocol interfaces and data transfers, but telecommunications involves problems that are very different from those related to local area networks. The correct approach would be the classification of the activity in this case as *partial experience*, which is discussed in the next section.

Full experience requires the capability to repeat previously successful activities.

11.2.3 Partial experience components

Partial experience refers to components that are in part similar to components developed in previous projects. An example of partial experience would be the development of a compiler by a team who had previously developed an assembler. The team would have accumulated experience in syntax analysis and error handling, but not in optimization or complex parsing. Another example (described at the end of the previous section) is the development of a telecommunications system based on the previous development of a LAN.

A partial experience component is a part of the software project that we can say we are familiar with, though we have not actually developed something similar in the past.

There is a reasonable degree of risk involved in the development of partial experience components, and it is the willingness to assume this risk that leads companies to expand their expertise gradually in evolutionary stages. However, in this instance too there is a danger of erroneous classification. Being partially familiar with a task is a subjective condition. There are few tasks within which we cannot find *something* we are familiar with. So the classification of a component as partial experience depends on the classifier. A possible solution is to require agreement by more than one estimator on the classification of components in this category, but, as we shall see later, this approach is recommended for many of the techniques used in estimation.

The main requirement in classifying a component as partial experience is the ability to identify both familiar and new elements within the component.

11.2.4 New development

New development is involved with the development of components when no relevant experience exists within the development team. This definition can be somewhat tempered based on the fact that computer companies seldom build automobiles, and automobile companies seldom build computers. So new development may have some previous experience to draw upon, and we will assume that the *basic skills* needed to perform the required tasks are available.

Not all research and development is evolutionary in nature. A perfect example is the United States space program, which was inspired by President Kennedy's prophetic declaration that by the end of the decade (the 1960s) the United States would land a man on the Moon. Nothing similar had ever been undertaken before – this was most certainly new development.

New development is obviously the most difficult class of components to estimate, and contains the highest degree of risk. Owing to rapid advances in computer science over the past few decades, computer projects are more apt to contain new development components than other branches of technology. This is especially true of software projects, and is one of the main reasons why computer projects have demonstrated such a poor track record in project estimation.

New development usually lacks a reliable basis for estimation, and requires the application of specific methods to enable adequate estimates to be made. This will be discussed in detail in the next section.

11.2.5 Project decomposition by level of risk

As we have seen, the initial decomposition of a software project identifies four major categories, with different degrees of development risk associated with them. After the first step of project

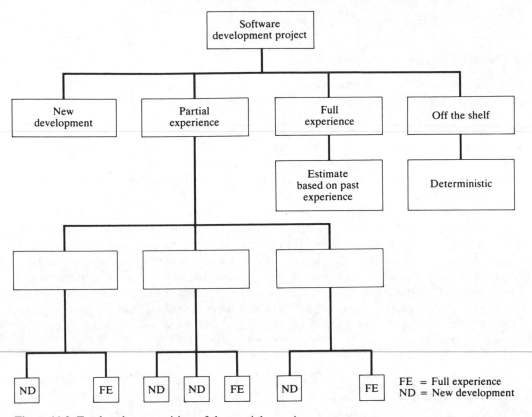

Figure 11.2 Further decomposition of the partial experience category.

decomposition, we end up with project components that either (1) we have available (off the shelf), (2) we know how to develop (full experience), (3) we are at least partially familiar with (partial experience), or (4) are completely new to us (new development).

The objective of the next step in project decomposition is to further identify familiar and unfamiliar tasks. This leads us to re-examine the partial experience category (see Fig. 11.2).

The partial experience category has been described as containing project components that are in part similar to components developed in previous projects. We therefore expect to be able to decompose these components further into smaller new development and full experience components. In some cases, off the shelf components may also be identified during further decomposition of the partial experience category.

By applying stepwise refinement, we can thus iterate and identify all new components of the project. In so doing, we have also identified all project components for which we can apply relatively reliable methods of estimation, based on our previous experience. This will increase the reliability of our overall project estimates.

11.3 ESTIMATING NEW DEVELOPMENT

When we do not have the benefit of experience to draw upon in preparing estimates, we must seek additional information in order to progress from the 'out of the hat' or 'ball park' estimate to something more reliable. Two common approaches are:

1. Prototype methods
2. Statistical methods

Both methods involve some common activities, such as the need to build something to base our estimates on. However, as we shall see, the prototype methods are more engineering oriented while the statistical methods are more scientific. For those who favor engineering over science, it should suffice to say that many prototypes never made it to the production shop.

11.3.1 Prototype methods

Software prototypes are different to prototypes in other branches of technology. An advanced prototype airplane may be very similar to the final production airplane, and may be used as a model for the construction of the production line. Software, however, is built only once (though it may be modified later). Once the software is developed, subsequent products can be immediately created just by copying the software that was produced. This is a unique feature of software (though written text is somewhat similar because of the ability to photocopy it).

The concept of prototypes assumes a slightly different meaning when applied to software. Software prototypes are reduced functional versions of the full product.

In addition to the reduced functionality of a software prototype, the development standards may be relaxed so that less formal development methods and standards are required. Also, the functionality that is retained in the prototype may be more crude than in the full product: for example the user interface may be less user-friendly. All this provides for a fast development cycle that quickly produces an initial version of the full software product. This procedure is commonly referred to as *rapid prototyping*.

The following example demonstrates the use of prototyping in the preparation of software development estimates.

Computer Developers Inc. (CDI) had been successfully marketing an expert system for lawyers that provided them with instant access to information on legal cases and precedents, laws and legal procedures, and lists of legal experts in various areas of law. The system acted as a very fast and reliable legal aide, and in some cases was even capable of suggesting solutions to legal problems.

Based on their success in the legal field, CDI management were contemplating broadening their share of the expert system market, and decided to evaluate the risk in developing an expert system for medical doctors. To enable them to evaluate the risk efficiently, the management of CDI needed estimates on the size and cost of the development of a medical expert system.

Clearly the medical expert system contained all of the project risk categories described in the previous section:

- Off the shelf components from the legal system (such as data retrieval and identification of experts)
- Full experience components (such as data maintenance and case history features)
- Partial experience components (such as recommendation logic and user interface)
- New development (such as medical diagnosis and drug interaction monitoring)

The complexity of the medical diagnosis component renders it difficult to estimate. Therefore building a computerized prototype medical diagnosis assistant would be effective in providing information on the amount of work necessary to develop a full version of the system.

The medical diagnosis prototype would exclude much of the user-friendly interface necessary to appeal successfully to doctors as potential users of the system. It would also exclude much of the required medical data and algorithms, and would be a standalone program that need not be integrated with the other features of the expert system.

The actual functionality of the prototype is dependent on the time and budget available for its development. Obviously the larger the budget and the longer the development time permitted, the more useful the prototype becomes as a tool for estimating the full system. In the extreme, the prototype would contain all of the functionality of the full system, and would thus provide an accurate estimate of the development resources required. This, essentially, is the same as developing the project first and estimating it after it is complete. This estimate is accurate but useless.

In many instances, the prototype is not a throw-away, and is later refined and incorporated into the full system. In such cases there is a risk of using substandard or poor quality software in the final product, as documentation may be lacking and coding and design practices may be inferior. This can be avoided if a decision is made before the development of the prototype to maintain development standards to the extent that would enable the prototype to be used later as part of the production software.

To summarize, a prototype of new development components is an excellent tool that can provide the additional information necessary to prepare reliable estimates. However, a prototype can be costly, and in fact the more supportive it is of a reliable estimate, the more costly it is to develop.

11.3.2 Statistical methods

Statistical methods employ sampling techniques in the estimation of project components. At the lowest level of project decomposition, representative units or modules are selected. These units are then actually developed and thus they provide information on the expected effort required for the development of the components they represent. This method includes the following basic stages:

1. Identify all new development software components.
2. Prepare an initial design of each component by identifying the software modules that will implement the component.
3. Divide the modules into similar categories, according to:
   - complexity (degree of difficulty)
   - function (such as communications, data base, human interface etc.)
   - type (operating system, library utility, service task etc.).
4. From each category, select one module that is representative of the others.
5. Implement the selected modules.
6. Based on the information derived from the implementation of the selected modules, estimate the resources required for each category.
7. Combine the estimates for each category, thus obtaining an estimate for all new development software.

For large projects, the selection of more than one module from each category will provide a more accurate estimate. The dilemma here is similar to prototyping. The more modules selected from each category, the more accurate the estimate. However, in the extreme we would be estimating a component based on the full development of that component. Once again, this would provide an accurate but useless estimate.

The selection of the module categories and the assignment of modules to these categories requires extensive experience in software development. The selection of representative modules also requires relevant experience. These activities are best carried out by three or four professionals who compare notes and attempt to reach agreement on the classification and selection decisions.

The initial design of the components, in stage 2, is a critical activity. Design is a major phase in software development, though the decomposition of the components into modules should suffice at this stage. Even this is no easy task, and for large projects may require a substantial effort. The initial design coupled with the implementation of the selected modules may sometimes be reusable in the full development of the system. This, however, is not assured, so that a separate prototype development budget should be allocated for these activities.

11.4 THE CONSTRUCTIVE COST MODEL (COCOMO)

The anecdote related at the beginning of this chapter illustrates the many factors that affect the extent of resources required to develop a software project. Clearly, a good development team will complete a project earlier and at a lower development cost than an average development team. Many other factors can be considered when estimating the cost of software development. The more common factors are:

1. Level of personnel
2. Level of complexity
3. Project size
4. Development environment
5. Reliability level

Similar factors were originally presented by Boehm (1981) and were included in his constructive cost model, later referred to as the COCOMO method, for the preparation of software cost estimates. Similar models, such as the one presented here, have since been further developed and modified, primarily in the selection of the effort formulae used by the model (see Jeffery and Low (1990), Anderson (1990) and Balda and Gustafson (1990)). The COCOMO model is an algorithm that takes into account the above five factors (and possibly others) and produces estimates associated with the quantification of risk. Several computer programs are available that perform much of the tedious work required by the model (further described in Section 11.5).

The COCOMO model starts from an existing estimate of the number of software lines of code to be developed. It then provides tools for the estimation of cost, schedule and the size of the development staff. The number of lines of code may be estimated using the project decomposition and statistical methods described at the beginning of this chapter.

The COCOMO model requires a set of formulae, one for each of the factors being considered. Examples of such formulae follow.

11.4.1 Level of personnel

A measure of the ability of a software engineer must take into account a wide range of performance. Sackman *et al.* (1968) have demonstrated a variation of 16 to 1 in experiments conducted on programmer performance.

Since Sackman conducted his experiments in 1968, the task of 'programmer' has evolved into many new professions such as coder, analyst, systems programmer, software engineer and others. The term 'software engineer' has come to refer to a college or university graduate who can assume responsibility for both design and coding (programming). Also, since 1968, the role of actual coding has diminished in the overall development cycle of complex software systems. As we have seen in Chapter 4, design, integration and testing take up most of the resources in the modern approach to project development. If the design is well done, then coding may require no more than 10 percent of the development resources.

We therefore expect that, to a large extent, the wide variation in programmer productivity observed by Sackman may have been due to a lack of methodical software development techniques at the time the experiment was conducted.

Unfortunately, a reasonable expected variation of software engineer performance is still measured in hundreds of percent. Assuming an orderly software development methodology is being used, a variation of up to 400 percent may be expected. This means that, on an average, we may expect an experienced, intelligent and motivated software engineer to produce up to four times as much as a beginner (or mediocre) software engineer.

The larger a project, the less impact individual performance will have, as this factor tends to average out based on personnel interaction and general statistical averaging theories.

Table 11.1 presents an example of the tabular function

$$PL = f(\Sigma EP, N, KSLOC)$$

which represents the personnel level (PL), using $KSLOC$ as a measure of the size of a project[3] (thousand source lines of code) and EP as the expected performance assigned between 1 and 4 for each engineer, summed over N, the total number of engineers on the project.

This function produces a value between 0 and 4 that serves as a factor to be applied to the cost of the development effort. A PL value below 1 indicates a good development team while a PL value above 1 indicates a weak development team. A PL value of 1 indicates an average development team, and will not cause the cost estimate to change.

Note that as the project size increases, the impact of the level of personnel on project cost variation lessens. However, an average personnel level of 1 produces a worst case factor for all project sizes, which in the above table is represented as a factor of 4.

Table 11.1 Cost multipliers for the level of personnel

	$PL = f(\Sigma EP, N, KSLOC)$		
$(\Sigma EP)/N$	$KSLOC < 25$	$25 < KSLOC < 300$	$300 < KSLOC$
4	0.33	0.50	0.75
3.5	0.45	0.65	0.81
3	0.66	0.85	0.90
2.5	1.00	1.00	1.00
2	2.20	1.80	1.50
1.5	3.50	2.50	2.20
1	4.00	4.00	4.00

3. Boehm (1981) uses KDSI (thousand delivered source instructions) in the various formulae he uses. However, project development costs are not based on the number of lines *delivered* but rather the number of lines actually *developed*. The two are often not the same, as delivered lines of code may originate from off the shelf components (see Section 11.2), and developed code may not be delivered for various reasons (e.g. test code). See also Ratcliff and Rollo's (1990) discussion on the ambiguity associated with KDSI.

Other similar functions may give more consideration to the contribution of the level of personnel by producing a wider span of values. In the extreme, we may assume that in some cases a development team with all level 1 engineers may never complete a large project. The actual numbers in the above table represent an improvement on a straight unfactored cost estimate. However, these numbers should be regarded as an example, and a refinement of the table should be based upon the actual experience accumulated in the organization within which the project is to be developed.

An additional improvement of Table 11.1 may also be achieved by refining the project size steps. Table 11.1 uses three project size steps, $KSLOC < 25$, $25 > KSLOC < 300$, 300, and $300 < KSLOC$. A more detailed set of step sizes may use 25, 100, 300 and 500.

We shall consider three examples based on three project sizes with three groups of engineers.

Consider the following projects:

- Project A with 10 000 estimated *SLOCs*
- Project B with 100 000 estimated *SLOCs*
- Project C with 500 000 estimated *SLOCs*

We shall assign the values

1. to beginner engineers
2. to average engineers
3. to high level engineers
4. to exceptional engineers

It is reasonable to expect most project engineers to be on a level of 2 or 3. Many projects permit one or two beginners and many projects will have one or two gurus. Note that in the case related in the introduction to this chapter, we can assume the team that was assembled comprised 3 and 4 level engineers.

For Project A we will assume 3 software engineers (this includes system designers, programmers etc.): none at level 1, 1 at level 2, 1 at level 3 and 1 at level 4.

For Project B we will assume 35 software engineers: 9 at level 1, 18 at level 2, 6 at level 3 and 2 at level 4.

For Project C we will assume 190 software engineers, 20 at level 1, 100 at level 2, 65 at level 3 and 5 at level 4.

Table 11.2 summarizes the calculation of the *PL* project cost factor, based on the values in Table 11.1.

The *PL* value for Project C is rounded to the closest value in Table 11.1. A linear interpolation between values of $(\Sigma EP)/N$ could also be used to determine the value of *PL* for Project C.

The results presented in Table 11.2 show that Project A is supported by a superior development team that brings the estimated project development costs down by one third. On the other hand, Project B has a weak development team that almost doubles the cost of project development. Project C has an average development team.

Exercise 4 at the end of this chapter deals with improved functions for factoring the level of personnel into the calculation of cost estimates.

Table 11.2 *PL* **cost factors calculated for three projects**

	A	B	C
KSLOC	10	100	500
N	3	35	190
ΣEP	9	71	435
(ΣEP)/N	3.0	2.0	2.3
PL	0.66	1.80	1.00

11.4.2 Level of complexity

The level of software complexity is a significant factor in the preparation of project estimates. It is obvious that some classes of software are much more difficult to develop than others. Generally, operating systems are more complex than typical data processing systems, so that the number of lines of code would not serve as an effective means of comparison for the development of two such systems. It is therefore reasonable to divide software components into classes by their level of complexity, and to assign different measures of complexity to each class.

Boehm (1981) chose three levels of program complexity: organic, semi-detached and embedded. We will consider the following four classes of complexity:

1. *System software*: this class of software includes any software that is close to the hardware, such as operating systems and communications software.
2. *Algorithmic software*: this class includes any software that is heavily dependent on complex logic and algorithms, such as scientific programs, sort utilities and fault tolerant software.
3. *Service software*: this includes basic utilities such as editors, word processors and graphics programs.
4. *Data processing software*: this class includes general data base applications, such as inventory programs, report generators and spreadsheets.

These four classes of software represent the main levels of software complexity. In some cases, it will not be immediately evident to which class some programs belong. In such cases we must assign the program to the class that is *closest* in complexity. An example might be the development of a compiler. The complexity of compilers is mainly due to the complex algorithms that are involved in such areas as syntax analysis, parsing, optimization etc. Therefore compilers would be classified as algorithmic software.

The following formulae are somewhat similar to those proposed by Boehm, except that *KSLOC* is used instead of *KDSI*, and four classes of complexity are used instead of three. Each formula produces the estimated number of software engineer months (*SEM*) based on the estimated number of lines of code and the class of software complexity.

System software: $SEM = 3.6 \times (KSLOC)^{1.20}$
Algorithmic software: $SEM = 3.2 \times (KSLOC)^{1.15}$
Service software: $SEM = 2.8 \times (KSLOC)^{1.10}$
Data processing software: $SEM = 2.4 \times (KSLOC)^{1.05}$

Similar functions were plotted by Fairly (1985), and the graphs demonstrate the divergence of the estimated effort (software engineer months) as the size of the project in lines of code grows. This means that in the preparation of estimates, the classification of software becomes more important as the size of the project grows. Above 100 000 lines of code it becomes significant, and above 300 000 lines of code the difference between the two extremes (system and data processing) can be over 200 percent.

Many projects contain software components that belong to different classes of complexity. The most efficient way to apply the above formulae is to decompose the software into components, assign each component to its class of complexity, and then to estimate each class of components separately. The resulting set of estimates is then combined to provide a single estimate for the overall project.

In the discussions above, software engineer months (*SEM*) refers to all types of software professionals involved in software development. It is important to note that an engineer month is not the same as a calendar month. It may take six weeks to achieve one engineer month of effort, due to the fact that engineers, similar to other employees, tend to be occasionally sick, they take vacations, and usually they do not work on national holidays. These topics are discussed further in Chapter 10.

11.4.3 The reliability factor

The required level of reliability in a software project can have a major impact on development costs. Reliability, similar to the complexity factor discussed previously, can also produce an increase in development costs of more than 200 percent.

Reliability is an expensive quality in computer systems, and can be achieved through hardware, through software, or through a combination of both. Reliability is also difficult to implement and should be heavily factored into development cost estimates. Fault tolerant systems require costly integration and test phases. This is due to the fact that fault tolerance and other levels of reliability are difficult to test.

Before considering reliability multipliers for the development of software, a decision must be made on the number of reliability levels that will be used. Boehm (1981) uses five reliability levels, based on the effect of system failure:

- Slight inconvenience
- Losses easily recovered
- Moderately difficult to recover losses
- High financial loss
- Risk to human life

It is comforting to find human life classified higher than high financial loss.

The basic approach is to divide the reliability of the system into levels that range from minimal (no specific effort devoted to reliability), to the highest level of reliability (maximum fault tolerance).

In order to introduce a reliability factor into the cost estimates for the development of a software project, an initial decomposition stage is required, similar to the method described in Section 11.2. However, the objective now is to decompose the system into classes of components by level of reliability.

After the initial decomposition, a table of reliability effort multipliers is then applied to each component and calculated for each level, yielding the reliability effort multiplier (*REM*). The values in the reliability table are based upon experience accumulated by the company or organization responsible for the development of the software project. A reliability effort function, similar to the one below, can be used to generate the reliability factor table.

$$REM = 0.75 + (L-1) \times 1.25/(2 \times N - L - 1)$$

Table 11.3 Reliability multipliers for five reliability levels

Level of reliability	Reliability multipliers
1. No effort required	0.75
2. Low	0.93
3. Data integrity preserved	1.17
4. High reliability required	1.50
5. Full fault tolerance	2.00

In this function, N is the number of reliability levels and L is the level of the multiplier being calculated. The reliability multipliers produced by this function for five levels are presented in Table 11.3.

In the above example the reliability effort multipliers grow by 0.18 from level 1 to level 2 and by 0.5 from level 4 to level 5. This indicates that as reliability becomes more critical to the project, the associated effort increases non-linearly. Actually, fully fault tolerant systems (level 5) require a major part of the development effort to be invested in the provision of reliability.

It is also worth noting that the above function introduces a range of close to 200 percent in the cost of implementing different levels of reliability (0.75 to 2.00). This means that a high reliability system could cost up to three times as much to develop as a system requiring no effort invested in reliability. In some cases the factor could even be higher.

After determining the reliability effort multipliers, these values are applied to the *SEM* estimates (refer to the previous discussion on project complexity) for each component within each class, thus factoring reliability into the estimates. The estimates for all components are then combined to produce an overall cost estimate for the project.

11.4.4 The development environment

Anyone who has ever attempted to make some minor home or car repairs has observed that tasks are easier to perform when the right tools are available.

How long does it take to mow the lawn? Well, it depends on the size of the lawn. However, it also depends on whether you are using a push lawnmower, or a motor-driven lawnmower (we have already seen that it also depends on the person behind the mower). Not surprisingly, this observation is also true of software development.

One of the most common contributors to the development environment factor is the use of high level languages. As programming languages become more efficient, it becomes less desirable to develop software in assembler languages, except for rare cases. Both productivity and reliability of code are many times higher when using high level languages as compared to assembler. This single consideration bears so much on the cost of software development that it is often factored into the development cost separately.

The programming language is but a single example of the effect the development environment can have on productivity. The hardware environment is also significant, as are the software tools that are available on the development hardware. If special purpose hardware is being developed for the project, then good debuggers and other software analysis tools become essential for effective testing and integration. Goldberg (1983) discusses the significant contribution of a good computer aided software engineering (CASE) environment to development productivity.

The basic algorithm comprises the following steps:

1. Decompose the software system using stepwise refinement, into subsystems and then decompose each subsystem into low level software modules.
2. Use a size estimation method (such as is described in Section 11.2) to estimate the size of each module. Then combine the estimates for each module, thus producing estimates for the size of each subsystem, and for the full system.
3. Determine effort multipliers for each module, using methods similar to those described at the beginning of this section. The effort multipliers used should at least include formulae for:
   - Level of personnel
   - Size of project
   - Reliability
   - Development environment
   - Module complexity
4. Apply the effort multipliers to each module using methods such as those described at the beginning of this section, thus producing estimates for each module.
5. Determine subsystem effort multipliers for each subsystem.
6. Combine the estimates for the modules in each subsystem with the subsystem effort multipliers, thus producing estimates for each subsystem.
7. Combine the estimates for all subsystems, thus producing an estimate for the whole system.
8. Review all factors that were considered on a module and subsystem level. Seek interaction between factors, between modules, and between subsystems, and allow for the interaction.
9. Seek additional costs that were omitted from the system estimate, such as market analysis, overhead etc., and combine them with the system estimate that was produced.
10. Have a second (and if possible a third) independent estimate prepared. Compare the estimates produced by each group, and examine any substantial differences. Resolve any differences and produce a single agreed project cost estimate.

This algorithm produces project development cost estimates taking all major factors into consideration. Step 10 also addresses individual errors of estimation by requiring major differences to be explained and resolved.

Step 1 refers to the term software *modules*, which is synonymous with the lowest level software decomposition unit.

Step 8 attempts to identify factors that have been partially or fully duplicated in the estimate. An example of full duplication would be the assignment of a complexity factor to a software component because of high reliability requirements, since the provision of reliability often requires complex logic. This would result in the estimate for the component being increased twice, each time for the same reason.

Additional factors may be included in Steps 3 and 5, based on the characteristics of the actual project being estimated. This could include such factors as the complexity of the programming language (if, for example, Ada was being used for the first time), or familiarity with target hardware (if special hardware is being developed and the integration phase would therefore be more difficult). A complete implementation of this algorithm should have all the above effort formulae included.

It is important to remember that the classification of the software components is *different* for each factor. This means that when applying the reliability multipliers to classes of components, these classes will most probably be different from those produced when the complexity multipliers are applied. Therefore each set of multipliers is applied individually to each decomposition component. This is where a computer could be most helpful and, as stated earlier, a number of COCOMO computer packages are available to perform these tedious tasks.

The COCOMO algorithm is heavily dependent on subjective decisions made by the estimator. This has led to the development of many variants of COCOMO, and the effort formula (see Jeffery and Low (1990), Anderson (1990) and Balda and Gustafson (1990)). The issue of deviation of subjective estimates by different estimators is addressed in Section 11.6.

11.5 FUNCTION POINT ANALYSIS

There is considerable controversy regarding the value of 'source lines of code' as a measure of project size (see Ratcliff and Rollo (1990) and Jeffery and Low (1990)). There is no common definition for the measure *SLOC*; it may or may not include test code or reused code, or in some cases even library code. Also, does *SLOC* really mean the same for assembler code and Ada code? Or Cobol code and C code? Can a single factor really be applied (see the COCOMO factors) to make all program languages comparable?

These questions can be sidestepped by directing the estimating process to project *problem size* instead of project *code size*. Function point analysis (FPA) is a method that produces project estimates based on the problem size.

Problem size is a measure derived from the initial project phases, in particular the requirements phase. The amount of functionality in the project determines the problem size, which is represented by a numerical value (the FPA value).

The FPA value of a project can be used to:

- Compare the complexity of projects
- Compare the relative effort required to complete a project
- Generate other project measures (such as $SLOCs$[4])

There are many variations of the FPA technique. Many of these variations attempt to adapt the technique to specific types of projects, or to increase accuracy by adding more project attributes to the FPA process.

11.5.1 The basic FPA steps

The basic FPA process includes eight steps. Two of the steps can be prepared independently of the project being estimated, as they are involved with determining lists of function types and complexity attributes to be used to classify the characteristics of the project.

The eight basic FPA steps are:

1. Determine a list of input/output dependent function categories. This may include:[5]
   - External input/inquiry functions
     - User inputs of data or controls
     - User inquiries requiring a response

---

4. Jeffery and Low (1990) describe a program called CLAIR used to convert *function points* (FP) to *SLOC*.
5. These function categories are similar to those suggested by Albrecht and Gaffney (1983).

- External output functions
  - Distinct data or signal output functions
- Logical internal file functions
  - Data or control information
- External interface file functions
  - Shared files, data and control information

2. The number of basic software functions of each type is identified. A function should be counted if it is expected to require special processing.
3. Each function counted in Step 2 is classified as:
   - *Simple*; minimal file accesses, few different data types and minimal user involvement.
   - *Average*; this classification is designated for functions between simple and complex. 'Average' can be subdivided into more than one intermediate classification.
   - *Complex*; many file accesses, many different data types and extensive user involvement.
4. A numerical weighted value is attributed to each classification set in step 3 (e.g. simple = 6, average = 8, complex = 10, or average can be extended over 7, 8 and 9). Each function category can have a different set of weights.

   The values of all weighted functions are added, providing the unadjusted FPA value (the *UFP*).
5. The attributes of the processing complexity are identified. These may include:[6]
   - Data communications functions
     - Data and control transmitted, local and remote
   - Distributed functions
     - Distributed data functions
     - Distributed processing functions
   - Performance
     - Performance objectives, such as the influence of throughput or responsiveness on development activities
   - Utilization of the configuration
     - The degree of usage of the hardware; communications lines
   - Transaction rate
     - The degree to which the transaction rate influences development
   - On-line data entry
     - The degree to which on-line data functions are handled by the system
   - End user efficiency
     - The required efficiency of the handling of on-line data functions performed by the end user
   - On-line update
     - The degree of updating required for logical internal files
   - Complex processing
     - The degree of influence of complex processing on development. This includes interrupt handlers, re-entrant code, complex algorithms, I/O etc.
   - Reusability
     - The degree to which the code must be developed as reusable for other systems
   - Installation ease
     - The degree to which installation ease impacts development

---

6. Albrecht and Gaffney (1983) suggest 14 complexity factors and Symons (1988) suggests an additional six.

Table 11.6 FPA values for different types of project

Project	UFP	CAF	AFP
Time and attendance system	1200	0.42	504
Access control system	680	0.87	592

- Operational ease
  - The required degree of ease in such functions as backup and restore, recovery, human interface etc.
- Multiple sites
  - The degree to which the system will be developed for different sites and different types of user
- Facilitate change
  - The degree to which the software must be developed to support functional changes easily

6. Each processing degree of influence for each complexity factor is designated based on one of the following values:

   0: non-existent
   1: insignificant
   2: moderate
   3: average
   4: significant
   5: strong

   and the total of all the complexity factor values is calculated, providing the total degree of influence (TGI).

7. The total degree of influence value is converted to a complexity adjustment factor (CAF). A simple conversion function may be:

$$CAF = \frac{TGI}{5 \times (\text{number of complex factors})}$$

8. The adjusted function point measure (AFP) for the project is then calculated as:

$$AFP = CAF \times UFP$$

An example of the values produced by function point analysis appears in Table 11.6. The values in the table demonstrate the importance of the function point value adjustment. A large commercial data processing system provides a much higher UFP than a real-time system, but the complexity adjustment produces a higher adjusted value for the real-time system. The conclusion is that even though the time and attendance system has almost twice the number of functions as the access control system, the complexity of the access control system indicates that it will require more effort to develop.

11.5.2 The application of FPA

There are many similarities between COCOMO estimation and function point analysis. Both methods use a similar weighting technique to adjust the initial estimates. However, FPA is only dependent on the functionality of the system being estimated, and not on any previously calculated estimates (e.g. lines of code, size of module).

As we have seen, the FPA measure is useful for comparing the effort of projects. It does not directly provide a method for estimating the cost of a project. Based on the assumption that there is a high correlation between cost and effort, a function can be applied to the FPA value to produce a cost estimate. A simple function can be based on past experience; for example a previous project with an *AFP* value of 1000 cost $1 500 000 to develop, and another previous project with an *AFP* value of 850 cost $900 000. If we assume a linear correlation, then if the current project being estimated produces an *AFP* value of 920, we will estimate its cost at $1 180 000.

More sophisticated methods of calculating effort (work hours) and code size (*KSLOC*) are presented by Albrecht and Gaffney (1983).

The COCOMO method can be applied together with function point analysis to achieve two important goals:

1. To assure that the estimates are reasonable (no major divergence of results)
2. To produce a more comprehensive set of estimates (comparison values and cost values)

The use of COCOMO in conjunction with function point analysis is discussed by Ratcliff and Rollo (1990), who conclude that 'a more fruitful long term objective would be the development of a new general estimation model for an operational paradigm', which would presumably provide a more comprehensive set of estimates. But COCOMO and FPA have been successfully combined within a comprehensive computerized estimation utility[7] that uses both techniques for the cost and size estimation of software projects. The attributes of the two techniques within this utility can be adjusted based on the experience gained during its use, and alternative models (sets of attributes for each model) can be stored separately and loaded into the utility as needed.

11.6 THE ESTIMATE AS A RANGE

If asked how long it would take to develop a single software module, an experienced programmer would probably respond 'It depends'. As we have seen, it depends on the programming language, on the complexity of the logic, on the individual programmer, and possibly on other factors. If pressed for a specific answer, the same programmer might respond that it could take anywhere between two days and two weeks. This is a valid answer.

Estimates are often presented as a *range*. A range is a helpful estimate in planning for the development of a project. Management will often be willing to accept an initial estimate that states that a project will cost no less than $400 000 and no more than $750 000. These types of estimate are frequently used in the planning stages of a project. As more information becomes available, the range becomes narrower, until eventually it becomes a single number.

The statistical theory behind this approach deals with the concept of *confidence intervals*. If a variable x has probability p of being between two values a and b, then we say that the interval (a, b) is a p-confidence interval for x.

As an example, if (2, 14) is a 95 percent confidence interval for the number of days it takes to develop a module, then we are 95 percent sure that the development of the module will take more than 2 and less than 14 days to develop.[8]

---

7. The referenced computer utility, *Before you leap* or *BYL*, is distributed by the Gordon Group, California.

8. Strictly speaking, the mathematical definition of probability refers to a function that produces a value between 0 and 1. However, in the real world, especially in the business world, probabilities are often expressed as percentages. In fact, in this author's own experience, percentages are to be preferred when presenting estimates to management as they are more easily grasped.

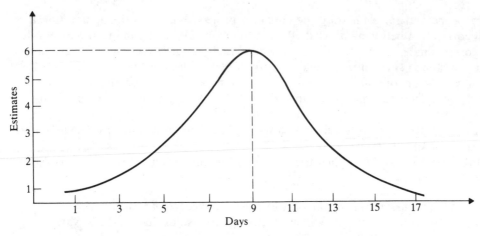

Figure 11.3 Normal distribution of estimates.

A word on being 95 percent sure. If we are 95 percent sure of something, then out of 100 instances, we expect to be right 95 times and wrong 5 times.

The range considered here will be the range of estimates for a given project attribute, such as *SLOCs*, development cost, size of development team, development time etc.

We will assume a normal distribution of estimates. This means that if 20 software professionals are requested to estimate the number of days required to develop a specific software module, we expect a result similar in distribution to the following:

1 person will estimate 2 days
2 will estimate 5 days
4 will estimate 7 days
6 will estimate 9 days
4 will estimate 11 days
2 will estimate 13 days
1 will estimate 16 days

Figure 11.3 presents a graph of the above numbers. The resulting curve is referred to in statistics as the graph of a *normal distribution* function.[9] The normal distribution is characterized by a bell-shaped graph with an even distribution of occurrences around the average. In the above example, the average estimate is 9 days, with as many estimating below the average as above. And, most importantly, both the frequency and distance of estimates below the average are similar to those above the average. Many frequently occurring events in nature occur as a normal distribution; for example the height of male (or female) students in a school class, or the number of rainy days in April (excluding England, where it is always 30).

Let us now consider a second possible set of responses by a group of software professionals to the same question:

1 person will estimate 7 days
4 will estimate 9 days

---

9. For the mathematically minded, strictly speaking, the normal distribution is a continuous distribution. For simplicity, we will also include the discrete approximation of the normal distribution.

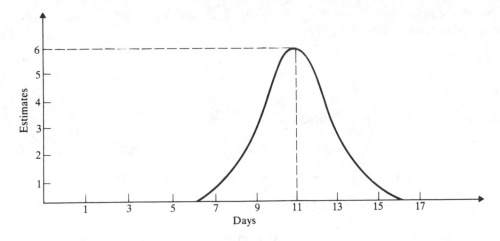

Figure 11.4 Normal distribution of estimates with small deviation.

10 will estimate 11 days
 4 will estimate 13 days
 1 will estimate 15 days

Figure 11.4 presents a graph of these new results. The curve, representing these results, undoubtedly also represents a normal distribution. However, the bell-shaped curve is thinner and taller than in the first example. In this case the divergence of responses was less than in the first example. Also, the average has moved: it is now 11 days.

All normal distributions are characterized by these two parameters, the average and the degree of divergence. The average is referred to as the expected value, μ, and the degree of divergence is referred to as the standard deviation, σ.

We shall use approximations[10] to calculate the normal distribution parameters of various software project estimates.

The first step is the calculation of a *worst case estimate* and a *best case estimate*. These can be calculated by a single person or by a group of people. If we estimate that the development of a synchronous communications driver would take at best four weeks, and at worst 12 weeks, then the best case estimate would be four weeks and the worst case estimate would be 12 weeks (this is not yet a confidence interval, because we do not yet know the probability of our estimate being correct). The two values, best case and worst case, approximate the two extremes of the normal distribution curve.

We now need to calculate values between the two extreme cases. The more estimates we can produce between the two extremes, the more accurate the normal curve will be. However, we will approximate with a single intermediate value, the *most likely* case. In the above example, if four weeks was the best case estimate and 12 weeks was the worst case estimate, we might conclude that seven weeks is a reasonable time for the development of the synchronous communications driver, so that seven weeks is the most likely case (note that the most likely case is an independent estimate and is *not* an average derived from the best case and worst case

10. Examples of approximations appear in Nienburg (1989). For a full discussion of these and other topics of statistics, refer to Fraser (1976).

estimates). In using the three estimates, best case, most likely and worst case, we will assign probabilities to each case as follows:[11]

P(best case) = 0.2
P(most likely) = 0.6
P(worst case) = 0.2

The discrete definition of the expected value μ is

$$\mu = E(x) = \Sigma x P(x)$$

Therefore, the approximation of the expected value in the previous example would be

$$\mu = E(x) = 0.2 \times 4 + 0.6 \times 7 + 0.2 \times 12 = 7.4$$

A simple approximation for the standard deviation would be the difference of the extremes multiplied by their probability:

$$\sigma = (\text{worst case}) \times P(\text{worst case}) - (\text{best case}) \times P(\text{best case}),$$

which, in the previous example, would produce:

$$\sigma = 0.2 \times 12 - 0.2 \times 4 = 1.6$$

We can use common normal distribution tables to discover that:

$(\mu - \sigma, \mu + \sigma)$ produces a 68 percent confidence interval
$(\mu - 2\sigma, \mu + 2\sigma)$ produces a 95 percent confidence interval
$(\mu - 3\sigma, \mu + 3\sigma)$ produces a 99 percent confidence interval

This means, that, in the above example, we can estimate the time to develop the synchronous communications driver as between 4.2 days and 10.6 days, and we are 95 percent confident of our estimate. We can also estimate the development time as being between 5.8 days and 9 days, but then we would only be 68 percent confident of our estimate.

One of the qualities of statistics is that the results can only be as good as the data on which they are based (a form of 'garbage in, garbage out'). It is therefore important to devote the necessary time and effort to the development of three effective estimates. A solid, though laborious, approach is to request a number of software engineers (say six) to prepare individual estimates for the worst, best and most likely cases. The worst case estimate and the best case estimate would be the two extremes produced, while the most likely would be either the average, the median or the most frequent (the mode).

11.7 ESTIMATING HARDWARE RESOURCES

Software must be designed to fit comfortably into its host environment. The host environment is comprised of the target hardware and its various attributes. Poor software design may result

---

11. Both Nienburg (1989) and Sodhi (1990) use the following similar approximation:
$$\mu = (\text{worst case} + 4 \times \text{most likely} + \text{best case})/6$$

in an overload of the CPU capacity, or it may exceed the available memory or mass storage capacity. This can sometimes, but not always, be remedied by expanding the target hardware, resulting in an increase in project cost.

Hardware resources are measured in units of the particular resource being considered: for communications, bits (or bytes) per second; for storage devices, kilobytes or megabytes (or even gigabytes), for a specific CPU, a percentage of the CPU load. A major resource that is heavily dependent on hardware, though it is not in fact hardware itself, is speed. Speed estimates describe our expectations regarding the performance of the system to be developed, and are often required in the early planning phase of the project.

We will consider methods for estimating the following three main resources:

1. CPU load
2. Data storage
3. Speed

Speed, though more an attribute than a resource, will be considered as a resource for the purpose of this discussion.

11.7.1 The CPU load

Estimation of the CPU load can be quite complex, especially in a multi-process environment, where at any given time more than one process may be competing for the CPU. This is similar to a service queue, in which a number of service requestors await service to be provided by one or more service providers. In our context, the service requestors are the processes and the service providers are the CPUs. The service queue problem is a common problem in operations research, and is handled with the aid of statistics. For a full discussion on queue theory refer to Gillett (1976).

We will consider the CPU load in a slightly more deterministic environment. We will assume that, at any given time, we can determine which demands can be made for CPU processing resources. Without this assumption the CPU load estimate cannot be calculated, and can only be derived by simulating the actual environment and observing the result.

The CPU load is estimated as a percentage. We say that a system has a 75 percent CPU load, meaning that 25 percent of the processing power is available for additional tasks.

The CPU load is always measured in a worst case situation. A 75 percent CPU load means that, at any given time, no more than 75 percent of the CPU is being utilized. This, however, is paradoxical, as in effect we know that at all times one hundred percent of the CPU is being utilized. We must therefore define what we mean by CPU utilization for purposes of estimation.

First, the CPU load is always measured within a specific *time window*. This means that within a specific interval of time (which, for example, may be 10 milliseconds long) we measure the amount of time utilized by the CPU. One of the main tasks, then, is the selection of an appropriate time window.

In determining the utilization of the CPU within the time window, we consider only those tasks that cannot be processed at any other time. In a system where diagnostics are performed in the background whenever the CPU has no other task to process, we would not consider the diagnostic tasks in the calculation of the CPU load.

A system that has a 60 percent CPU load in a 10 millisecond window can accept an additional 4 millisecond task if that task can tolerate a maximum 10 millisecond delay.

As an example, we will consider data input from a communications port. If the port has a data transfer rate of 1200 bits per second, then a byte can be available at the input port

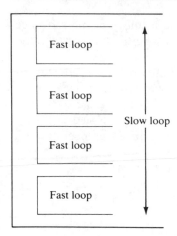

Figure 11.5 Real-time executive with slow and fast loops.

approximately every 7 milliseconds, and we must be ready to retrieve a byte from the port before the next byte becomes available. The communication port driver can therefore tolerate a maximum 6 millisecond delay (assuming 1 millisecond processing time).

CPU load estimates are most often required in real-time systems. They are rarely required in commercial data processing systems. Real-time systems are frequently characterized by a basic system loop, often referred to as the main loop, or the executive. This is a low level task that loops endlessly, executing a set of synchronous tasks that drive the system. In many cases, the low level loop is actually part of the operating system that can be configured based on the required cycle time for the loop. This low-level loop may be selected as the time window for the calculation of the CPU load. If the main loop comprises even lower level *fast loops*, then the smallest fast loop may be selected as the time window (see Fig. 11.5).

The following set of steps describes the method for calculating the CPU load. This method requires an initial decomposition of the system into its major software tasks and the estimated execution time for each task.

1.   Determine the lowest level system loop, and derive from that the time window to be used for estimating the CPU load
2.   Perform a timing analysis of the system and identify all tasks that may require processing within the time window
3.   Combine the estimated execution times for all tasks identified in Step 2
4.   Divide the result of Step 3 by the size of the time window

Note that Step 2 requires the identification of any task that *may* require (not just request) CPU time within the time window. This includes operating system tasks.

Consider the following example. A computerized intensive care monitoring system includes the following main components

1.   Data input from monitoring equipment
2.   An alarm
3.   A user interface component
4.   An executive loop for reading the monitor equipment

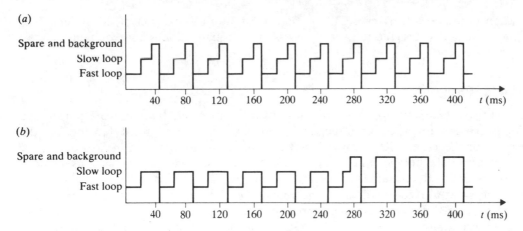

Figure 11.6 Real-time executive with slow and fast loops: (a) timing analysis perception; (b) actual execution timing.

The executive loop consists of:

1. A main loop that reads two complex inputs that also require some logic processing every 400 ms. These tasks are estimated to take 60 ms each.
2. A fast loop that reads two inputs every 40 ms. These tasks are estimated to take 10 ms each.

There are 10 fast loops within the main loop. We will select a time window of 40 ms. In calculating the worst case, within the time window, we will first consider the fast loop tasks. They immediately use up 20 ms of the 40 ms available. That means that of the 400 ms main loop, only 200 ms are left for other tasks. Of this, 120 ms are required for the two main loop tasks, which can be accommodated easily. If we divide the main loop tasks evenly between the fast loops, then an additional 12 ms will be required from the time window, for a total of 32 ms.

We can assume that when the alarm task is executed, all other tasks are aborted, so that we need not consider the execution time for this task. The user interface component is not a real-time activity (compared to the monitoring equipment input tasks), and we can assume that the user interface will be handled by the main loop spare of 80 ms, in the background. The executive loops are relatively simple, and are estimated to require less than 1 ms, and will therefore also be excluded from the calculation.

The CPU load for the intensive care monitoring system is

$$32/40 = 0.80$$

which means that the CPU load is 80 percent within a 40 ms time window. This example is illustrated in Fig. 11.6.

An interesting situation arises when the CPU load calculation provides a result greater than 1.00. This means that the CPU load is more than 100 percent! The obvious conclusion then is that the processor is incapable of performing the tasks required. In such cases there are two possible remedies: either the system requirements should be reduced or a faster processor should be used.

If a 100 percent CPU load poses a problem, a 90 percent CPU load is usually no less of a problem. This is due to the fact that the CPU load is rarely accurately estimated. Also, the changing requirements during project development often increase the CPU load. Another consideration is the need to reserve CPU resources for future expansion of the system. It is always good practice to design a software system so that initially it does not require more than a 60 percent CPU load.

11.7.2 Data storage

We will use the term *data storage* to cover both software storage and data storage. Data storage utilization is essentially a design issue, and frequently has but limited bearing on the requirements for the system. Requirements may consider data storage from the aspect of cost, because inefficient data storage design may require excessive storage facilities, such as memory and disk drives. Such unnecessary facilities translate into terms of added cost.

Requirements may also address data storage from the *spare* perspective. A requirement that the system must provide 30 percent spare memory or disk space may have considerable impact on data storage design, especially in a system where operational memory consumption is close to the limit.

By and large, data storage utilization is not visible to the user, and is therefore mainly determined during the design phase. However, initial rough estimates are required at early phases of the project to assure that the target hardware configuration is capable of supporting the software system being developed.

Measures of the amount of software to be developed, as discussed earlier in Section 11.1, may be lines of code (*KSLOC*s), or Kbytes of memory. Memory storage is estimated only in units of Kbytes. The first step involves system decomposition, similar to the stepwise estimation method described in Section 11.2. This time the objective is to estimate the amount of memory required by each module at execution time.

The low level software components are combined into concurrent memory resident groups of modules. Then other factors are also considered, such as dynamic memory allocation, operating system requirements and various memory-resident buffers and tables.

The following method produces memory estimates based on the worst case memory utilization during system execution.

1. Decompose the system into low level modules and estimate the memory requirements for each module at execution time.
2. Identify the indirect memory requirements of each module with respect to:
   - dynamic and static memory work areas
   - memory resident tables
   - buffers
3. Identify the set of memory modules with the largest combined memory requirements that will be memory-resident at any given time.
4. Review the correlation between the memory modules and remove duplicate memory requirements.
5. Repeat Steps 3 and 4 until the largest expected memory utilization is identified.
6. Identify system level memory requirements, such as:
   - memory resident tables
   - file buffers
   - stack size
7. Calculate the total operating system memory utilization.
8. Combine the results of Steps 5, 6 and 7 to produce the total memory storage estimate.

Step 7 should exclude memory requirements that have already been considered in Steps 5 and 6 (e.g. the same file buffers should not be considered both in Step 2 and in Step 6).

The use of overlays can reduce memory requirements, but this is achieved at the expense of additional resources, such as disk I/O, CPU load and execution speed. The trade-off between memory and speed is a common factor in most software systems.

Estimates of mass storage requirements are less critical than estimates of memory requirements. Computer memory is much more limited than disk storage. Disk storage is often restricted only by the cost of the disk storage device.

Estimates of disk storage utilization must take into account the following disk storage consumers:

1. Fixed operating system and service utilities
2. Variable operating system requirements (overlay and swap areas, system files etc.)
3. Project software
4. Data files

For the purpose of this discussion, we will include service packages, such as data bases and communication programs, as part of the operating system. Information regarding the operating system disk utilization is commonly provided by the operating system vendor. If, however, the operating system is being developed as part of the project, then it must be estimated either as a separate system, or as part of the project software (as a subsystem).

Variable operating system requirements are dependent on the specific operating system configuration and on the project software. As an example, disk space for overlays is both a function of the operating system and of the actual software design. Advanced operating systems often provide utilities for estimating disk overhead (both in terms of storage and access) when using overlays. Swap areas for multi-user applications can usually also be sized based on standard operating system utilities. These utilities are commonly part of the operating system tuning or configuration tools.

Estimates for the disk requirements of the project software are straightforward and are produced by the system decomposition. The total of all estimates for each module produces the disk requirements for all project software being developed.

The preparation of estimates for all data file sizes is a tedious task, and is based on the size of individual records and the maximum number of records for each file. This becomes more complicated when records are of variable length. In such cases, maximum or average record sizes should be used. All data files have an overhead, which includes indexes and directories. These must also be factored into the estimate, and are heavily dependent on the data base or file system being used.

In many cases, mass storage data estimates need not be based on a worst case scenario. This is primarily because of the relative ease with which additional mass memory can be added to the configuration. Therefore, in many cases the average mass storage requirements may suffice. Obviously, there are some cases in which a worst case scenario must be used, such as when mass storage utilization grows very fast.

Design estimates for data storage requirements must also make allowances for spare. This is especially true of memory estimates, where the design should provide for about 33 percent spare. This spare memory must be available to cover errors in estimation, changes in the requirements and future development.

11.7.3 Speed

The speed of a system is measured in terms of response time. This is often based on a very stringent set of requirements that define system response to specific events.

An example might be the requirement that the user interface must respond to user input in no more than three seconds. It is extremely frustrating having to wait in front of an automatic bank teller machine for a response to a request. Many such teller machines have alleviated the frustration of having to wait by providing background noise that sounds as if money is mechanically being counted, or at least as if something is happening. A simpler solution is to display a flashing message that says 'Transaction being processed'.

Hatley and Pirbhai (1988) differentiate between *external timing* and *internal timing*. Internal timing is a design issue, while external timing is a requirements issue. External timing, then, would refer to response time. Hatley and Pirbhai suggest a diagram (which they call a *timing requirements picture*) that assists in the analysis of the system timing constraints.

In their analysis of internal timing, Hatley and Pirbhai include activities that are not directly related to response time. We will consider here only the timing issues that are directly related to response time, as viewed externally by system users.

Response time can be perceived as system feedback generated by an external event; this is illustrated in Fig. 11.7. It is therefore reasonable to divide response time into three basic components:

1. The time from the end of the occurrence of the event until the event is identified by the system
2. Event processing time
3. The time from the conclusion of event processing to the beginning of the external response

Note that response time does not include the time it takes to perform the events on both ends; it includes only the interval of time between the two events (see Fig. 11.8).

When estimating response time, the perspective then becomes one of input, processing and output. The input component refers to the time it takes for the system to receive information regarding the end of an event and to identify it.

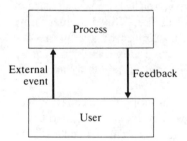

Figure 11.7 Response time perceived as feedback.

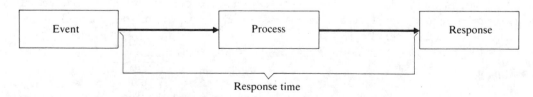

Figure 11.8 The response time interval.

Table 11.7 Example of a response time distribution table

Response time (seconds)	Percentage
0–3	20%
3–6	60%
6–9	39%
9–15	1%

The output component refers to the time it takes the system to take the result of processing and to communicate it to the external response generator.

The event processing component includes all activities within the system that are required to generate the response. This also includes delays caused by higher priority activities, and by external devices, such as disk drives, that must be accessed for relevant information.

Response time is usually provided both as a worse case response and an average response.

In the previous example, the automatic teller responds to key input by the user. The last keypress of a transaction (usually *enter*) starts the response time interval. The screen display or the cash dispenser end the interval as soon as they begin to operate. As we have seen, the system designer may 'cheat' by responding with a 'please wait' message before the real response is ready. This is a perfectly valid practice, and does make the system appear more user-friendly. However, a flashing message that announces 'Please wait, now processing request' can also become irritating if it is displayed for too long.

An average automatic teller response to a balance inquiry may require a response time of 5 seconds. On some occasions, when the teller system is at peak utilization, the same inquiry may take 15 seconds. The average response time would then be 5 seconds, and the worst case response time would be 15 seconds. Although a 15 second response delay may be irritating to the user, it may be acceptable to the bank if it does not occur too often. It is therefore necessary, when presenting response time estimates, to include an estimate of the percentage of time in which the worst case can be expected to occur. We may state, for example:

1. Estimated average response time: 5 seconds
2. Estimated worst case response time: 15 seconds in 1 percent of transactions

A more detailed description of the estimated response time is frequently required. In the above example, 10 percent of the response delays may take 14.5 seconds, which would not be acceptable, but which may fit into the above figures. In such cases a distribution table would be preferred (see Table 11.7).

11.8 NON-DEVELOPMENT OVERHEAD

Good estimates are based on the most current and comprehensive data available. It is therefore important to update all project estimates periodically. This should at least be done at major project milestones, such as the software requirements review, the preliminary design review and the critical design review. Updated estimates should be part of the required deliverables at these reviews.

After the end of the design phase, estimates should be revised before integration begins, and then again before testing begins. Also, any unexpected event that occurs during the development cycle may require the recalculation of estimates. An example of such an event may

Table 11.8 Overhead of non-development activities

	Overhead
Management	0.1
Configuration control	0.02
Software quality assurance	0.03

be the substitution of an off the shelf component for a new development component, or a major unscheduled project delay.

Also, any changes to the project requirements specification must always be accompanied by an analysis of the impact of that change on the project schedule. All changes, with very few exceptions, require cost changes. Even the removal of a requirement will produce a change of the estimated project cost.

A certain amount of change to the requirements specification is often taken into account during the preparation of project estimates. This is included in the estimate in the form of a *safety factor*. The safety factor can also be used to compensate for other circumstances, such as errors of estimation and unexpected delays.

Commonly used safety factors range from 20 percent to 40 percent, depending on the degree of confidence in the estimates, the expectancy of requirements changes and the possible delays that could occur.

Similar factors are also sometimes used to include non-development activities into the estimates, such as project management, configuration control and quality assurance. However, the extent of these tasks is also dependent on other project characteristics. A very small project may not require any direct management, while a large project would be doomed without it.

Table 11.8 presents overhead factors for non-development software project activities. The numbers in Table 11.8 indicate that a software project with a team of 100 engineers would require approximately 10 full-time managers. This includes such tasks as project manager, deputy project manager, team leaders (who may devote part of their time to development work) etc. In a small three person project, one of the team members would be expected to devote about one third of his or her time to the management of the project.

Similarly, in a software project developed by a team of 100 engineers, we would expect to assign two configuration control engineers and three software quality assurance engineers. A more general statement would be that in a 100 work year project, two work years would be devoted to configuration control and three work years would be devoted to general quality assurance.

The numbers in Table 11.8 may be slightly influenced by project size and by the factors discussed in Section 11.4. A complex project will require more overhead than a relatively simple project.

The total project overhead for these activities totals about 15 percent. It is important to remember that this refers only to *direct* project overhead, and does not take into account time invested by high level management, secretaries etc.

11.9 SUMMARY

This chapter illustrates how estimation is applied in the prediction of uncertainties. Any unknown quantity can be estimated, while known quantities do not need to be estimated. For the software project manager, there are many unknown quantities that must be estimated. These are associated with such areas as:

1. Project development costs
2. Project development schedule
3. The size of the project development team
4. The amount of software to be developed
5. The required hardware resources

Stepwise estimation, often referred to as the 'divide and conquer' approach, divides a large problem into numerous smaller problems, and is used in most estimating techniques. The basic approach is to decompose the project into well-defined components, and then to iterate step by step until only small units remain that can then be more easily estimated.

The initial decomposition of a software project identifies four major categories, with different degrees of development risk associated with them. The first step of project decomposition produces project components that either (1) we have available (off the shelf), (2) we know how to develop (full experience), (3) we are at least partially familiar with (partial experience) or (4) are completely new to us (new development). Specific estimation techniques can then be applied for each different type of project component.

Another method, called the constructive cost algorithm (COCOMO), consists of 10 basic steps. These steps cover the decomposition of the project into components, the application of effort formulae to each component and the combination of all the data produced into a single project cost estimate.

Function point analysis (FPA) produces project estimates based on the problem size. The amount of functionality in the project determines the problem size, which is represented by a numerical value (the FPA value). The FPA value of a project can be used to:

- Compare the complexity of projects
- Compare the relative effort required to complete a project
- Generate other project measures (such as *SLOCs*)

Estimates are also often presented as a *range*. A range is a helpful estimate in planning for the development of a project. The statistical theory behind this approach deals with the concept of *confidence intervals*, which provides a probability that development costs will fall into a given range.

Methods for estimating CPU load, data storage and speed are based on decomposition of the software into estimable modules. These estimates are then combined with a safety factor. Commonly used safety factors range from 20 percent to 40 percent, depending on the degree of confidence in the estimates and the expectancy of requirements changes.

Good estimates are based on the most current and comprehensive data available. It is therefore important to update all project estimates periodically. However, no matter which method of estimation is used, it is always important to remember that an estimate can only be as good as the data on which it is based.

EXERCISES

1. Analyze a warehouse inventory system being developed by a company that has previously developed a department store inventory system. Using stepwise estimation, decompose the system into the four categories of components. Then decompose the partial experience components into full experience components and new development components. Specify any assumptions made.

2. Further develop the problem in Exercise 1, and prepare a plan for the estimation of new development components using statistical sampling. Define a group of categories, and assign each new development component to its relevant category. Select representative modules from each category for implementation. Explain the rationale behind the assignment of categories and the selections made.

3. Based on your experience, assign reasonable numbers of *KSLOCs* to each component in Exercise 2. Assume one development person for each 5 *KSLOCs*. Assume that 10 percent of the personnel are level 1, 30 percent level 2, 45 percent level 3 and 15 percent level 4. Compute the *PL* factor for the development project. Discuss the impact of the *PL* value on project development costs.

4. Review Table 11.1, which is concerned with the calculation of the *PL* factor. Suggest a different table of values, based on additional *KSLOC* levels and a wider range of multipliers. Discuss the reasons you chose the numbers in your table. Recalculate the values in Table 11.2, based on the table you have proposed.

5. Decompose the warehouse inventory system described in Exercise 1 into components by level of complexity. Based on the *KSLOC* numbers assigned in Exercise 3, calculate the *SEM* for each class of components and combine the results to produce an estimated number of *SEMs* for the whole project.

6. Decompose the warehouse inventory system described in Exercise 1 into components by level of reliability. Use five reliability levels to factor reliability into the *SEM* estimate calculated in Exercise 5.

7. (a) Suggest a five level table of multipliers for the level of the development environment, based on three levels of project size:

$$KSLOC < 25, 25 < KSLOC < 300, 300 < KSLOC$$

(b) Suggest a table of multipliers to factor subsystem complexity. Discuss whether project size should also be considered.

8. Calculate the cost estimate for the warehouse inventory system described in Exercise 1 using the results of Exercises 3, 5, 6 and 7.

9. Consider the application of the function point analysis algorithm to the warehouse inventory system described in Exercise 1. What are the advantages and what are the disadvantages in using the FPA method? Compare FPA to COCOMO for this specific project.

10. Class assignment: based on the different individual results produced for Exercise 8, calculate 68 percent and 95 percent confidence intervals for the range of the development cost for the warehouse inventory system.

11. (a) Review the CPU load example in Section 11.6. Assume that the equipment input is driven by interrupts. Each interrupt has an overhead of 0.5 ms. What is the CPU load?

(b) What would the CPU load be if the fast loop had three inputs instead of two? Discuss the implications of the result.

Albrecht, A. J. and Gaffney, J. E. Jr. (1983). Software function, source lines of code, and development effort prediction: a software science validation. *IEEE Transactions*, SE-9 (**6**), November.

Ambriola, V., Bendix, L. and Ciancarini, P. (1990). The evolution of configuration management and version control. *Software Engineering Journal*, Vol. 5, No. 6.

Anderson, O. (1990). The use of software engineering data in support of project management. *Software Engineering Journal*, Vol. 5, No. 6.

Balda, D. M. and Gustafson, D. A. (1990). Cost estimation models for the reuse of prototype software development life-cycles. *ACM Sigsoft, Software Engineering Notes*, Vol. 15, No. 3, July.

Balzer, R. (1985). A 15-year perspective on automatic programming. *IEEE Transactions on Software Engineering*, SE-11, No. 11, November.

Bennatan, E. M. (1987). *Artificial Intelligence in Software Engineering – a survey of projects and initiatives*. Desarrollo De Sistemas Informaticos (DSISA) S.A., Madrid.

Boehm, B. W. (1981). *Software Engineering Economics*. Prentice-Hall, Englewood Cliffs, NJ.

Boehm, B. W. (1988). A spiral model of software development and enhancement. *Computer*, May.

BSI (1991). *British Standard 5750*, British Standards Institution, 1991, London.

Carlow, G. D. (1984). Architecture of the space shuttle primary avionics software system. *Communications of the ACM*, Vol. 27, No. 9, September.

Cobb, R. H. and Mills, H. D. (1990). Engineering software under statistical quality control. *IEEE Software*, November.

Cohen, B., Hartwood, T. W. and Jackson, M. I. (1986). *The Specification of Complex Systems*. Addison-Wesley, Reading, MA.

Cox, B. J. (1990). Planning the software industrial revolution. *IEEE Software*, November.

DeMarco, T. (1979). *Structured Analysis and System Specification*. Prentice-Hall, Englewood Cliffs, NJ.

Dijkstra, E. (1972). *Notes on Structured Programming*. Academic Press, New York.

DOD-STD-2167 and DOD-STD-2167A (1988a). *Military Standard, Defense System Software Development*. US Department of Defense (1984, 1985 and 1988).

DOD-STD-2168 (1988b). *Military Standard, Defense System Software Quality Program*. US Department of Defense.

Fairly, R. (1985). *Software Engineering Concepts*. McGraw-Hill, New York.

Francis, B. (1993). The search for client/server security, *Datamation*, 1 May.

Fraser, D. (1976). *Probability and Statistics, Theory and Application*. Duxbury Press, Mass.

Frenkel, K. A. (1985). Toward automating the software development cycle. *Communications of the ACM*, Vol. 28, No. 6, June.

Giegold, W. C. (1982). *Practical Management Skills for Engineers and Scientists*. Lifetime Learning Publications, Belmont, CA.

Gillett, B. (1976). *Introduction to Operations Research: A Computer-Oriented Algorithmic Approach*. McGraw-Hill, New York.

Goldberg, A. (1983). *Proceedings of the 1983 ACM Computer Science Conference*, ACM, pp. 35–54.

Hatley, D. J. and Pirbhai, I. A. (1988). *Strategies for Real-Time System Specification*. Dorset House, New York.

IEEE (1984). *Software Engineering Standards*. The Institute of Electrical and Electronics Engineers, Inc., New York.

IEEE (1987a). *Standard for Software Project Management Plans*. The Institute of Electrical and Electronics Engineers, Inc., New York (IEEE Std-1058.1-1987).

IEEE (1987b). *Software Engineering Standards*. The Institute of Electrical and Electronics Engineers, Inc., New York.

IEEE (1990*a*). Draft of *Standards for a Software Quality Metrics Methodology*. The Institute of Electrical and Electronics Engineers, Inc., New York.

IEEE (1990*b*) *Standard for Software Productivity Metrics*. The Institute of Electrical and Electronics Engineers, Inc., New York (IEEE Std-1045-1990).

IEEE (1990*c*). *Standard for a Software Quality Metrics Methodology*. The Institute of Electrical and Electronics Engineers, Inc., New York (IEEE Std-1061-1990).

IEEE (1993). *Software Engineering, IEEE Standards Collection*, The Institute of Electrical and Electronics Engineers, Inc., New York.

Inmon, W. H. (1993). *Developing Client/Server Applications*, John Wiley & Sons, New York.

ISO (1990). *Quality Management of Quality Assurance Standards*. The International Organization for Standardization (Standard 9000–3).

Jackson, M. A. (1975). *Principles of Programming Design*. Academic Press, New York.

Jeffery, D. R. and Low, G. (1990). Calibrating estimation tools for software development. *Software Engineering Journal*, Vol. 5, No. 4, July.

Kaposi, A. A. and Myers, M. (1990). Quality assuring specification and design. *Software Engineering Journal*, Vol. 5, No. 1, January.

Laplante, P. A. (1990). The Heisenberg uncertainty principle and its application to software engineering. *ACM Sigsoft, Software Engineering Notes*, Vol. 15, No. 5, October.

Macro, A. and Buxton, J. (1987). *The Craft of Software Engineering*. Addison-Wesley, Reading, MA.

Madden, W. A. and Rone, K. Y. (1984). Design, development, integration: space shuttle primary flight software system. *Communications of the ACM*, Vol. 27, No. 9, September.

Microsoft (1992). Designing client–server applications for enterprise database connectivity, *Microsoft Technical Notes*, Vol. 3, No. 14.

Nienburg, R. E. (1989). *Effective Skills for Technical Managers*. Learning Tree International, Los Angeles, CA.

Overmyer, S. P. (1990). The impact of DOD-STD-2167A on iterative design methodologies: help or hinder. *ACM Sigsoft, Software Engineering Notes*, Vol. 55, No. 5, October.

Parnas, D. L. (1972). On criteria to be used in decomposing systems into modules. *CACM*, Vol. 14, No. 1, April.

Paulk, P. C., Curtis, B., Chrissie, M. B., and Weber, C.V. (1993A). *Capability Maturity Model for Software* Version 1.1, Software Engineering Institute, Carnegie Mellon University, CMU/SEI-93-TR-24.

Paulk, P. C., Curtis, B., Chrissis, M. B., and Weber, C. V. (1993b). *Key Practices of the Capability Maturity Model*, Version 1.1, Software Engineering Institute, Carnegie Mellon University, CMU/SEI-93-TR-25.

Peter, L. J. and Hull, R. (1970). *The Peter Principle*. Pan Books, London.

Pinto, J. K. and Mantel, S. J. (1990). The causes of project failure. *IEEE Transactions on Engineering Management*, Vol. 37, No. 4, November.

Polack, A. J. (1990). Practical applications of CASE tools on DOD projects. *ACM Sigsoft, Software Engineering Notes*, Vol. 15, No. 1, January.

Pressman, R. S. (1992). *Software Engineering, A Practitioner's Approach*, third ed. McGraw-Hill, New York.

Ratcliff, B. and Rollo, A. L. (1990). Adapting function point analysis to Jackson system development. *Software Engineering Journal*, Vol. 5, No. 1, January.

Riggs, J. L. and Jones, D. (1990). Flowgraph representation of life cycle cost methodology – a new perspective for project managers. *IEEE Transactions on Engineering Management*, Vol. 37, No. 2, May.

Rochkind, M. J. (1975). The source control system. *IEEE Transactions*, Se-1 (**4**).

Sackman, H. *et al.* (1968). Exploratory experimental studies comparing online and offline programming performance. *Communications of the ACM*, Vol. 11, No. 1, January.

Shaw, M. (1990). Prospects for an engineering discipline of software. *IEEE Software*, November.

Silver, H. (1986). *Technical Marketing and Proposal Preparation*. HSA Publication, California.

Sinha, A. (1992). Client–server computing, *Communications of the ACM*, Vol. 35, No. 7, July.

Sodhi, J. (1990). *Computer Systems Techniques*. TAB Professional and Reference Books, Pennsylvania.

Symons, C. R. (1988). Function points analysis: difficulties and improvements. *IEEE Transactions*, SE-14 (**1**).

Tahvanainen, V. and Smolander, K. (1990). An annotated CASE bibliography. *ACM Sigsoft, Software Engineering Notes*, Vol. 15, No. 1, January.

Ullman, E. (1993). Client/server frees data, *Byte*, June 1993.

Ward, P. T. and Mellor, S. J. (1986). *Structured Development for Real-Time Systems*. Yourdon Press, New York.

Warnier, J. D. and Orr, K. T. (1977). *Structured Systems Development*. Yourdon Press, New York.

Wesselius, J. and Ververs, F. (1990). Some elementary questions on software quality control. *Software Engineering Journal*, Vol. 5, No. 6, January.

Wilson, D. N. and Sifer, M. J. (1990). Structured planning: deriving project views. *Software Engineering Journal*, Vol. 5, No. 2, March.

Yourdon, E. and Constantine, L. L. (1978). *Structured Design*. Yourdon Press, New York.

Zimmer, B. (1991). Implementing productivity managers. *IEEE Software*, January.

Brooks, F. P. (1982). *The Mythical Man Month*, Addison-Wesley, Reading, MA.

BSI (1986). *Quality Vocabulary*. British Standards Institution (Standard BS4778).

Bureau of Business Practice (1981). *The Art of Motivating People*. Prentice-Hall, Englewood Cliffs, NJ.

Herzberg, F. (1987). One more time: how do you motivate employees? *Harvard Business Review*, September–October.

Kocagolu, D. F. (1990). Toward a paradigm for engineering and technology management. *IEEE Transactions on Engineering Management*, Vol. 37, No. 4, November.

Loucopoulos, P. and Champion, R. E. M. (1990). Concept acquisition and analysis for requirements specification. *Software Engineering Journal*, Vol. 5, No. 2, March.

Putnam, L. (1980). *Software Cost Estimating and Life Cycle Control*. IEEE Computer Society Press.